EXPEDITION OF THIRST

EXPEDITION

OF THIRST

Exploring Breweries, Wineries, and Distilleries across the Heart of Kansas and Missouri

—

PETE DULIN

 University Press of Kansas

Published by the University Press of Kansas (Lawrence, Kansas 66045), which was
organized by the Kansas Board of Regents and is operated and funded by Emporia
State University, Fort Hays State University, Kansas State University, Pittsburg State
University, the University of Kansas, and Wichita State University.

Map illustration by Eric Schotland Design.

Library of Congress Cataloging-in-Publication Data

Names: Dulin, Pete, author.
Title: Expedition of thirst : exploring breweries, wineries, and distilleries
    across the heart of Kansas and Missouri / Pete Dulin.
Description: Lawrence, Kansas : University Press of Kansas, 2017. | Includes
    bibliographical references and index.
Identifiers: LCCN 2017026681 | ISBN 9780700624928 (paperback : alkaline paper)
    | ISBN 9780700624935 (ebook)
Subjects: LCSH: Breweries—Kansas—Guidebooks.
    | Breweries—Missouri—Guidebooks. | Wine and wine
    making—Kansas—Guidebooks. | Wine and wine making—Missouri—Guidebooks.
    | Distilleries—Kansas—Guidebooks. | Distilleries—Missouri—Guidebooks.
    | Kansas—Guidebooks. | Missouri—Guidebooks. | Kansas—Social life and
    customs. | Missouri—Social life and customs. | BISAC: TRAVEL / United
    States / Midwest / West North Central (IA, KS, MN, MO, ND, NE, SD).
    | COOKING / Beverages / Beer.
Classification: LCC TP577 .D85 2017 | DDC 663/.3—dc23
LC record available at https://lccn.loc.gov/2017026681.

British Library Cataloguing-in-Publication Data is available.

Printed in China

10 9 8 7 6 5 4 3 2 1

The paper used in this publication is acid free and meets the minimum
requirements of the American National Standard for Permanence of
Paper for Printed Library Materials Z39.48-1992.

CONTENTS

AUTHOR'S NOTE

Expedition of Thirst involved more than 1,500 miles of travel across the prairie and Flint Hills of eastern Kansas and the rolling hills, plains, and Ozarks region of western Missouri. Highway and winding country roads lead past a parade of natural beauty. The landscape between each point offers a rich kaleidoscope of seasonal imagery. En route to these regional breweries, wineries, and distilleries, look out the window and admire the hills, valleys, bluffs, farm ponds, quiet Main Streets, and busy cityscapes.

This travel guidebook explores 150 destinations in eastern Kansas and western Missouri. Few relevant businesses exist in the western half of Kansas; meanwhile, coverage of the eastern half of Missouri's breweries, wineries, and distilleries would significantly expand the scope of the book beyond its original premise. Besides, my liver can only handle so much research.

The routes covered on this expedition follow major interstates, highways, and roads in the territory. The entries in this guide list businesses on or near these routes. No assumptions are made about the point of departure. To organize listings in each section, business entries on routes that pass through Kansas City, for example, begin there and proceed outbound. Entries along I-70 West run from Kansas City to Hays, Kansas, along I-70 East from Kansas City to Columbia, Missouri, along I-35 South toward Wichita, Kansas, and along US 24 to its easternmost point.

Each entry is an introduction to the owners and artisans, a sense of the place, and highlights on beer, wine, and spirits. Expeditionary notes on local history, culture, and personalities are woven through these entries. Hopefully, these observations add layers of interest for travelers on the road and readers curled up at home with this book, thirsty for knowledge.

It's the twenty-first century. GPS-based applications on mobile devices are common and (mostly) reliable tools used to navigate in the city, suburbs, and country. For practical purposes, detailed maps of destinations and specific geographic areas are not listed in this guidebook. Directions are included for listings in some rural areas as well as locations that merit specific detail. If GPS or wifi is inaccessible, make a quick phone call. Let the business know you're coming, and ask for directions. More often than not, you'll be speaking with the owner. These locally owned breweries, wineries, and distilleries are family-run businesses— they look forward to your visit and value your patronage.

Ask questions on your travels. Learn about the grapes in the vineyard, the hops and malts used in brewing, and the method used in distilling. It's interesting to learn how each business operates and how each applies its craft. Sampling at the taproom or tasting room is only one way to learn through the senses. The brewer, vintner, distiller, tour guide, or friendly face at the bar is usually happy to share details about how the beer, wine, and spirits are made.

Have fun on your expedition. Drink responsibly. Know your limits. Respect the judgment of the person pouring behind the bar. Bring home souvenirs and stories and enjoy the exploration.

If you see me on your travels, don't be a stranger.

Pete Dulin

ACKNOWLEDGMENTS

Thank you to Kim Hogeland, acquisitions editor at the University Press of Kansas. *Expedition of Thirst* was a great book concept. It's also been a grand adventure.

A salute goes to my trusty red Ford Focus. I literally couldn't have completed this expedition and written this book without my car. In fact, one night I resorted to sleeping under a fuzzy blue blanket in the Focus. By the way, never assume there won't be four conventions at the same time in Springfield, Missouri, that will sell out every hotel and motel room. Remember to make advance reservations.

Thank you to the many people I met at regional breweries, wineries, and distilleries who answered my questions, poured samples, and showed midwestern hospitality. My gratitude goes to Margaret and Dick Burkhalter and longtime friend Jim Miles for opening their homes to me while I was on the road.

Years ago, I traveled with my uncle Mike Wagner and aunt Tawee Wagner in the back seat of their car through northern California. We drove past a vineyard lined with grapes in the heat of summer. Being an instigator of antics, Mike stopped the car and encouraged me to run to the vines and grab a bunch of grapes. Old enough to know better but young enough to obey my elder, I stepped out of the car, dashed across the dusty road, and quickly grabbed what I could with both hands. As I ran back to the car, Mike began pulling away. Tawee shouted, "Go, go, go!" I dove through the open rear door into the back seat. Catching my breath, I looked at the haul of mostly grape leaves and a small cluster of grapes. Sure enough, they were unripe and sour. That experience ended my career as a grape thief, but it wasn't the last of my adventures. Thanks, Mike and Tawee.

MISSOURI

35

65

NSAS CITY

63

24

BOONVILLE

70

40

COLUMBIA

50

SEDALIA

JEFFERSON CITY

9

65

EAST

JOPLIN

SPRINGFIELD

BRANSON - 44 MI SOUTH

CHAPTER 1

INTRODUCTION

Travel is fatal to prejudice, bigotry, and narrow-mindedness, and many of our people need it sorely on these accounts. Broad, wholesome, charitable views of men and things cannot be acquired by vegetating in one little corner of the earth all one's lifetime.—Mark Twain

Expedition of Thirst is a guide and an account of travels to other places, people, and their craft. Spanning the eastern half of Kansas and western half of Missouri, the exploration covers the crafts of brewing, winemaking, and distilling. To seek, find, and sample the handiwork of the makers is the most fundamental point. As a journey of purpose, the expedition goes beyond quenching thirst by sipping wine, imbibing whiskey, or quaffing beer. Traveling also satisfies a thirst for knowledge and adventure. Heading across the Midwest, the opportunity to learn and expand views transcends the page and inhabits personal experience. Each mile waiting to be traversed is an invitation. *Expedition of Thirst* begins a quest to understand how place, people, and craft are interconnected.

Above Ancient Seas

Bob DesRuisseaux stands on the edge of a grassy bluff. He studies rows of grapevines that lead toward Prairie Fire Winery. He owns and operates the business with his wife Julie on Bacchus Ranch in Paxico, Kansas, in Wabaunsee County. DesRuisseaux wears a tan long-sleeved shirt, worn blue jeans, and a broad-brimmed hat that shades his eyes from late afternoon sun. Behind us, the bluff slopes toward Hudson Ranch Road and Interstate 70 in the distance. Westbound traffic heads toward Manhattan, located deeper in the Flint Hills. Automobiles and semitrailers headed east will pass through Topeka in roughly twenty minutes before reaching Lawrence and Kansas City. The sound of highway traffic never reaches our ears.

A stout winemaker with silvery hair and a broad smile, DesRuisseaux provides an impromptu overview of the landscape. He gestures toward Buffalo Mound, a 1,270-foot mountain peak in the distance, and other surrounding ridges. Prairie Fire's vineyard of Chambourcin, Vignoles, and other varieties grows on a high ridge. Wind flows in patterns through specific contours of his acreage that differ from adjoining ridges and valleys. Cool wind complements blankets of sunlight throughout the seasons. Grapevine-laden hills maintain a temperature seven to eight degrees warmer than adjacent slopes. This geospecific overlay of wind, sun, and soil creates a microclimate on southeast slopes that infuses character into Prairie Fire's wines.

We walk downhill to the tasting room. DesRuisseaux names wildflowers such as blue false indigo and primrose. He explains how prairie grasses form root systems eight to ten feet deep. These roots are the foundation to growth in these lands. Annual controlled prairie fires cull weeds and invasive species, fostering the growth of native grass in a timeless cycle. The root system and rocky soil beneath the grassy slopes provide good drainage for grapevines that "don't like their feet wet." Much like native grass, grapevines push into the earth and seek rich nutrients deposited from an ancient seabed.

Glancing at the boundless sky, swell of the Flint Hills, and sweep of the plains, it is bewildering and captivating to realize that much of Kansas and vast swaths of the central and upper Midwest were once inundated by the Western Interior Sea. A shallow sea up to nine hundred meters deep covered the middle third of North America during the late Cretaceous period about one hundred million years ago. The central lowlands of Kansas and its neighboring states once formed the bottom of this sea. The former presence of ancient waters and its remnants still defines this place and what grows here and throughout the Midwest.

DesRuisseaux bends and picks up one of the many hefty rocks that will be cleared from a hillside as more grapevines are planted in coming seasons. The rock in his hands—as are those in a larger collection behind the tasting room—is studded with the fossils of seashells and creatures of the sea. Flint, limestone, and deposits of fossils and minerals left behind hundreds of millions of years ago continue to enrich the soil that feeds native flora and grapevines introduced to the region.

The conversation with DesRuisseaux offers insight into the livelihood of grape-

Vineyards planted in the Flint Hills in Paxico, Kansas, form a backdrop as Prairie Fire Winery owner and winemaker Bob DesRuisseaux surveys the land above the tasting room. Photo by the author.

growers and winemakers throughout Kansas and Missouri. Not all grapegrowers are winemakers, and vice versa, but they are innately connected to what story the land has to tell in Kansas and Missouri. That story begins with rocks, minerals, and soil, the sculpture of geography subject to the timeless dance of weather patterns and the agricultural ministration of human hands. The grapegrower is attuned to the cycle of planting, caretaking, and harvest. The winemaker applies craft and skill to divine the potential of grapes sourced from the vineyard. Producing wine involves the vintner's intuition, experience, and application of science, but it all begins with stewardship of the land.

Of Oak and Clay

To the east, several ancient seas submerged much of Missouri's landscape during separate geological periods. The Absaroka Sea covered vast areas of the state, particularly the northern half known as the glaciated till plain, and southwest near the Mississippi Highlands along the state's bootheel. The Absaroka Sea rose and regressed five times in the state before it subsided during the Pennsylvanian period about 320 million years ago. The Ozark Mountains rose above the waters as part of the Appalachian land mass that extended toward the eastern seaboard.

Long gone are the glaciers that tilled the Midwest and the briny waters that formed an expansive watershed between the Rockies and Appalachians. Left behind are rich, varied strata of limestone, sandstone, silt, shale, clay, granite, and other rocks. What is the connection between these rock-strewn remnants of a bygone sea and beer, wine, and spirits produced in Kansas and Missouri? The answer involves Missouri white oak and clay of the region.

The majority of American oak barrels used in the beer, wine, and spirits industry are made from Missouri white oak sourced from the Ozarks region. Compared to more porous red oak, the wood cells of white oak trees contain a plasticlike sealing substance called *tylose*. This substance makes the wood waterproof and increases resistance to rot and decay.

Missouri white oak has been the preferred wood for modern barrels that store beer, wine, and spirits in the United States for more than a hundred years. This preference holds true for winemakers in California and Kansas, spirit houses in Kentucky and Missouri, and breweries barrel aging beer in Portland, Wichita, and Kansas City. Accordingly, several of the nation's most prolific cooperages are based in central Missouri. One man in particular helped to launch Missouri's barrel-making industry.

Thomas Walton Boswell founded T. W. Boswell Stave Company in 1912 to produce white oak barrels from staves—vertical wooden planks. Tough Missouri mules hauled logs from the Ozark forests to the mill. By the 1920s Boswell owned and brokered production for thirty-six stave and sawmill operations across southern and midwestern states. Boswell's son J. E. renamed the company in 1936 as Independent Stave Company and renovated its plant in Lebanon, Missouri. Missouri cooperages continue to lead the industry, working with breweries, wineries, and distilleries around the world.

In addition to the structural integrity of oak barrels, the wood affects the flavor and aroma of the liquid it contacts. The cellular structure of white oak permits small amounts of oxygen to permeate barrel staves and diffuse its contents. Chemical reactions help soften tannins from wood and stabilize the liquid's color. Curing oak before barrel construction also imparts aroma and flavor.

Andy Rieger and Ryan Maybee are cofounders of Kansas City–based J. Rieger & Co. Head distiller Nathan Perry produces the distillery's vodka, gin, whiskey, and other spirits. The fifty-three-gallon barrels that store whiskey in their East Bottoms facility are made from Missouri white oak. Approximately 1,400 barrels rest on racks as the whiskey ages.

Based in Kansas City's East Bottoms, J. Rieger & Co. stores and ages its bourbon whiskey in Missouri white oak barrels at its distillery. Credit: Samantha Levi Photography.

According to Rieger, the distillery's barrels are made from wood that has been seasoned for a period of twenty-four to sixty months after the staves are cut to shape and prior to the barrel being built. Toasting and charring barrel staves also introduce a range of flavors and affects the mouthfeel of the spirit. Exposure to heat converts compounds in the wood and coaxes out aromas such as vanilla, caramel, nut, and smoke.

Rieger pointed out that Missouri's soil has a high clay concentration. Clay is abundant in Ozark soil where forests of white oak are found. That dense clay is packed with nutrients—a result of age-old seas and geological forces transforming layers of earth. Rieger added that white oaks grow slowly in clay-rich soil and gradually absorb nutrients. The oak trees grow stronger and high in compounds that impart great flavor to alcohols when aged properly over several years. As a storage container, a white oak barrel and its liquid contents are connected to the land and a particular place that imparts character as part of the distiller's craft.

Water and Chemistry

Sometime in the 1850s, Kentucky businessman Ben Holladay settled in Weston, Missouri, thirty-three miles northwest of Kansas City. He saw opportunity in a limestone spring that had been discovered decades earlier by explorers Lewis

Tom Nichol, former master distiller at Tanqueray and recipe collaborator on J. Rieger & Co.'s Midwestern Dry Gin, rolls a barrel at the Kansas City distillery. Credit: Samantha Levi Photography.

and Clark. Ben and his brother David Holladay opened Holladay Distillery in 1856 near the spring. The spring's mineral-infused waters were ideal to use in the mash that produced bourbon similar to the spirits in Holladay's home state. After the bourbon aged, fresh limestone spring water was added to it to dilute the bourbon and bring it to a desirable proof for bottling. Fresh spring water is still used in this time-tested process to produce Holladay's bourbon.

Similarly, Copper Run Distillery in Walnut Shade, Missouri, also benefits from close access to natural limestone-rich water in the Ozarks that directly affects the quality of its spirits. Limestone is loaded with calcium-bearing carbonate minerals. Water from a limestone spring is rich in minerals, such as calcium, and has a high pH, which promotes fermentation. Most importantly, the limestone filters out impurities such as iron that can cause whiskey to have a bitter taste.

A distillery's water source and its quality play an integral role in the chemistry involved with producing spirits. Historically, breweries in Germany, England, and Belgium also chose locations with access to abundant water that bore qualities well suited to brewing specific styles of beer. Modern brewers assess water

The hand-dug cistern at Holladay Distillery in Weston, Missouri, contains more than forty-five thousand gallons of fresh limestone spring water for use in its spirits. Photo by the author.

quality reports to determine optimum sites and how best to treat water for brewing. In fact, the founders of Tallgrass Brewing Company in Manhattan, Kansas, and Walnut River Brewing in El Dorado, Kansas, chose locations in part due to the purity and qualities of local water.

Throughout the Midwest, the natural resources of a place play a key role in the time-tested methods used by makers of beer, wine, and spirits. Yet land, sun, and water alone are not enough to create these beverages. Practitioners of the craft matter as well.

Immigrants Produce Wine in the New World
Wild varieties of grapes such as Catawba, Concord, and Norton have long grown along riverways and the surrounding lands of Kansas and Missouri. In 1724, American Indian tribes supplied French explorer Captain Etienne Venyard de Bourgmont with wild grapes. His party ventured beyond the Missouri and Kansas Rivers into what is now the northeastern corner of Kansas. Eight decades later, Meriwether Lewis, William Clark, and their Corps of Discovery encoun-

Grapes hang on the vine before fall harvest at Holy-Field Winery in Basehor, Kansas. Photo by the author.

tered vast quantities of grapes growing along Missouri River banks below the bluffs. Despite the abundance of grapes, the origins of the wine industry in these territories only began with the migration of Germans to the area.

German immigrants sought a "new Rhineland" where they could grow grapes, produce wine, and raise families in America. In Missouri, German immigrants settled in Saint Louis and founded towns such as Hermann. Others traveled south to what are now designated as the Ozark Mountain and Ozark Highland wine regions. Throughout the mid- to late 1800s, Germans and other immigrants continued west on the Missouri River or by land. Their destination was the frontier town on the Missouri River that became Kansas City, the arid territory that became Kansas, and beyond. Settlers established farms and vineyards in river valleys and on hot, sunny plains. Winemaking grew beyond its tether to the farm's vineyard and became a commercial industry.

In *A History of Wine in America*, author Thomas Pinney notes that German brothers Adam and Jacob Brenner migrated to Kansas in the 1860s and settled in the northeastern corner of the state. Winding curves of the Missouri River bound the edge of Doniphan County and deviate from the state's otherwise rectilinear borders. Riverbanks and nearby lands provided a rich supply of native grapes. Jacob planted Central Vineyards in 1864, followed a year later by his brother establishing Doniphan Vineyards. In 1869 Jacob's son George planted Bellevue Vineyards adjacent to the vineyards of his father and uncle. The vineyards grew native grapes and domestic varieties from other states. By 1883 the combined vineyards totaled more than one hundred acres of vines and were capable of producing more than sixty thousand gallons annually. Unfortunately, the Missouri River flooded the town of Doniphan in 1890 and contributed to the demise of the town and vineyards.

Elsewhere, Frenchman Isador Labarriere grew grapes and produced wine in the 1870s in Douglas County, Kansas. In Miami County, Swiss immigrant John Ulrich "Wine" Smith and his wife Martha moved from Ohio to Kansas City, relocated to Ellsworth, Kansas, and finally settled in Paola to establish prolific vineyards and produce wine. According to records in 1873 from the Kansas State Board of Agriculture, vineyards were established in fifty counties in the state. Production accounted for 35,000 gallons. By 1880, Kansas wineries produced a whopping 226,000 gallons of wine.

By the mid-1880s Missouri produced more wine by volume than any other state. The bulk of the wine production was along the Mississippi River Valley around Saint Louis and in the Ozarks region. Before Prohibition went into effect in 1920, Missouri was the second-largest wine-producing state in the nation. Along with native Catawba, Concord, and Norton grapes, hybrids such as Vignoles, Seyval, and Chambourcin were added to vineyards and flourished.

Winemaking and its sister industries of distilling and brewing first began in the Midwest with the bounty of land and water in Kansas and Missouri. Yet these industries would not have flourished without the labor, skill, technological advances, and vision of the first generations of Americans. A nation of immigrants and colonists became pioneers, westbound migrants, settlers, farmers, skilled artisans, and architects of agriculture-based industries.

Reconstitution

Several people in Missouri's wine industry played key roles in saving Europe's wine industry in the nineteenth century. In the mid-1800s, a deadly infestation began to devastate vineyards in France and other countries. French botanist Jules Émile Planchon theorized that phylloxera, a tiny aphidlike insect that feeds on roots of *Vitis vinifera* grapes, was the cause of the blight. *Vitis vinifera* grapes produce most of the world's best-known wine varieties, such as Cabernet Sauvignon, Pinot Noir, and Sauvignon Blanc. At the time, these grapes weren't commercially grown in the Midwest. The vines couldn't withstand the cold climate and seasonal temperature changes in fall and winter.

Charles Valentine Riley, Missouri's state entomologist and leading expert on phylloxera, confirmed Planchon's theory. French grapegrowers Leo Laliman and Gaston Bazille suggested a possible solution: if European *Vitis vinifera* could be grafted with aphid-resistant American vines, then the problem might be solved. Viticulturist Thomas Volney Munson, who devoted much of his career to collecting and documenting native American grape species and bred new varieties from them, was consulted about the proposed solution. He then provided native Texan rootstocks for grafting tests that confirmed the solution.

Afterward, Missouri growers and nurserymen George Hussman of Bluffton, Austrian-born Isidor Bush of Saint Louis, and Hermann Jaeger from Newtown County, a trained Swiss viticulturist living in the Ozarks, led the effort to furnish massive volumes of rootstocks and cuttings. These American grapevines enabled the French to reconstitute their afflicted vineyards, an effort known as the "Reconstitution."

Temperance and Intolerance

Despite burgeoning wine production in the mid- to late 1800s, intolerant moral and political opponents of alcohol in Kansas weren't so enamored by the industry. Opposition to the production, sale, and consumption of alcohol in Kansas has roots dating back to the 1830s. Steadily, new laws were passed over several decades as communities took a more restrictive stance.

The temperance movement, led in Kansas by fierce, hatchet-wielding Carrie Nation, the Women's Christian Temperance Union, and other groups, gained steam in municipalities after the Civil War and into the mid-1870s. Temperance strangled the growth of alcohol production and sales across the nation. The momentum of Kansas winemakers as well as brewers came to an abrupt halt when Kansas became a "dry state."

In 1880 Kansas voters approved an amendment to the state constitution that prohibited the manufacture and sale of intoxicating liquors statewide, effective on January 1, 1881. Kansas was the first state in the nation to enact such a prohibition on alcohol. This statewide ban preceded national Prohibition by forty years.

From the early 1800s until the onset of Prohibition, brewers, winemakers, and distillers continued to operate and prosper in Missouri. In fact, some entrepreneurs relocated to the Show-Me State from Kansas. For example, brewer John Walruff moved his business from Lawrence to Weston. Post-Prohibition, these industries quickly returned and ramped up operations in Missouri. A dis-

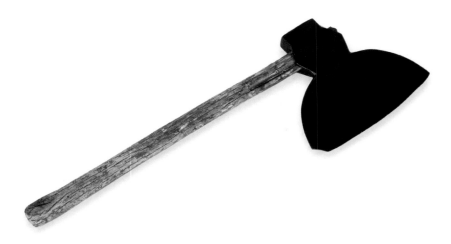

Carrie Nation used this hatchet to bust up saloons, circa 1901. From the collection of the Kansas Historical Society.

parity in growth, density of alcohol-manufacturing businesses, and volume produced between Kansas and Missouri continues to the present day.

More than a century would pass before it became legal again to manufacture alcohol in Kansas. The formation of the Kansas Grape Growers and Winemakers Association in 1987 helped to represent industry interests on legislative issues. Changes in the state's laws also opened doors for the wine and distilling industries in Kansas.

Chuck Magerl, founder of Free State Brewing Company in Lawrence, Kansas, was the modern pioneer who initiated efforts with state lawmakers to update and amend the Kansas State Constitution. Once it was legal, Magerl took a risk by opening his brewery in 1989 and subsequently launched a brewing renaissance in the state.

Bearing Witness

The word *craft* is often overused and misused, much like *artisan*, *local*, and *organic*. These words have value but can lose their currency as meaningful terms. *Craft* implies that something is handmade with skill in small-scale production. That applies equally to a local winemaker's semisweet Vidal Blanc with citrus aroma and pineapple notes and to the brewer's coffee stout.

Not all wine, beer, and spirits on the market are produced in the small-batch sense of craft. Seeing the vineyard, brewhouse, or pot still in person can underscore the authenticity and value of the craft and its maker. Asking questions

Free State Brewing founder Chuck Magerl (left) and former head brewer Steve Bradt. Magerl's brewery in Lawrence was the first to open in Kansas, post-Prohibition, in more than a century. Photo by the author.

also sheds insight on the differences between their operation and factory-scale producers.

Taking an expedition to meet the makers is an opportunity to behold, understand, and support their craft. We bring ourselves closer to the origins of stories told by winemakers, distillers, and brewers through the voice of agriculture and industry. Terroir is its regional accent and the maker's craft is its patois. To travel and be present in their tasting rooms, tours, and taprooms is to bear witness to their stories and labors.

Visiting these businesses slakes the thirst for knowing more and gaining experience through adventure. Talking and tasting firsthand helps to broaden the senses and expand the palate. Or it simply confirms preferences. After all, winemakers are fond of the phrase "Drink what you like. Like what you drink."

The men and women presented in these expedition notes uphold traditions of craft that predate the existence of the United States itself. They follow in the footsteps of others who drew from the resources of eastern Kansas and western Missouri lands. Each bottle and pour passes along a distant message and cultural lineage from the past. These makers also update traditions and advance the craft with modern ideas, techniques, and technology.

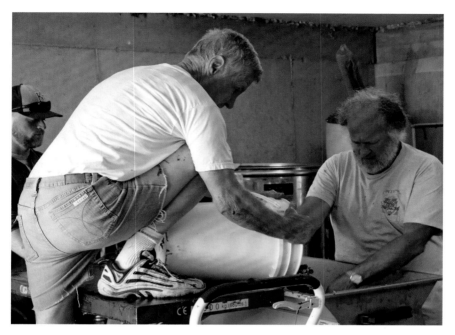

Workers load grapes from the fall harvest at Holy-Field Winery in Basehor, Kansas, into a crusher-destemmer. Photo by the author.

Local Brings Us to This Place

You can't get it just anywhere. That statement proposes a reason for why we eat and drink as local residents do when we travel. There's something about the exclusivity of food or drink tied to a place that has great appeal. The notion seems almost quaint in a time when on-demand products and services appease our whims. The scarcity or inaccessibility of a great seasonal beer or limited vintage of wine makes it all the more desirable.

Yet being local or hard to obtain shouldn't be the only criterion.

John McDonald, founder of Boulevard Brewing Company, once said, "You don't support local because it is local, but because it is good." If it isn't good, then why seek it out? Of course, *good*—not to be confused with *quality*, which may be measured and tested against criteria—is a matter of taste and preference. Again, drink what you like and like what you drink.

There

Travel is more than the sum of consuming, documenting, and rating another place. *There* matters. The sights seen. The people who live and work in a place unlike home are part of the experience. Discovering the similarities and differ-

Guests enjoy craft beer made with farm-sourced ingredients at Miami Creek Brewing Company's taproom in Drexel, Missouri. Photo by the author.

ences, the familiar and strange, is an opportunity to take the measure of what exists elsewhere. In doing so, travel prompts self-reflection about our willingness to risk, the value of creature comforts, and the identity of the people and place we left.

We can traverse great distances by jet, ship, and automobile, or virtually by accessing distant places via the internet. Too often we fixate on the exotic locale and overlook the richness of local treasures. *Expedition of Thirst* presents 150 reasons to change that tendency.

When traveling, we're open to a different rhythm and the newness of people, sights, and experiences. We physically move our bodies from home to another place miles away. There's an exchange of molecules and energy across time and space. We're interacting and immersed. No matter how modern travel has become, it is this process of seeking, finding, and connecting in person that is the underpinning of discovery. Bonding over a glass of wine, a sip of spirits, or a pint of beer taps makes the adventure even more memorable.

The road awaits.

KANSAS

CHAPTER 2

CENTRAL AND EASTERN KANSAS, I-70 WEST

Interstate 70 cuts across the heart of Missouri and Kansas, connecting prairie to peaks as it stretches westward past the Flint Hills toward the Rocky Mountains. This chapter follows this busy interstate from Kansas City, Missouri, to Hays, Kansas, at its westernmost point. Numerous wineries and breweries await in cities and towns for travelers ready for refreshment.

Rowe Ridge Winery

11255 Leavenworth Road, Kansas City, KS 66109
913-721-9776
roweridge.com

Marc and Pamela Rowe, hobby winemakers, developed a vineyard in 2005 on their Wyandotte County property and opened the winery two years later. Rowe Ridge's five-acre vineyard has more than three thousand vines with seven grape varieties, including Chardonel, Seyval Blanc, Saint Vincent, Chambourcin, Norton, Concord, and recent plantings of Valvin Muscat.

Pamela, the vintner, also handles recordkeeping, sales, tasting room operations, and other business duties. Marc, a retired firefighter, concentrates on vineyard management and bottling. Rowe Ridge's wines are made with grapes only from their vineyard. For its fruit wines, the winery sources fruit from To-

Vintner Pamela Rowe produces wines made with estate-grown grapes at Rowe Ridge. Photo by the author.

peka and regional orchards. The tasting room is a bright, sunlit space above the production area of the winery. Wine flight tastings include samples of six wines and a logo glass.

Highlights: Semisweet and sweet wines include Traminette, Saint Vincent, and jammy Concord. Apple-pear, delicious chilled or served as a warm mulled wine, pairs well with spicy food. Blackberry fruit wine, made with three hundred pounds of fruit for each fifty-gallon batch, floods the palate with ripe berry and lingering sweetness. Dry wines include fruit-forward Chardonel with citrus flavors, light acid, and dry finish; Seyval Blanc; and medium-bodied Chambourcin's spicy, earthy tones and berry flavor. Saint Vincent hints at berry and offers a peppery, spicy finish. Dark purple in color, Norton swaggers with earthy, robust spice notes and dry finish.

Grinders High Noon

206 Choctaw Street, Leavenworth, KS 66048
913-651-1000
grinderspizza.com/high-noon

Grinders High Noon is part of the Grinders family of restaurants launched in 2004 by STRETCH, a Kansas City–based artist, restaurant owner, and developer. The restaurants are known for New York–style pizza, Philly cheesesteaks, sandwiches, salads, "death wings," and a selection of premium craft beer from Kansas City, across the United States, and breweries worldwide. Each space has its own STRETCH-designed decor and character with live music featured regularly.

Unlike its sister operations, Grinders High Noon in historic Leavenworth operates a craft brewery. Head brewer Marco Leyton, a homebrewer and former head brewer at 75th Street Brewery, manages production on the seven-barrel system. "Beer is only one aspect of our restaurant," says general manager Dave Staab. "Your experience is important to us. From our made-from-scratch kitchen to live bands to brewery, Grinders High Noon truly has something for everyone."

Highlights: Core beers include porter, honey wheat, pub ale, IPA, pilsner, and cream ale. The brewery also features a rotation of barrel-aged beers.

Holy-Field Vineyard and Winery

18807 158th Street, Basehor, KS 66007
913-724-9463
holyfieldwinery.com

In 1994, Michelle Meyer and her father, Les Meyer, first opened the doors to Holy-Field Vineyard and Winery—named after Holyfield Road, which is now known as 158th Street. Native and French hybrid varieties such as Cynthiana, Saint Vincent, Valvin Muscat, Vignoles, Chardonel, Chambourcin, Seyval, Melody, and Traminette were planted in 1986 and grow in a seventeen-acre vineyard within the thirty-acre property. Annual harvest production totals ten thousand gallons of wine produced from ten grape varieties.

"We are bonded Kansas Winery number five. We weren't the first Kansas winery, but we are the oldest," said Michelle. "We started our vineyard with four hundred grapevines. Every year we planted more vines." Eventually, the volume

Holy-Field Vineyard and Winery has won seven awards at the Jefferson Cup Invitational, more than any other winery in Kansas. Photo by the author.

of grapes exceeded the capacity of the vineyard's wholesale buyers. The Meyers applied for a winery license.

"Our vineyard is the agriculture behind the wine. The wine is our value-added product," said Michelle. "In 1998, my father retired from his business, and later in 1998 I resigned my full-time position. We didn't decide to open a winery on a whim. We had years of passionate viticulture and winemaking experience. The winery was the evolution of our vineyard. We are proud to offer a Kansas agricultural product."

Inside the tasting room and gift shop, visitors might find Cooper, a huge Landseer Newfoundland with white hair and watchful brown eyes, lounging by the doorway. Hundreds of medals and awards hang on a wall in the tasting room and make a definitive statement. Holy-Field has won seven awards at the Jefferson Cup Invitational, more than any other winery in Kansas. At this annual competition in Missouri, more than seven hundred wines are preselected and judged. Winning wines exemplify top viticulture and winemaking throughout wine regions of America.

Unlike many other Kansas wineries, Holy-Field uses only grapes from its vineyard. Grape harvest and crush begins in late August and continues through September. In 2016, nine tons of grapes were harvested in the first week alone

Michelle Meyer and her father, Les Meyer, co-own Holy-Field Vineyard and Winery, the oldest winery in Kansas. Photo by the author.

by staff and volunteers. A one-day haul in mid-September is roughly half that amount. Pressure mounts to bring the harvest in as the season's end draws close.

Michelle, tall and lean with sun-bronzed skin and a broad smile that showcases dazzling white teeth, strolls out of the wine production cellar on an interception route. Guests are not normally allowed in the area. A busy crew of workers unload and weigh crates filled with the morning's grape harvest. "We were the first in Kansas to plant and make wine from the Valvin Muscat grape," says Michelle. "It's an amazing hybrid with over-the-top, fruity, floral character and truly a wine for all types of wine aficionados."

Young assistants pass a crate to elders in grape-stained shirts, who load clusters of purple-skinned grapes into a crusher-destemmer. The machine breaks the fruit open to expose skin and pulp without crushing tannin-loaded seeds and stems. Skins, seeds, and solids are removed so that unwanted color and tannin doesn't affect the pulp that will produce white wine. In pulp that is used for red wines, skins are kept to add flavor, color, and tannin. The harvested and processed grapes are punched down, or pressed. Later, yeast is added and fermentation begins to produce alcohol in the next stages of the winemaking process.

Highlights: Bestselling Tailgate Red, a blend of Saint Vincent and Chambourcin, is a fruit-forward semisweet style. Saint Vincent offers low tannin, cherry notes, and smoky hints from aging in oak barrels. Corky's Barrel, a dry blended red, honors its namesake wine mascot and Newfoundland depicted on the label. Chardonel, a dry white wine, dances with crisp fruity flavor. Vignoles leans sweet with honey and stone fruit flavors. Private tastings are available for parties of fifteen or more. Visitors also come to Holy-Field to attend seasonal events, music performances, dinner theater, and festivals, and enjoy wine on the gazebo.

Travel tip: From I-70, take exit 224 for KS 7 toward US 73 Bonner Springs/Leavenworth. Turn right on KS 7/US 24/US 40 West/US 73 North and proceed for 1.5 miles. Take US 24/US 40 West/State Avenue W ramp and proceed on this route for 2.7 miles. Turn right on 158th Street and make an immediate left into the driveway.

Crescent Moon Winery

15930 246th Street, Lawrence, KS 66044
785-550-5353
moonandwine.com

Cheryl and Keith Hand were inspired to establish Crescent Moon by past travels to Europe and the encouragement of a fellow Kansas grapegrower and winemaker. "My husband and I were both in the US Army and traveled in Germany and France," said Cheryl. "We wanted to do something with our ten acres." Ten acres isn't much for a crop farm. The Hands connected with Greg Shipe of Davenport Orchards and Winery in Eudora, Kansas. Cheryl said, "Greg got us into growing grapes and then we learned how to make wine." The couple began planting their vineyard in 2009 on property located near the western edge of Leavenworth County just north of Lawrence. They established the winery in 2011 and opened their tasting room in October 2014.

Keith and Cheryl Hand (pictured) opened their tasting room in October 2014. The winery and tasting room is near Ted Grinter's famous sunflower field in Lawrence. Photo by the author.

The Hands, who both work as nurse practitioners, first began making wine from Edelweiss grapes sourced from vines at the Heimhof Winery and Vineyard in Leavenworth. Heimhof was one of the first Kansas vineyards to open post-Prohibition and one of the oldest operating wineries in Kansas until it closed. Crescent Moon now grows Edelweiss, Seyval Blanc, Chardonel, Vignoles, Noiret, Norton, Chambourcin, and Grüner Veltliner grapes. This last variety, used for white wine, is commonly grown in Austria, Slovakia, and the Czech Republic. Normally it takes three to five years for newly planted vines to produce fruit ready for harvest and wine production. The Hands waited longer to begin selling Crescent Moon wines at their tasting room because they wanted the wines to age.

The tasting room, winery, and vineyards are located on lush fields near a pond. Bullfrogs get skittish and plop across the water when disturbed. Guests are welcome to help with the autumn harvest, stroll the grounds, and settle in a lawn chair with a bottle of wine and glasses close at hand.

Highlights: Free tastings are available on weekends during business hours or by appointment. Edelweiss, a winter-hardy grape variety, has a silky mouthfeel, sweet honeyed aroma, and distinctive character that suggests notes of caramel and hard candy. Crisp, dry, and unoaked Chardonel, derived from parent grapes Chardonnay and Seyval Blanc, is Cheryl's favorite wine. Vignoles is a semisweet white with notes of honey and pear and crisp acidity. Cheryl noted that, as one of the last grapes harvested each season, "Vignoles is a persnickety grape that doesn't grow well. It splits easy. We're happy to get whatever we can." Crescent Moon's Chat Noir, made primarily with Frontenac grapes, is blended with four other grapes to produce a dry red with smoky-sweet layers of berry flavor and smooth finish. Bestselling Starry, Starry Night is an award-winning blackberry dessert wine made from Noiret and Norton grapes that is fortified with brandy made from Crescent Moon's Noiret grapes. It is superb with dark chocolate, cheesecake, cheese, and nuts.

Travel tip: From I-70, take exit 212 for 222nd Street and turn right. Turn left on Woodend Road and proceed 1.4 miles. Turn left on US 24 West/US 40 West and proceed 1.6 miles. Turn right on 243rd Street and then left on Levee 27/Stilwell Road, which turns north and becomes 246th Street. While in the area, visit Ted Grinter's famous sunflower field (24154 Stillwell Road, Lawrence, KS; krisgrinter.blogspot.com), during the forty-acre farm's summer bloom. The Kaw Valley Farm Tour takes place during the first full weekend of October.

Davenport Orchards and Winery

1394 East 1900 Road, Eudora, KS 66025
785-542-2278
davenportwinery.com

C. W. and Mary Davenport moved to Lawrence in 1949, settled on a farm west of town, grew crops, raised cattle, and ran a meat market until 1960, when C. W. retired. To keep busy, the Davenports bought land in the Kaw Bottoms east of Lawrence and planted seventy-four acres of peaches and six acres of apples for a pick-your-own apple orchard business.

The Davenports' grandson Greg Shipe, who worked the farm during summers, has since taken over operations. Greg began planting grapes in 1990 because his wife, Charlee, thought "they looked so pretty." In August 1997, Greg and Charlee established the winery and it now has a twenty-four-acre vineyard with only five acres of apples on the property. "Grapes do better," said Greg. "People don't can or freeze fruit as much. You can grow grapes and bottle wine."

Davenport's tasting room is housed in a red building near the production facility, tractors, and quarter-mile-long rows of grapevines. A series of personal

Greg Shipe of Davenport Winery mans the tasting room. Photo by the author.

license plates stamped with VINTNER, old ballcaps, and other memorabilia are mounted on the tasting room walls. Greg Shipe is lean and wiry with a patient professor's tone. "From 1901 to 1902, Kansas had 5,668 acres of grapes and produced 173,000 gallons of wine," he said, citing figures from the biannual Kansas Board of Agriculture report for those years. According to the state's last official count in 2010, there were 342 acres of grapes in Kansas and 107,419 gallons of wine were produced.

Davenport has used only Kansas-grown grapes to produce its forty different wines. Doing so has required growing a large volume of grapes, some more than others among the seventeen varieties in the vineyard. Shipe has planted one thousand vines of Fredonia, a grape used to make the winery's bestselling Charlotte's Red. He sells out of the sweet cotton-candy-tasting wine annually and plans to plant more vines.

Highlights: Aged twenty-two months in American oak barrels, the 2012 Chambourcin is smoky with blackberry notes and a dry, tannic finish. The 2012 Matrot Norton, a dry red aged thirty months in medium-toasted American oak barrels, delivers a spicy, peppery finish. Matrot's wine label depicts the Matrot Castle and Winery, built in 1883 by Parisian Seraphin Matrot, which houses Davenport's satellite tasting room (6424 Southwest Huntoon, Topeka, KS; topekawine.com) in Topeka. Bluesman, a Norton aged in a no. 2 charred oak barrel, is juicy with prominent berry flavor, light body, and smooth finish. Artist Alexander Odood created the artwork for the Bluesman label as well as for Jazzman, a smoky, light-bodied Saint Vincent—the grape varietal named "after the patron saint of winemakers and growers." Mandolin is available as an off-dry or sweet red wine. The latter has caramel and butterscotch notes that linger on the nose and tastes like pie cherries.

Travel tip: From I-70, take exit 212 for 222nd Street. Turn left (west), following 222nd Street as it turns south and proceed for 6.5 miles as it becomes East 2172nd Road/Main Street. Turn right on West 10th Street/North 1400 Road/Old K-10 for 2.2 miles. Turn right on East 1900 Road. BlueJacket Crossing Winery is also located in the area. Lawrence is a short drive away on K-10.

BlueJacket Crossing Winery

1969 North 1250 Road, Eudora, KS 66025
785-542-1764
bluejacketwinery.com

Pep and Basuki Selvan-Solberg established their eight-acre vineyard on a twenty-acre property in 2002. The initial planting began with five hundred vines of a native variety of grape known as either Norton or Cynthiana. Later, Pep added more Norton, Saint Vincent, Seyval, Chambourcin, Fredonia, Léon Millot, Vignoles, Traminette, and Melody vines. Today, BlueJacket Crossing Winery is home to four thousand vines.

Anjali Peruman, who manages the tasting room, first met the winery's founders years ago in Eugene, Oregon, where they all lived. Peruman said, "Pep earned a master's degree in architectural engineering in Eugene." Later, he moved to a town south of Napa and Sonoma, where he ran a construction company, and built many projects for area wineries. The Selvan-Solbergs returned to Kansas to be near family. Instead of ranching cattle, Pep decided to start a winery and

Betty's Blush followed by Wolf Red are top-selling wines at BlueJacket Crossing Winery. Photo by the author.

used his skills to construct a home, production cellar, and tasting room on the property. Selvan-Solberg learned aspects of the trade from Holy-Field Winery and also taught himself about winemaking.

BlueJacket Crossing offers tours only during the Kaw Valley Farm Tour in October. The winery hosts music and other events at the tasting room. Volunteers assist with the harvest each fall season and enjoy lunch with sangria for their efforts. In the tasting room, guests may try award-winning wines and enjoy a bottle on the patio. Bring snacks.

Highlights: Tastings include samples of eight wines. Reservations are required for groups of six or more. BlueJacket Crossing won a prestigious Jefferson Cup for its 2009 Seyval Reserve, a silver for Betty's Blush, and a silver for the Off-Dry Vignoles. The winery's 2009 Off-Dry Vignoles also earned a gold medal at the 2011 Finger Lakes International Wine Competition. The Vignoles packs in grapefruit, pineapple, and mango notes, a burst of initial sweetness despite no residual sugar, and a parting dry finish. Betty's Blush is the top seller, followed by Wolf Red. Traminette, blended with some Valvin Muscat grape, blooms with apricot-pear floral aroma and a crisp lime finish. Off-Dry Vidal Blanc's touch of sweetness accompanies aromas of tropical passionfruit, melon, and kiwi. Seyval Blanc's crisp, dry white sings with pear-apple notes.

Free State Brewing Company

636 Massachusetts Street, Lawrence, KS 66044
785-843-4555
freestatebrewing.com

". . . because without beer, things do not seem to go as well . . . "
—Diary of Brother Epp, Capuchin Monastery, Munjor, Kansas, 1902

Free State Brewery founder Chuck Magerl grew up in the sixties. During that era, the Beatles grew to prominence, NASA landed a rocket on the moon, the struggle for civil rights roared, and the Vietnam War bruised the ideals of a nation. Magerl, his extended family, and friends had lively discussions about topics of the day. The power of community and connecting over food, beer, and conversation remained with Magerl, a former homebrewer and cofounder of the Community Mercantile natural foods grocery co-op in Lawrence. Magerl recalled the value of these social connections and spaces when he first imagined Free State Brewing Company.

Since its launch in 1989, Free State Brewing's brewpub has been a top-draw destination for food, beer, and socializing in downtown Lawrence, Kansas. Photo by the author.

Founded in 1989, Free State was developed as a brewery and restaurant where family, both biological and extended, could gather someplace besides home or the office. Sharing beer and food has always facilitated social exchange. That purpose remains true today at the oldest operating brewery in contemporary Kansas history.

State prohibition once stymied the manufacture of alcohol in Kansas for more than a century. Brewery historian and author Cindy Higgins writes in *Kansas Breweries and Beer: 1854–1911* that Kansas once had more than ninety commercial breweries before state prohibition commenced in 1881. More than half of them were established before 1870. Post-Prohibition, the state was slow to update its laws concerning the manufacture and sale of alcohol.

As a pioneer in 1989, Magerl launched Free State Brewing in the heart of downtown Lawrence after working avidly with state legislators in Topeka to amend the code of alcohol laws. The changes allowed brewpubs to produce and sell beer on the premises. The brewery also opened a bottling plant in east Lawrence in 2012 to boost its production capacity and bottle for distribution in Kansas, Missouri, and Nebraska.

Led by former director of brewing operations Steve Bradt, Free State's beers have won numerous awards. Bradt, a veteran national competition beer judge, developed and refined many of Free State's earliest beers, such as Copperhead Pale Ale, that remain core beers today. Head brewer Geoff Deman has introduced dynamic seasonals—such as the award-winning Garden Party, a lager brewed with juniper, basil, and cucumber—that appeal to long-time craft beer fans and seekers of fresh flavor experiences. As a forerunner of modern craft brewing, Free State focuses on producing a portfolio of quality craft beer rather than chasing trends with scores of new releases to attract fickle beer consumers.

Drinking at Free State's brewpub is a satisfying way to enjoy their year-round, seasonal, and experimental beers. Generations of customers also dine there on burgers, sandwiches, steak, seafood, salads, and daily specials.

Highlights: The production brewery in east Lawrence (1923 Moodie Road) offers free tours that include three beer samples on the second Saturday of every month at 2 p.m. Flagships include light, refreshing Free State Golden; full-bodied Ad Astra Amber, with slight malty sweetness; hop-forward Copperhead Pale Ale—so named after Bradt stepped on a venomous snake and was bitten on the ankle; and silky Oatmeal Stout. Seasonals include Brinkley's Maibock, Winterfest, Oktoberfest, and Stormchaser IPA, an American-style ale with a citrusy hop bouquet and grapefruit-orange flavors. Old Backus Barleywine Ale's sweet malt is elevated by fruit notes and crisp hop finish. Ask about seasonal and brewery-only beers at the brewpub.

23rd Street Brewery

3512 Clinton Parkway, Lawrence, KS 66047
785-856-2337
brew23.com

Anchoring a retail hub on the southwest side of Lawrence, 23rd Street Brewery is a local favorite for hearty pub fare, social gatherings, and fans cheering the University of Kansas Jayhawks. Established in 2004 and originally named 75th Street Brewery like its former sister brewpub in Kansas City, the business was renamed in December 2006.

Brewmaster Russell Brickell worked with former brewmaster Bryan "Bucky" Buckingham (now at Cinder Block Brewery in Kansas City) before taking the helm. As brewer, Brickell said, "I keep the beer styles simple, pure, and not too experimental. A fresh batch is made every four to six weeks and is usually consumed within a month."

The unusual fifteen-barrel brewhouse was built high above the main bar, dining room, and kitchen. The elevated design creates a striking visual but makes it challenging to coordinate delivery of supplies, clean equipment, and manage the brew cycle in the cramped space. The large brewpub is known for its specialty burgers and entrées such as fish and chips, meatloaf, sirloin, and chicken fried steak. A full range of pasta, sandwiches, salads, sides, and appetizers is available to rock Jayhawk appetites.

Highlights: Eating, drinking, socializing, and cheering for favorite sports teams is the pastime here. Year-round flagships include Wave the Wheat Ale; popular Rock Chalk Raspberry Wheat; 2007 Great American Beer Festival silver medalist Crimson Phog, an Irish ale with a red hue; and The Bitter Professor IPA with grapefruit-tangerine notes and crisp citrus flavor. Seasonals include Big Leaf Porter, Hawktoberfest, and Morning Cowbell Coffee Milk Stout.

Unusual in its configuration, 23rd Street Brewery's fifteen-barrel brewhouse was built above the main bar, sports-themed dining room, and kitchen. Photo by the author.

Kugler's Vineyard

1235 North 1100 Road, Lawrence, KS 66047
785-843-8516
kuglersvineyard.com

In 1996, Tony and Kay Kugler planted native and hybrid grapes on two acres of their property in Lawrence. Under the name Kugler's Winery, they produce wines from Concord, Niagara, Seyval Blanc, Vidal Blanc, and Cynthiana. Their wine is available to purchase year-round from the winery and at local liquor stores.

Glacial Hills Wine Trail

glacialhillswinetrail.com

This Glacial Hills Wine Trail is a brief day trip from Topeka, Lawrence, and Kansas City. Trail stops include Glaciers Edge Winery in Topeka, Crescent Moon Winery in Lawrence, Crooked Post in Ozawkie, and Jefferson Hill Vineyards and Guesthouse in McLouth. When guests visit the wineries, they will receive a card that is stamped after the first visit to each winery. After the card is stamped by each winery, the cardbearer will receive a gift.

Glaciers Edge Winery

1636 Southeast 85th Street, Wakarusa, KS 66546
785-862-5421
glaciersedgewine.com

Glaciers Edge owners Mike and Lisa Steinert are rejuvenating their vineyard, established in 2014, due to past drought. In this agricultural industry, grape-growers and vintners face challenges from weather, pests, and other factors that impact their business pursuits, but find ways to persevere.

Glaciers Edge currently grows Norton, Noiret, Traminette, Muscat, Vidal, and Catawba grapes. Past plantings of Vignoles have been replaced with Seyval. Chambourcin was removed and Baco Noir was added, as well as Crimson Cabernet. Overall, they have 2,500 vines and a wide variety of wines available. From the novice to the experienced wine drinker, Glaciers Edge welcomes all.

"We are unassuming, easygoing, instructional, and nonthreatening to the novice wine drinker, yet informative and unique to the experienced wine drinker," said Mike. "We like to try to do things that are maybe against the grain and provide a quiet, laidback experience."

Highlights: Catawba, Norton, and Cranberry are top sellers. Catawba, a sweet white with tartness for balance, has a floral nose with grapefruit notes. Tart Cranberry is popular especially around the holidays. Norton is more fruit-forward, with a pleasing dry finish. Noiret's initial berry is followed by a complex finish of smoke, tobacco, and chocolate notes with black pepper.

Lori Henderson of Crooked Post Winery, near scenic Lake Perry on the Glacial Hills Wine Trail, offers wine samples in the tasting room. Photo by the author.

Crooked Post Winery

7397 K-92 Highway, Ozawkie, KS 66070
785-876-9990
crookedpostvineyard.com

"Wine is bottled poetry." This line by Robert Louis Stevenson, author of *Treasure Island*, is etched on a barrelhead mounted on the wall of Crooked Post's tasting room. Rather than relax in retirement, Kevin and Lori Henderson started growing grapes in 2006 for other Kansas vineyards on farmland near Lake Perry, a picturesque area that might inspire poetry. Smoky Hill, Davenport, BlueJacket Crossing, Crescent Moon, Prairie Fire, and Middle Creek wineries have all sourced grapes from the Hendersons' vineyard. In May 2014, the Hendersons began producing their own wine from French-American hybrid grapes under the label Crooked Post, a reference to the fence posts hewed from hedge wood on the property.

"We built this place as a destination for vacation getaways and a place to just relax on a day trip," said Lori. The winery's location near Lake Perry and winding highways across Jefferson County make it a popular stop for neighbors, lake visitors, and motorcyclists cruising through the surrounding farmland. The tasting room is housed in a building inspired by Italian architecture and style, overlooking fifty-six acres with 5,300 vines planted in two locations. Located next to the tasting room, a nine-hundred-square-foot event room is also a draw for area gatherings.

The Hendersons do not spray for insects, and they use minimal chemical compounds in winemaking and grape growing. They allow natural insect predators to take care of unwanted insect species.

Highlights: Tastings are free. Guests may purchase wine and beer by the glass and relax in the tasting room or on the front patio. Seyval Blanc, a grape that produces a dry, mineral-tasting white wine, is a French hybrid that was brought to the area in the 1920s, Lori noted. The winery grew seven tons of this grape in 2015 and 2016. Fion Gael, Crooked Post's sweet fifty-fifty blend of Seyval Blanc and Cayuga White, "flies off the shelf." *Fion gael* means "white wine" in Scottish Gaelic but may be pronounced refreshing in any language. Cayuga White, a descendant of Seyval Blanc and available as a dry or semisweet wine, is similar to a crisp Chardonnay with a citrus aroma. Cabernet Franc jumps with juicy berry flavor. Sweet-tart Saint Vincent, a lively Chianti-style red with cherry and smoky overtones, is also ideal in sangria. Perry Sunset, a rosé made from a proprietary blend, is as smooth, sweet, and relaxing as a sunset lake cruise. Wood-fired pizzas made in-house from scratch are available on Friday, Saturday, and Sunday evenings, as well as cheese trays and popcorn.

Travel tip: From I-70, take exit 224 for KS 7 toward US 73 Bonner Springs/ Leavenworth. Turn right onto KS 7 North/US 24 West and merge onto US 24 / US 40/State Avenue West. Proceed 11.1 miles. Turn right onto KS 16 West (4th Street/McLouth Road) and continue 16.1 miles. Turn right on US 59 North, go one mile, and turn left on KS 92/Jefferson Street. Proceed 9.9 miles. The winery and tasting room, located one mile west of Ozawkie, is one mile from Lake Perry and Old Town Campground.

Jefferson Hill Vineyards

12381 Washington Road, McLouth, KS 66054
913-796-6822
jeffersonhillvineyard.com

Don and Maxine Bryant transformed a 1920s dairy farm into Jefferson Hill Vineyards, a five-acre Kansas farm winery, café, and bed-and-breakfast in the sweeping hills of Jefferson County in northeastern Kansas. The owners primarily focus on the bed-and-breakfast, but wine tastings are offered on weekends and tours by appointment. Dining at Café de Vine is by reservation only. Guests may relax on a large veranda around the building and in nearby gazebos.

Highlights: Wines include Harvest Moon White, semisweet Jefferson Red with hints of red fruit and blackberries, and Indian Summer's sweet blend of grape and locally sourced elderberry. Dream Catcher, a blend of grapes and black currants, is sweet and earthy, balanced by tannin and a sharp finish.

Travel tip: From I-70, take US 40 West (or US 40 North if coming from Lawrence) to KS 16 West. Turn right onto KS 16 West/West 4th Street/McLouth Road. Proceed 10 miles. Turn right onto KS 92 East/South Union Street and proceed 4.5 miles. Turn left onto 118th Street. Turn right onto Washington Road.

Topeka's Beermuda Triangle

Happy Basset Brewing Company, Norsemen Brewing Company, and The Blind Tiger Brewery and Restaurant form the three points of Topeka's Beermuda Triangle. These three breweries collaborated in 2016 to brew Topeka Beermuda Triangle, an amber-colored lager with the aroma and flavor of caramel malt and medium bitterness from hops. The beer was brewed, fermented, and conditioned on the brewing system at Blind Tiger. Since this limited-edition beer was released, no mysterious disappearances have been reported in the Triangle, but appearances by craft beer fans are welcome.

The Blind Tiger Brewery and Restaurant

417 Southwest 37th Street, Topeka, KS 66611
785-267-2739
blindtiger.com

Kansas led the nation by enacting a series of regressive alcohol prohibition laws decades before national Prohibition took effect in 1921. The local and statewide laws didn't make life better for manufacturers, saloons and taverns, or imbibers of alcohol during the era. Ingenious Americans who owned illegal drinking

Blind tiger *was a code phrase used by businesses during Prohibition to communicate to custom-ers that illegal booze was available. Photo by the author.*

establishments developed a Prohibition-era custom to communicate with their clientele: restaurants and other establishments displayed stuffed or china tigers to alert potential patrons to the availability of bootleg alcohol after-hours. In the South, a "tiger" referred to a rip-roaring party. These Prohibition-era tigers were "blind" because the authorities, at least officially, didn't know they existed. Post-Prohibition, the blind tiger is a reminder of less-tolerant days.

The Blind Tiger Brewery and Restaurant opened in May 1995 as Topeka's first craft brewery. In February 2007 Jay Ives acquired and updated the menu and service at the struggling business. Now Blind Tiger thrives thanks to Ives's stewardship and the skill of brewmaster and co-owner, John Dean. Most of the beer produced by the fourteen-barrel brewhouse is consumed on the premises, with approximately 10 percent distributed in and around Topeka.

Dean is well respected in the brewing industry and has advised many re-gional brewers. He began as a homebrewer in the 1990s and learned the craft from others and self-study. His focus on quality over quantity is evident when tasting Blind Tiger's beers. "I decided not to make cheaper beer, but made the

Blind Tiger brewmaster and co-owner, John Dean, earned the award for World Champion Brewpub and Brewer, Large Brewpub Division, at the 2014 World Beer Cup. The brewery has earned twenty-one national or international awards. Photo by the author.

best I could. You can't make great beer with mediocre ingredients. Homebrewing helped me to learn the fundamentals. It's hands-on without a lot of instruments," he said. "At the next level, you start adding science for consistency."

During Dean's tenure since he joined the company in 2001, the brewery has earned twenty-one national or international awards. Dean earned the award for World Champion Brewpub and Brewer, Large Brewpub Division, at the 2014 World Beer Cup. Blind Tiger's Munich Dunkles won the gold award at the 2014 World Beer Cup, and the Maibock won a silver, making it second-best among worldwide competition.

Dean and his brewhouse team have 250 recipes in their repertoire. He sums up the difference between German and American brewers this way: "In Germany, their way of thinking doesn't stray. Beer has tasted that way for hundreds of years." However, "in America, it's the opposite. We're constantly changing, making it up, inventing."

Blind Tiger's restaurant serves barbecue, steak, pasta, and homestyle food that draws a regular crowd. Seating is available in the family-friendly dining room, bar, lounge, outdoor deck, and atrium. The brewhouse and fermenters are visible to guests intrigued by the brewing process.

Highlights: Flagship beers include Raw Wheat, County Seat Wheat, Raspberry Wheat, copper-colored Holy Grail Pale Ale, coffee-infused Tiger Paw Porter made with Brazilian beans from PT's Coffee Roasting Company, and malty, slightly sweet Tiger Bite Midwest-style IPA. Try their seasonal Maibock (available in May) and Top Gun IPA, named after the fighter pilot school in Miramar, California.

Norsemen Brewing Company

830 North Kansas Avenue, Topeka, KS 66608
785-783-3999
norsemenbrewingco.com

Opened in the heart of the NOTO Arts District in North Topeka, Norsemen's taproom is located next to its seven-barrel brewhouse. The brewery's origins go back more than five years as a homebrewing group dubbed Fat Back Brewery, with members Jared Rudy, Adam Rosdahl, and Andy Sutton. Jared's wife, Emily Rudy, and Adam's wife, Melissa Rosdahl, later got involved with the group. They connected with local brewers' guilds and industry professionals to learn and refine their craft, brew, and drink beer.

In May 2015, the Rudys and Rosdahls formed Fat Back Brewing Associates Corporation and proceeded with plans to develop Norsemen Brewing Company, named after a local school mascot. The brewery opened in mid-October 2016 with the spirit of Vikings and the pride of north Topekans.

In addition to the taproom, spaces include the Midgard Mezzanine, an intimate area overlooking the main room, and Halls of Valhalla, a banquet room that seats 160 people.

Highlights: Year-rounders include Fat Back Lager, a crisp Vienna-style lager with toasted malts and mild hops, Odin's One-EyePA, a hoppy pale ale, and Shield Maiden Wheat, an American wheat beer with a touch of rye for peppery flair. Attempted Conspiracy is a Russian imperial stout with chocolate undertones and smooth, dry finish. Andy's Sensual Saison is a fruity farmhouse ale with a not-so-subtle acronym. Seasonal Oktoberfest Märzenbier is full-bodied, rich, and toasty.

Happy Basset Brewing Company

6044 Southwest 29th Street, Topeka, KS 66614
785-783-3688
happybassetbrewingco.com

Located in the Villa West Shopping Center, the Happy Basset brewery and eighty-seat taproom was named after founders Marne and Eric Craver's two basset hounds. Eric, a longtime homebrewer, works full-time as an HVAC technician while Marne works for Mars as a food scientist. Though the brewery has no kitchen, guests are welcome to bring snacks and purchase food from food trucks as available.

Highlights: Flagship beers on tap consist of Yellowbrick Blonde, Hoppy Basset, Purebred Porter, and 785 Ale. Generally, at least eight rotating varieties are on tap, including raspberry wheat, milk stout, Scotch ale, Irish red, bourbon stout, unfiltered wheat, saison, strawberry blonde, barleywine, and pumpkin ale.

Prairie Fire Winery

20250 Hudson Ranch Road, Paxico, KS 66526
785-636-5533
prairiefirewinery.com

Bob and Julie DesRuisseaux built a "Little Château on the Prairie" in the Flint Hills, twenty minutes west of Topeka. The couple founded the winery in January 2008 with a mission to promote economic, environmental, and social sustainability. Using Prairie Fire as a hub, the couple promotes wine, food, and goods from their winery and other Kansas producers.

More than six thousand vines line the slopes of their sixty-acre ranch and winery. Julie manages the tasting room, housed in a spacious building with a wood deck at the top of a grassy hill. Regional, national, and international guests traveling on I-70 stop to learn about and taste some of the nearly two dozen wines available. Behind the tasting room, a slope rises to the summit of a bluff that overlooks the valley.

Bob DesRuisseaux has been making, studying, collecting, and teaching about wine for over twenty-five years. He graduated from the winemaking program of the University of California, Davis, studying enology and viticulture. He founded

Prairie Fire Winery's tasting room near I-70 draws thousands of visitors annually, who sample, purchase, and drink wine on scenic slopes that overlook the Flint Hills. Photo by the author.

the Kansas Wine Institute to foster quality winemaking and grapegrowing education, and to conduct research on grapes and wine specific to Kansas.

A nearby walking trail circles around the bluff lined with native wildflowers. Scores of wine lovers, cross-country travelers, and visitors walk their pets here for the view. DesRuisseaux offered an impromptu lesson on the grapevines—Chambourcin, Cabernet Franc, Vidal, Rougeon, Riesling, Grüner Veltliner, Vignoles, Marquette, Zweigelt, and Noiret. "Chambourcin, our best seller, is the most widely planted grape in Kansas. It's a grape hybrid that originated in Loire, France," said DesRuisseaux.

Grapevines thrive here because of the rich organic soil in the Flint Hills. The network of roots and mineral-rich soil, built on layers of an ancient inland seabed studded with limestone and flint, have proven suitable for certain native and hybrid grapevines that can withstand cold Kansas winters. "Sunlight along the southeast aspect of the slopes helps warm up the vines in winter," DesRuisseaux observed, "and the sun burns off the dew in summer."

Because of the position of the slopes on this land, cold air flows away from rows of vines stitched across the hills. DesRuisseaux said, "It is seven to eight degrees warmer here than the surrounding area. The slopes have good drainage, too." The contours of the land, weather patterns, soil, and the growers' deep knowledge of the grapevine varieties all factor into the quality of the wines produced at Prairie Fire.

Guests enjoy wine outdoors on grassy slopes and also stroll up the bluff to view Prairie Fire's vineyards under the expansive Kansas sky. Photo by the author.

Highlights: Bestsellers include semidry Storm Chaser White and dry red Chambourcin. Lightly floral Vidal Blanc has fruit-forward notes of pineapple, melon, pears, and figs. Rougeon, a French-American hybrid grape, produces a dry red wine with stone fruit and dark cherry aromas and mild tannin. The winery also produces sparkling wines made by *méthode champenoise* such as Vidal Blanc Brut and sweeter Vidal Blanc Doux. Local sausage, cheese, art, and gifts are also available. Guided tours are scheduled on a regular basis, weather depending.

Oz Winery

417 Lincoln Avenue, Wamego, KS 66547
785-456-7417
ozwinerykansas.com

Oz Winery's name comes from the children's novel *The Wonderful Wizard of Oz*. The tasting room and gift shop are based in downtown Wamego. The winery's production space is on-site but hidden from view. Married couple winemaker Noah Wright and pastry chef Brooke Balderson, a Wamego native, co-own the shop.

Forty percent of the grapes used, such as Seyval, Norton, Vignoles, and De Chaunac, are grown in Kansas, with the remainder sourced from New York, California, and other states. The winery annually produces five thousand gallons combined of reds, whites, blush, dessert, limited-edition, and sparkling wines. Private tasting parties are hosted in a separate room. A wine club is also available.

Wamego is home to several bed-and-breakfast operations and motels, making the town a convenient spot for a weekend getaway to shop, kayak on the Kansas River, visit the Oz Museum, and explore the annual Tulip Festival in April.

Highlights: Tastings (free) include samples of two wines. Wine flights include three or five wines. Bestsellers include Fraidy Cat Moscato and Squished Witch, a semisweet red. The minerality of Poppy Fields Pinot Gris is softened by honeysuckle notes. Wicked Deeds, a floral Riesling, blossoms with Golden Delicious

Travelers interested in The Wonderful Wizard of Oz *(and Kansas wine) will delight in this Oz-themed winery and tasting room. While in Wamego, visit the Oz Museum. Photo by the author.*

apple notes and finishes with a crisp mineral bite. Flying Monkey, a spicy Zinfandel with raspberry and vanilla nose, and the jammy Angry Trees, made from Chambourcin, demonstrate the wide range available. Colorful labels featuring Oz-related artwork add to the appeal for Oz collectors.

Tallgrass Brewing Company

5960 Dry Hop Circle, Manhattan, KS 66503
785-537-1131
tallgrassbeer.com

Brewery tours (limited to fifteen people per group; first come, first serve) are available on select Saturdays. Contact the brewery in advance for tour dates. A guided tour (ages twenty-one and up) includes a souvenir glass and five 4-ounce beer samples.

Tallgrass Tap House

320 Poyntz Avenue, Manhattan, KS 66502
785-320-2933
tallgrasstaphouse.com

Tallgrass founder Jeff Gill, an avid homebrewer and former geologist, made a decisive commitment in response to a question from his wife, Tricia. In April 2006, Tricia asked her husband, "What do you want to do with the rest of your life?" Jeff wanted to open a microbrewery.

In early 2007, they established Tallgrass Brewing Company in Manhattan, Kansas. They wanted to settle and raise a family in the Flint Hills surrounded by the Tallgrass Prairie. The area's water quality was also highly suitable for brewing beer. The initial brewery was built on Green Valley Road. The original copper-clad brewhouse arrived in June 2007, and the first beer (pub ale) was brewed in August 2007 in time for a grand opening celebration.

Tallgrass declared its "Canifesto" in 2010 and began packaging its beers exclusively in cans instead of bottles. Not only was the shift environmentally responsible, it saved the company money on shipping costs. Canned beer is also a more portable, lighter-weight package for consumers. Sales skyrocketed. The company's original brewery reached its brewing capacity in 2013 at sixteen thousand barrels per year.

In early 2015 Tallgrass moved into its newly built, $7 million, sixty-

Tallgrass Brewing Company, the largest craft brewer in Kansas, is a must-visit tour destination for craft beer fans. The $7 million, sixty-thousand-square-foot brewery, built in 2015, quadrupled its capacity. Courtesy of Tallgrass Brewing Company.

thousand-square-foot brewery, quadrupling its capacity as the state's largest craft brewer. The brewery features a four-vessel, automated fifty-barrel brewhouse and three thousand square feet dedicated to developing a barrel-aging program. The brewery's annual production capacity is one hundred thousand barrels. Brewmaster Greg Papp oversees production of nearly thirty thousand barrels per year. Tallgrass Brewing distributes in seventeen states.

The brewery built Tallgrass Tap House, an eleven-thousand-square-foot brewpub, to foster craft beer culture in downtown Manhattan. The brewpub has 285 seats, including room for 75 people on the rooftop deck overlooking downtown. Head brewer Chris Chalmers oversees the ten-barrel brewhouse. The brewpub offers a full selection of upscale pub food for lunch and dinner. The Tap House was named the 2016 Best Beer Bar in Kansas by the Brewers Association and CraftBeer.com.

Firkin Fridays take place on the first Friday of each month at 6 p.m., when the brewery taps a new firkin release. A firkin is a cask beer with flavors added and then aged for a few weeks before tapping.

Highlights: The website lists current beers on tap. Year-round favorites include 8-Bit American pale ale, Buffalo Sweat oatmeal cream stout, Zombie Monkie ro-

Tallgrass Taphouse, a popular spot for dining and exploring brewpub-only beer releases, was named the 2016 Best Beer Bar in Kansas by the Brewers Association and CraftBeer.com. Photo by the author.

bust porter, Moro St. Wheat, and Top Rope IPA, an American IPA. Ask about beers available in the Explorer Series.

Little Apple Brewing Company

West Loop Shopping Center, 1110 Westloop Place, Manhattan, KS 66502
785-539-5500
littleapplebrewery.com

Established in 1995, the Little Apple Brewing Company, a high-volume steak-house and brewery, adopts the nickname of Manhattan, Kansas. The "Little Apple" refers to the Manhattan borough of New York City and the city's moniker as the Big Apple. The brewery, also known as LABCo for short, is located away from Kansas State University's collegiate crowd in Aggieville and downtown.

Kelly Loub and chef Russ Loub built Little Apple Brewing into a hub for the community, where regulars and newcomers indulge in easy-drinking beer, USDA Prime steaks, farm-to-market specials, and lively conversation. Photo by the author.

Regular customers include regional travelers, local professionals, residents, and families.

Little Apple is primarily operated by Kelly Loub and chef Russ Loub, who was trained at Johnson and Wales University. The Loubs share ownership with cattle breeders Galen and Lori Fin. Taking a farm-to-fork culinary approach, chef Loub shops at the weekly farmers' market for regional produce to complement premium meat and seafood entrées and specials on the menu. The restaurant is known for its USDA Prime-certified Angus beef aged thirty days and for its hearty pub food.

The brewery shows appreciation for its dedicated patrons with fun events and recognition programs. Irishman Peter Gavigan was the 2014 Beer Drinker of the Year. Customers submit an application for the annual honor and the chance to earn a free weekly growler for a year. To win, Gavigan advised, "You have to suck up to the judges." Retired biology professor and homebrewer Spencer Tomb was the first member of LABCo's Mug Club. He also earned the honor of being inducted into Little Apple's Beer Drinker Hall of Fame and was the first honorary Beer Drinker of the Year. Tomb also inspired a turn of phrase at the brewpub. A "Spencer" refers to an extra partial beer pour into your glass on the house to "keep the conversation going" when patrons aren't ready to leave just yet. At the bartender's discretion, a Spencer might arrive if you're blessed with the gift of gab and the stars are aligned. Oktoberfest and Saint Patrick's Day are lively times to join in festivities, but there's no need to wait for seasonal events. Any trip to Manhattan is a good reason to visit Little Apple Brewing.

Highlights: A single five-ounce taster costs $1.50. A flight ($7) includes seven tasters. XX Black Angus Stout uses six malts and Pacific Northwest hops to produce a rich, creamy flavor with roasted notes. Bestselling Wildcat Wheat Ale, light and slightly sweet, blends domestic malted barley and white wheat with American hops for a refreshing sipper. Amber-colored Riley's Red Ale, named after Fort Riley, nicely balances malt and hops with a slight bite on the finish. Malty, caramel flavor defines the Bison Brown Ale.

Travel tip: The luxurious, reasonably priced Bluemont Hotel (1212 Bluemont Avenue, Manhattan; bluemonthotel.com) is conveniently located near downtown along with several hotels, motels, and bed-and-breakfast options. Other top local eateries include Bourbon and Baker, Harry's, 4 Olives Wine Bar, and historic breakfast café The Chef.

Blue Skye Brewery and Eats

116 North Santa Fe Avenue, Salina, KS 67401
785-404-2159
blueskyebrewery.com

Blue Skye Brewery owner Monte Shadwick sought to create a pub on historic Santa Fe Avenue in Salina where friends and neighbors could gather. He recruited homebrewer John Goertzen, a rugged firefighter for more than two decades, as head brewer. Lt. Goertzen juggles time between his service at Fire Station 1, brewing at Blue Skye, and parenting his three children.

The brewery occupies the former fifty-one-year-old Anderson's Leather retail shop, which closed in May 2008 after a devastating fire. The renovated space includes the brewhouse, dining room, main bar, wood-fired pizza oven, and kitchen. The seven-barrel brewhouse produces 350 barrels annually with distribution around Salina as well as Lawrence to the east and McPherson to the

Salina residents and tourists gather at Blue Skye Brewing for its wood-fired pizza, brewpub fare, and beers like Fire Engine Red Irish Ale. Photo by the author.

south. Blue Skye is packed with diners and fans of local beer on a regular basis. The menu of pizzas, salads, burgers, appetizers, fish tacos, and fish and chips pairs easily with the selection of beers.

When ordering a Mugler's Revenge IPA at Blue Skye, raise a glass to the beer's namesake, brewer Peter Mugler, and his independent spirit. Mugler, an immigrant from Alsace, France, became a legal US resident in Kansas in the late 1800s. With support from the US Brewers' Association, Mugler challenged the state of Kansas in a lawsuit regarding a state's right to close down a brewery if the state government felt it would prevent injury from use of its product.

Previously, the people in Kansas had adopted the following article to the state's constitution on November 2, 1880: "The manufacture and sale of intoxicating liquors shall be forever prohibited in this State, except for medical, scientific, and mechanical purposes." The statute went into effect in May 1881. It reinforced a moral and legal shift in Kansas toward local temperance laws and state prohibition of alcohol that had been building since the 1850s.

Mugler spent $10,000 in 1877 to construct a brewery on Third Street in Salina and began to manufacture and distribute beer. He continued to make and sell beer in 1881 without a permit after the liquor ban. Multiple charges were brought against him and he was indicted in November 1881. Mugler's attorney argued against the state's authority "to prohibit the manufacture of intoxicating liquors for personal use or for the purpose of export." A second argument protested the devaluation—from $10,000 to $2,500—of Mugler's building, which had been designed specifically for brewing and was unsuited for other uses. The case progressed from the Supreme Court of Kansas to the US Supreme Court and ended in a decision against Mugler in 1887.

The monumental ruling affirmed the state's police power to enforce legislation dealing with the state's health, morals, and safety of its population, and the state's powers of eminent domain over private property. Not only did Mugler lose his enterprise, the legal decision prompted other Kansas alcohol manufacturers to close, switch to other operations, or establish breweries in Missouri. The state's prohibition on alcohol wouldn't be amended for more than a century.

Modern brewers and fans of craft beer know that brewing is a boon for the local economy and social development of community. Generations later, Peter Mugler deserves a toast for his efforts to uphold individual liberty and economic opportunity. While you're at it, toast John Goertzen and fellow brewers for breathing new life into locally brewed beer.

Head brewer and local firefighter John Goertzen uses Kansas-grown wheat when brewing each style of Blue Skye beer as a nod to Kansas farmers. Photo by the author.

Highlights: Bestselling Fire Engine Red, an Irish ale with red hue, is a tribute to firefighters everywhere. Golden-colored and light-bodied with mild maltiness, B-17 Blonde is named after the first Air Force bomber to be based at Salina's Smoky Hill Army Field. Dirty Ol' Stout is a light creamy oatmeal stout with dark coffee and chocolate notes. A portion of Kansas-grown wheat is used in every Blue Skye beer, a nod to wheat farmers in the state.

Visit Salina

Salina is home to the Rolling Hills Zoo, which has a rare white camel and more than a hundred wildlife species; the Smoky Hill Museum; and the Eisenhower Presidential Library and Museum. Before leaving town, pop over to the six-seat counter at the Cozy Inn, established in 1922, and order a dozen Cozies. These onion-laden sliders are similar to White Castle's, which was founded in Wichita in 1921, and are cooked on the same cast-iron grill that has been in use since the restaurant opened.

Smoky Hill Vineyards and Winery

2771 Centennial Road, Salina, KS 67401
785-825-8466
kansaswine.com

Smoky Hill Vineyards' original owners in 1991 were two world-traveling engineers who had retired and opened the winery. By 2009 it had become one of the largest grape-producing wineries in Kansas. After one owner retired, the remaining owner operated Smoky Hill with his son until they sold the operation in 2013 to current owner George Plante. Plante learned the recipes, acquired the trademark and equipment, and built a tasting room and winery in its current location. The tasting room is a modest space with wines and medals on display.

The winery's large refrigerated rooms, similar to a wine cellar, store pressed juice from various grape harvests between twenty-eight to fifty-four degrees. Plante describes the space as a "grape grain elevator" that enables him to store raw juice for up to one year and "make wine as needed." Grapes are sourced from the original three-acre estate north of Salina, eight acres in the city, and three acres in nearby Lindsborg, Kansas. Plante plans to develop another twenty acres for grape growing.

George Plante displays a few of Smoky Hill Winery's award-winning wines sold at more than four hundred liquor stores across Kansas. Photo by the author.

Winery manager Bart Hettenbach and Plante's son-in-law Brock Ebert oversee the winery's operations. Smoky Hill's wines are sold at more than four hundred of the seven hundred liquor stores across Kansas and online via vinoshipper.com.

Highlights: Heartland Red Velvet is a new dry red blend made with Noiret, Norton, and Chambourcin that isn't overly tannic. The Noiret took first place in the 2016 Finger Lakes International Wine Competition. River Valley Red, a rich sweet wine made from Concord grapes, is ruby in color and pairs well with burgers, brats, light cheese, and fruit. Top-selling Sweet Lady, a white wine made from Catawba, is light-bodied and floral. The popular Christmas wine is a seasonal semisweet blend. The winery sells seven thousand bottles of the Christmas wine annually. Premium Auslese, a German-style late harvest semisweet white wine, is a nod to the German roots of the wife of the winery's founder.

Travel tip: From Lawrence/Kansas City, take I-70 West to exit 250A. Merge onto I-135 South/US 81 South. Take exit 90 for Magnolia Road. Turn right on

Magnolia Road. Turn left on South Centennial Road. Look for tan storage buildings with dark green roofs. The winery and tasting room is the building on the end with a gravel drive.

Three Rings Brewery

536 South Old US 81, McPherson, KS 67460
620-504-5022
threeringsbrewery.com

Owners and brewers Ian Smith and his father, Brian Smith, founded Three Rings Brewery in June 2016 inside of a former car detail shop in McPherson, roughly forty minutes due south of Salina. The brewery's name is an homage to a beer stein owned by famous German theologian and Protestant reformer Martin Luther. According to legend, the stein had three rings around it that Luther said stood for the Ten Commandments, the Creed, and the Lord's Prayer.

Three Rings Brewery taps into the roots of the owners' family's brewing tradition dating back more than five hundred years. The Smith family completed some genealogical research during the brewery's planning stages. Ian's twelfth great-grandfather Berend Brauer was a brewmaster in Einbeck, Germany, during the early 1500s. Einbeck was known for its "bock" style of beer. Brewed since 1325 and considered the most famous beer of the Middle Ages, Einbeck bock was widely available throughout Germany.

"Our grandfathers were involved in the development of this beer style," said Brian. The German surname Brauer translates to *brewer*. "The family's brewing history goes back even before the year 1500 at least one generation, and possibly many more." Historical records show that Martin Luther's favorite beer style was Einbeck. Luther had a cask of it at his wedding, provided by Berend Brauer.

"We enjoy the creativity and science in brewing and wanted to pursue that as a career, with the eventual goal of opening a place of our own," said Ian. "We wanted to have beer available to people for good times and bad times. Celebrating life with them every day through our beers." Ian, a homebrewer with a decade of experience, runs the seven-barrel brewhouse. He decided he wanted to open a brewery after visiting the Anheuser-Busch plant in Fort Collins, Colorado. He graduated with a food science degree from Kansas State University in Manhattan. Ian completed part of his summer internship at Boulevard Brewing prior to working at Tallgrass Brewing while earning his degree. Brian, a thirty-plus-year veteran of the bakery and food science industry, is a corporate quality manager for Grain Craft flour mill in Wichita.

Three Rings Brewery taps into the family's German brewing tradition dating back more than five hundred years. Credit: Atelier Design & Print LLC.

Highlights: Taproom visitors are able to sample the beer. Currently, the brewery sells its craft beers by filling kegs and growlers at the taproom, but cannot sell beer by the glass. Flagships include bestselling Yankee Rose Blonde Ale, Misty Mountain Hops Pale Ale, citrusy hop-forward Vertigo IPA, Foggy Dew—a Weizenbock, or wheat-style beer—and Bulldog Stout, with characteristic chocolate-coffee notes. Seasonal release Witch Hunt Oktoberfest uses German hops, malt, and yeast to yield a malty, amber-colored beer for fall. Three Rings's beer is distributed in McPherson, Hutchinson, Salina, Lindsborg, and Abilene. See their website for locations.

Travel tip: Take I-70 to exit 250A and merge onto I-135 South/US 81 South toward Wichita. Proceed 30 miles. Take exit 65 and turn right on Pawnee Road. Turn left onto 14th Avenue/Old US 81. Keep right to continue on Old US 81 South. The brewery is on the west side of McPherson and is located off the road north of the McPherson airport. While in McPherson, grab a bite at local restaurants Marigold's, Woodies BBQ Shack, or Main Street Deli.

Fly Boy Brewery and Eats

105 North Main Street, Sylvan Grove, KS 67481
785-526-7800
facebook.com/Fly-Boy-Brewery-Eats
-404835609680696

Clay Haring, a pilot and homebrewer, and his wife, Linda Haring, a schoolteacher, opened Fly Boy Brewery and Eats in downtown Sylvan Grove in October 2014. In a town with fewer than three hundred people, the microbrewery and restaurant is the heartbeat of the community. The owners know many of the friends, neighbors, and regulars who dine and drink here.

Clay's great-grandfather, a German immigrant, brewed beer in Nebraska until the brewery burned down. Clay revives the family craft at Fly Boy. The building was once a turn-of-the-century hardware store, Sylvan Grove opera house, and Masonic lodge with a basketball court. "The community needed a restaurant, a place to go," said Clay, who dusts crops for a living. "The building was up for sale. We spent six months to restore it and opened up the brewery. We employ high school kids and mothers."

With a lack of local restaurants and even nearby fast food restaurants, Fly Boy is a welcome addition to the town for locals who don't feel like cooking and want to get out of the house. For travelers, it is a cozy spot worth visiting off the interstate. The brewery pulls in customers from Salina, Hays, Wichita, and Great Bend, Kansas.

Best-selling dishes include the P51 Mustang burger, a beef patty topped with beef brisket and American cheese, and served with fries. Besides hearty dishes like the fourteen-ounce ribeye, chef Grant Wagner prepares adventurous specials such as grilled salmon with couscous, pickled cherries, bacon lardons, spinach, and caper sauce. The chocolate chip cookie oven-baked in a skillet and served with vanilla ice cream and chocolate syrup alone is worth the drive.

Highlights: Hotel Oscar Whiskey is a sweetish golden ale brewed with honey and orange. Aviator Ale, Nutty Navigator (a bold peanut butter porter), Barnstormer Brown Ale, and Tailspin IPA are flagships featured on tap. Gear Up Honey Wheat is brewed with German hops. Haring's seasonal fruit beers include summertime Rhubarb Missions, a refreshing rhubarb-raspberry wheat. Lomcevak, a stout bolstered with chocolate and coffee, is named after a daring aerial maneuver in which the aircraft enters a vertical climb, reaches near-zero speed, and begins a series of tumbles. The term comes from a 1958 air show in Brno,

Fly Boy Brewery, established by pilot Clay Haring and his wife, Linda, draws Sylvan Grove residents and travelers with its P51 Mustang burger, beers, and chocolate chip cookie oven-baked in a skillet. Photo by the author.

Czechoslovakia, when journalists asked about Czech aerobatic pilot Ladislav Bezák's aerial tumble maneuver and the mechanic jokingly suggested they were *lomcevaks*, a word that means headache. It's also a Czech slang name for a shot of a strong drink.

Travel tip: From I-70, take exit 209 toward 6th Road. Turn right on 6th Road and proceed north 7.5 miles through serene countryside. Continue on the road for 3.7 miles as it becomes KS 181 North. The road becomes Main Street once you arrive at the outskirts of Sylvan Grove.

Rosewood Wine Cellar

1901 Lakin, Great Bend, KS 67530
620-603-6410
Rosewood Winery
1171 Southwest 20 Road, Pawnee Rock, KS 67567
620-982-4487
rosewoodcreations.com

Executive director Tammy Hammond founded Rosewood Services, an enterprise that includes a ranch, winery, furniture store, greenhouse, arts studio, and wine retail shop, in 1998. Rosewood Services was created to teach work skills and provide employment opportunities to client-employees, or people on staff with developmental disabilities. Rosewood is "the only winery in North America designed and developed to employ individuals with developmental disabilities," said Hammond.

Head winemaker Alex Hammond uses grapes from Rosewood's vineyard and other growers to produce small batches of wine in Pawnee Rock. Employees hand-bottle and label twenty-five thousand bottles annually under the label Rosewood Creations.

Rosewood Winery employs individuals with developmental disabilities. Employees hand-bottle and label twenty-five thousand bottles annually under the label Rosewood Creations. Courtesy of Rosewood Winery.

The Wine Cellar in Great Bend is a rustic, ranch-style retail shop that sells Rosewood Creation's line of more than thirty wines as well as specialty foods and gifts. All products are made by employees and help to sustain employment for people with disabilities. Each wine is named after one of the horses involved in the award-winning equestrian therapy program at Rosewood Ranch.

Highlights: Free tastings (up to three wines) at The Wine Cellar, plus a taste of the award-winning signature wine Boots Made for Walking Blackberry Cabernet Sauvignon. Reds include the dry, medium-oaked Angel with a Gun Amarone, Chicka Star Buck Malbec Bonarda blend, and One Time Jackie, a Black Cherry Pinot Noir. Selections among whites include Boo Koo Shine, a fruity, floral Torrontés; zesty Shining Spark Riesling Chenin Blanc; and Sheza Lady Principle, a peach-apricot Chardonnay that won gold at the 2014 Kansas Grape Growers and Winemakers Association "Taste of Kansas." The wines are also sold in retail locations throughout Kansas.

Travel tip: Rosewood Creations Winery is approximately nine miles west of Great Bend and five miles north of Pawnee Rock. This winery is nearly an hour's drive southbound from I-70. Directions to the Rosewood Wine Cellar retail shop: From I-70, take exit 225 for KS 156 and turn left, heading west toward Ellsworth and Great Bend. Proceed on KS 156 West for 48 miles to US 56 and turn right. Follow US 56 for 3.7 miles to Kansas Avenue and turn right. On Kansas Avenue, turn left on the third cross-street onto Lakin Avenue.

Beaver Brewery at Mo's Place

1908 Elm Street, Beaver, KS 67525
620-587-2350
facebook.com/beaverbrewery

Look for the Beaver Grain Corporation grain elevator in the unincorporated town of Beaver, Kansas. Next to the grain facility is a metal building known as Mo's Place Grill and Brewpub. The original owners, Leonard and Linda Moeder, retired in 2014, and the bar and grill remained closed for more than a year. New owners Dale Kaiser and Austin Bell purchased the business and reopened it in 2016 to the delight of locals within a fifty-mile radius who visit for fresh beer, burgers, and grilled foods.

Burgers are made from meat sourced from the Ellinwood Packing Plant. Try a fried bologna sandwich or signature Tommy Rocket, a grilled six-ounce burger topped with a seared all-beef hot dog, sautéed jalapeño peppers, and American and pepper jack cheeses.

Highlights: Beaver Creek Brown uses three types of malt barley to produce a mildly sweet brown ale. Lights Out Stout is smooth with chocolate notes and a silky finish. Other beers include Elm Street Porter, Crazy Hawk Red Ale, Ol' Farmstead IPA, and seasonal Gun Barrel Java, a Russian imperial stout with coffee added after fermentation.

Travel tip: From I-70 West, take exit 225 for KS 156 toward Ellsworth/Great Bend. Turn onto KS 156 and continue for 25.5 miles. Turn right onto Avenue T and continue 3.8 miles. Turn right onto Northeast 160 Avenue/Northeast 160th Avenue/1st Road. After 3 miles, turn left onto Northeast 190 Road and proceed 10 miles. Turn right on Elm Street.

Volga Germans in Kansas

From 1870 to 1900, approximately one hundred thousand Volga Germans emigrated to Kansas, the Dakotas, and Nebraska. These ethnic Germans once lived along the River Volga in the southeastern region of Russia. Many immigrants settled in and near Hays. One of these, Russian-born Bernhard Warkentin, introduced Turkey Red wheat, a type of hard winter wheat, to Kansas. The wheat prospered and replaced the predominant softer variety of wheat and altered the state's agricultural destiny. The influence of Volga German culture and prominence of wheat as an agricultural product is still evident in the city of Hays and its two breweries.

Gella's Diner and Lb. Brewing Company

117 East 11th Street, Hays, KS 67601
785-621-2739
lbbrewing.com

Gella's Diner draws its name from the Volga German heritage of the immigrant community in Kansas that traces back to the late nineteenth century. Rather than a name, *Gella* is a Volga German term that means "you know" or "don't

Lb. Brewing Company's name refers to "liquid bread," or beer, the sustenance that Volga German field workers once drank when they couldn't stop working to eat bread for lunch. Photo by the author.

you agree?" Used at the end of a statement, the word is intended to ensure the listener agrees. Agreement and understanding in conversation is helpful when building social bonds. It makes sense that this powerful German word identifies this Kansas diner, where people dine, converse, and bond over food and beer.

The diner alone is a worthwhile destination, with a wide variety of brewpub soups, salads, sandwiches, and entrées such as ribeye and fried chicken. Volga German influences are upheld in its sauerkraut soup and smothered bierrock—bread dough stuffed with seasoned beef, cabbage, sauerkraut, and cheddar cheese, baked, and smothered in a creamy cheese sauce. Lb. Brewing Company operates within the diner. Its name is a reference to "liquid bread," or beer. When settlers and farmers didn't have time to interrupt work and eat lunch with bread, sometimes they drank nutritious, refreshing beer made from Kansas wheat.

Backed by fifty-three local investors, Gerald Wyman, a former homebrewer and cattle rancher, and Chuck Comeau, a successful furniture designer and real estate developer, opened the microbrewery and diner in 2005. Since then the brewery has won numerous awards for beers based on Wyman's beer recipes at the Great American Beer Fest (GABF). In 2013, the brewery and Wyman were named Small Brewpub and Small Brewpub Brewer of the Year at the twenty-seventh annual GABF, the first Kansas brewery to receive the honor.

Highlights: Ten house brews are on tap seven days a week. American Hefeweizen, an American-style wheat beer with yeast and floral flavor, won a 2013 GABF gold medal and GABF medals in 2008 and 2012. Grapefruit Radler's blend of American pale ale infused with zesty citrus and Cascade hops is refreshing in hot weather. Seasonals include malty Oktoberfest Lager; Winterfest Ale, made with warm winter spices; Christmas Ale, a brown ale made with fermented honey and cinnamon; and crisp, citrusy German-style Kölsch. The $6.50 sampler includes eight 4-ounce pours of your choice. Growlers (32 ounces and 64 ounces) of beer, handcrafted root beer, and cream soda are available. Check the website for current beers on tap.

Defiance Brewing Company

2050 East 8th Street/Old Highway 40, Hays, KS 67601
785-301-2337
defiancebeer.com

Numerous craft breweries have opened and thrived to the west of Hays in Colorado, and to the east in Lawrence, Manhattan, and Kansas City. Defiance Brewing Company founders Matt Bender, brewmaster Dylan Sultzer, and Kenny Gottschalk founded the brewery here in part because of the city's location. "People don't associate western Kansas with beer," said Bender. "We're the only production brewery in this part of the state."

The lack of competition was an opportunity to be first to market as a local brewery, and presented a clean slate to help shape the taste for craft beer in Hays. "Our taproom is a playground for different beer styles," says Sultzer. "It helps to educate people and build a craft beer culture."

As millennials, Bender, Sultzer, and Gottschalk chose the brewery's name to signal an intention to follow their own path. Bender said, "As a company, we're youthful and whimsical but we take beer styles seriously." "We like to have fun," said Sultzer. "We're the younger side of the brewing generation." The vibrant, edgy design of the brewery's cans reflects Defiance's irreverence and youthful energy. Artist John Stadler creates the colorful artwork that illustrates the spirit of each beer's name.

Defiance Brewing cofounders Kenny Gottschalk, Matt Bender, and Dylan Sultzer brought locally made craft beer to western Kansas. Photo by the author.

Brewer Jared Englert and brewer/ambassador Travis Reynolds assist with managing brewhouse operations. Designed as a twenty-barrel production brewery for distribution, Defiance began producing beer in December 2013 and commenced shipping beer to market the next month in western Kansas and Wichita. The brewery's beer is distributed throughout Kansas and Nebraska, most of Missouri, and parts of Pennsylvania.

Highlights: Tours are available on Saturdays by appointment. In the taproom, guests can choose from ten to twelve selections that include year-round flagships and brewery-only experimental beers, such as Pie Face Winter Warmer and Francy Pants Rhubarb Sour. Some styles are sold in 750-milliliter bottles available only at the taproom. Best-selling beers include Thrasher, a year-round session IPA with notes of apricot, citrus, and tropical fruit, and Gutch, a malty English mild red amber ale with hints of hazelnut and toffee that finishes with citrus and spice. Fuzzy Knuckles, an imperial stout brewed with cacao nibs and locally sourced Union Station coffee, is full-bodied and robust. Distinct floral and spice notes emerge from Origami Spaceship, a seasonal Belgian-style saison balanced by the bite of hops.

Shiloh Vineyard and Winery

16079 M Road, WaKeeney, KS 67672
785-743-2152
shilohvineyard.com

Wheat farmers Treva and Kirk Johnston planted their first vines in 2008 and in the same year founded the Shiloh Vineyard and Winery on their family farm, which dates back to the 1920s. The tasting room is actually a restored chicken coop from that era. A barn has been converted into an event space for weddings and other gatherings. Initially, the plan was to plant and grow five acres of grapes and sell them to another winery three years later. When the winery client folded

Farmers Treva and Kirk Johnston transformed their 1920s-era family farm into a vineyard, winery, and event space graced by the natural beauty of Kansas. Courtesy of Shiloh Vineyard and Winery.

its business after two years, the Johnstons decided to produce and sell wine made from its grapes themselves.

Kirk's degree in agronomy from Kansas State University and years of farming experience proved helpful in the transition to grapegrowing and winemaking. After the initial planting of Vidal Blanc and Norton grapes, the vineyard is now also stocked with Noiret, Chambourcin, Brianna, and Petite Pearl.

Highlights: Dry whites include Brianna, a crisp wine with pineapple aroma and flavor. Vidal Blanc is dry with balanced fruit and acidity. Aromatic notes and tastes of apricot and nectarines are followed by hints of lemon and tangerine. The winery offers semisweet versions of both wines. Old Barn is a rich dry red wine lush with black currants and cherries and spiced with notes of black pepper and toasted oak. Noiret's refined character reveals distinct black pepper with moderate tannins and hints of raspberry, blackberry, and mint. Sweet fruit wines include apple, peach, and plum. The apple wine uses fruit direct from Shiloh's orchard.

Travel tip: From I-70, take exit 127 toward US 283/US 40 WaKeeney/Ness City. Turn left on US 283 and follow four miles to M Road. Turn right on M Road.

CHAPTER 3

SOUTHEASTERN KANSAS, I-35 SOUTH TO US 69 SOUTH

Overland Park, the second-largest city in Kansas after Wichita, anchors the north end of this route. Downtown Overland Park provides a natural starting point to sample wine at Aubrey Vineyards Tasting Room and then eat and drink at local restaurants before heading south on US 69 into the countryside.

Aubrey Vineyards Tasting Room and Outlet Store

7932 Santa Fe Drive, Overland Park, KS 66204
913-909-2926
aubreyvineyards.com

Though closed to the public, Aubrey Vineyards is located along Kenneth Road in southern Overland Park near Loch Lloyd. The owners acquired two hundred acres of surrounding farmland in 2010 and planted 3,100 grapevines on five acres two years later. Steady breezes and slopes of fertile, loamy, well-drained soil with low clay content offered prime conditions for growing. The vineyard more than doubled in size with additional plantings. The first harvest commenced in fall of 2015. Cabernet Sauvignon and Chardonnay grapes are sourced from Lake

Aubrey Vineyards's tasting room and outlet store is located inside Vinyl Renaissance & Audio. Guests may sample and purchase wines, including several Jefferson Cup Award winners. Photo by the author.

County, California, shipped by refrigerated truck, and pressed and fermented in Overland Park.

The vineyard is named after Aubrey Township, which likely derived its moniker from François Xavier Aubry, a famous French Canadian trail merchant and explorer. The winery's tasting room and outlet store is inside Vinyl Renaissance & Audio, a record store in downtown Overland Park. The shop offers free tastings and sales by the bottle.

Highlights: Oaky, robust Cabernet Sauvignon, spicy and dry Chambourcin, a dry floral Chambourcin rosé, the floral honey notes of Trail Rider White, semidry and foxy Catawba, crisp citrus flavors of Vidal Blanc, and balanced acidity of Traminette with kiwi, honeydew, and starfruit flavors. The 2013 Chambourcin, Chambourcin Rosé, and Trail Rider White earned silver at the 2015 Jefferson Cup.

Brew Lab

7925 Marty Lane, Overland Park, KS 66204
913-400-2343
brewlabkc.com

Brew Lab opened in 2013 as a homebrew supply store and brew-on-premises retail shop. The business was founded by Clay Johnston, Justin Waters, Kevin Combs, and Matthew Hornung. For a fee, homebrewers and first-timers can learn the fundamentals of brewing, use ingredients in stock, and produce a beer with guidance from a brewer on staff. In 2016, the business announced an expansion that included a brewery, taproom, and gastropub kitchen. Brew Lab relocated (from 8004 Foster Street) to a larger retail space two blocks away in downtown Overland Park near the farmers' market.

The brewery opened in 2017 with a three-barrel system that produces beer under the Brew Lab brand. Brew Lab's taproom has nearly two dozen taps that feature their house flagship beers, experimental beers, and guest beers from other breweries. As a special feature, a tap is dedicated to serving a beer on rotation from a homebrewer that has scaled up their recipe. The homebrewed beer tap spotlights the name of the brewer and beer name.

Brew Lab continues to operate as a homebrew supply store and brew-on-premises retail shop. Customers may eat, drink beer, and watch beer being brewed in a craft beer setting. If inspired, they can learn how to brew beer as well.

White Wind Winery and Vineyard

20000 West 47th Street, Shawnee, KS 66218
913-294-4900
whitewindwines.com

Established in 2010, White Wind Winery and Vineyard is a small-production, 1.5-acre winery that does not have a tasting room. Vintner Gilbert Hermes does sell directly to the public via his website and at the Overland Park Farmers' Market (7950 Marty Street) on Saturdays (April–November). Contact the winery to confirm appearances.

Highlights: Bandit Red, a semisweet red with raspberry and cherry flavors, is a strong seller among White Wind's five wines. Mischievous is a semisweet white with melon and citrus notes.

Somerset Ridge Vineyard and Winery

29725 Somerset Road, Paola, KS 66071
913-294-9646
somersetridge.com

Somerset Ridge founders Dennis and Cindy Reynolds saw potential in the limestone ridge that rises along the Miami County property once owned by Dennis's parents. As trailblazing Kansans, the Reynoldses launched Somerset Ridge as the first winery in the county since statewide prohibition was implemented in 1881. Since then, a cluster of new wineries have emerged in this historically vibrant winemaking region now known as the Somerset Wine Trail.

Planting at Somerset Ridge began in 1998, and the winery was established three years later. Somerset Ridge acquired the property next door in 2005 and expanded operations. To date, the winery encompasses more than forty acres and is home to more than eight thousand grapevines and thirteen varieties. The winery produces more than six thousand cases annually, making it one of the largest producers in Kansas. Sustainability is important to these pioneers and stewards of the land. No pesticides or synthetic fertilizers are used in production.

Somerset Ridge Vineyard and Winery's tasting room in Paola, Kansas, is a popular destination to sample, purchase, and enjoy wine and locally produced goods. Photo by the author.

During warm weather months, guests gather at Somerset Ridge to enjoy wine in the courtyard near the vineyards with live music and an on-site food truck. Photo by the author.

Somerset Ridge's wines are produced from three types of *Vitis vinifera*—Cabernet Sauvignon, Cabernet Franc, and Chardonnay—as well as native Norton and hybrids such as Chambourcin and Marquette, a descendant of Pinot Noir. White grape varieties include Chardonel, Traminette, and La Crescent, a hybrid from the University of Minnesota known as the "Riesling of the Midwest."

A trip to the tasting room is a delightful escapade. Live musicians and local food trucks such as El Tenedor make appearances on weekends during warmer months. An outdoor courtyard and patio provides a charming setting for lunch with a date.

Highlights: Ruby Red is a Bordeaux-style Meritage blend of estate-grown Cabernet Franc and other red grapes. Aged in American oak barrels, this gold medal winner and Jefferson Cup finalist is loaded with complex raspberry and blackcurrant fruit. Citron, a dessert wine, emulates limoncello as a blend of white wine, brandy, and organic lemon for a refreshing citrus sipper. Other bestsellers include Aphrodite, a crisp, dry French-style rosé; Flyboy Red, their soft-bodied dry red from Cabernet Franc and Marquette finished in stainless steel; Buffalo Red, a semisweet red wine that tastes like a fruity glass of sangria; and Oktoberfest, winner of the national 2010 Jefferson Cup.

Travel tip: Follow I-35 South to US 69 South/Overland Parkway. Continue on US 69 South to KS 68 West exit toward Louisburg. Turn right on KS 68 West, proceed 3.9 miles, turn left on Somerset Road, and continue straight for 2.3 miles.

Somerset Wine Trail and Louisburg Cider

The Somerset Wine Trail includes Somerset Ridge Vineyard and Winery, Night-Hawk Vineyard and Winery, and Middle Creek Winery. The Miami County Trolley (miamicountytrolley.com, 913-306-3388, $20/person) travels to these wineries on its route. Contact the trolley for pickup and dropoff points, which include local bed-and-breakfast operations at Casa Somerset and Canaan Oaks. Stop at nearby Louisburg Cider Mill (louisburgcidermill.com) for fresh cider, dry goods, and edible provisions.

NightHawk Vineyard and Winery

16381 West 343rd Street, Paola, KS 66071
913-849-3415
nighthawkwines.com

As part of the Somerset Wine Trail, NightHawk is a scenic stop in a century-old walnut grove. The tasting room is a popular destination for wine lovers, bridal parties, and anyone on a weekend outing. The winery has seating on the outdoor patio and grounds under shade trees. Local musicians such as guitarist Dan Bliss perform on the weekends.

Owners Don and Cathy Warring built a 1,700-square-foot straw bale home on the property with help from friends and neighbors. The five-acre vineyard is supplemented by Kansas-grown grapes. Don handles vineyard duties as viticulturist and grower. Cathy, the vintner, also oversees tasting room operations.

"Wineries in Kansas only began to come back in the early 1990s," said Don. "It takes twenty-five years to figure out what grows well here with limestone and

NightHawk Vineyard and Winery, part of the Somerset Wine Trail, entices guests to relax with a glass and bottle of wine on the winery's landscaped grounds after a tasting room visit. Photo by the author.

clay soil, humidity, and heat. Compared to California, it is difficult to grow grapes here because of weather, insects, and fungus. You have to have passion for it. Kansas winemakers and growers are a great group of people."

Highlights: At the 2013 Kansas Grape Growers and Winemakers Association Conference, Sunrise Blush, made with Frontenac grapes, earned a "Best in Class" award. Chambourcin won Kansas Wine of the Year at the conference. Melody is a white grape with a floral bouquet. Baco Noir is a Chianti-like, medium-bodied red available as a semisweet and dry wine.

Travel tip: If driving from US 69, take the 359th Street exit west for approximately five miles. Turn right on Somerset Road and go north for two miles to 343rd Street. Turn left and go west a quarter mile. If proceeding from Somerset Ridge Winery, then turn left out of the parking lot. Go straight south on Somerset Road for five miles. Turn right at 343rd Street. The winery is a quarter mile west on the south side of 343rd.

Middle Creek Winery/ Graue Vineyards

New Lancaster General Store and Winery
36688 New Lancaster Road, Paola, KS 66053
913-377-4689
middlecreekwinery.com
newlancastergeneralstore.com

Native Kansans Stephen and Kristin Graue and their daughter Ann are kind, industrious people with a natural knack for hospitality. On my visit, Kristin poured samples of a sangria-style wine slushie—a welcome offering in blazing summer heat—and peppered conversation with notes about their properties.

In 1994 the Graues acquired land in Louisburg with an old horse barn and abandoned vineyard. By 2010 they had converted the barn and land into Middle

Stephen and Kristin Graue of Middle Creek Winery established their tasting room in the New Lancaster General Store. The building dates back to 1874 and is listed on the National Register of Historic Places. Photo by the author.

Creek Winery, planted what would grow to be 2,600 vines, begun production of more than a half dozen wines, and opened the winery to the public. Now they produce up to eight thousand bottles of wine annually from Kansas-grown grapes, honey, and fruits. An old sorghum press and remnants of peach orchards are still on the property.

The original vineyard on the 1850s-era homestead was made with hedge posts. The Graues installed taller posts to facilitate vine growth. They learned about winemaking processes from agricultural programs offered by the University of Missouri and Kansas State University. In recent years, they reduced public access to Middle Creek Winery. In 2012 they bought the historic New Lancaster General Store in Paola, restored it, and reopened the retail store in 2014.

Listed on the National Register of Historic Places, the general store was originally built in 1874 and has housed a post office, a creamery, and a telephone office. It was once a gathering place for the Kansas Anti Horse Thief Association and a place for farmers to bring in their produce and eggs. Now visitors from the area and tourists pop into the tasting room and general store for local foods, arts, and crafts.

The Graues produce wines from Chardonel, Vignoles, Cayuga, Saint Pepin, Muscat, Orange Muscat, Norton, Chambourcin, and Traminette grapes. The winery also produces wine from Kansas apples and peaches.

Highlights: Cheyenne Red is a bestselling semisweet blend. Made from peaches sourced from Middle Creek and Sunflower Orchard in Miami County, the seasonal sweet peach wine earned a gold medal from the Kansas Grape Growers and Winemakers Association. Semidry Noiret has notes of pepper and earth, plus tannin from oak aging. Norton undergoes a secondary fermentation that produces a softer taste than the typically foxy native wine. Made primarily from Chardonel grapes, Sunflower White is a dry oak-barrel-aged wine with the color of hay. Peach and sangria wine slushies are a surefire way to beat the Kansas heat.

Miami Creek Brewing Company

**14226 Northwest County Road 14001,
Drexel, MO 64742**
816-892-0297
miamicreek.com

Homebrewer Will Reece and his wife, Chrissy, opened Miami Creek Brewing in late 2016 on the family farm, split between ten-acre and eleven-acre plots. Will

Will Reece of Miami Creek Brewing produces small-batch beer and cider using fruit, herbs, and wild hops grown on his Drexel, Missouri, farm near Miami Creek. Photo by the author.

produces small-batch artisan beer and cider using seasonal local produce as available. He has planted thirty varieties of apples, plus plum, pear, peach, apricot, and nectarine trees. Blackberries, fresh herbs, and wild hops grow on the land nestled next to a stretch of Miami Creek.

Will also operates a small on-site coffee roasting business that fulfills orders through coffee subscriptions. A farmer in Kona, Hawaii, handpicks green coffee beans and ships them to the Miami Creek farm, where Will roasts them and ships orders to customers.

Miami Creek Brewing's rich pantry of raw ingredients is incorporated into its beers. Will and assistant brewer Carl Jacobaus produce batches on a one-barrel and a seven-barrel system in the brewhouse. The brewhouse and tasting room, located in a metal barn on a concrete pad, is surrounded by serene farm acreage on the southern edge of Drexel in Bates County.

Highlights: Beer flights and growlers are available. Year-round beers include Royal Honey Pale Ale, made with local Cooper's honey, and Kona Coffee Stout. Rotating seasonal beers include Lemon Thyme Saison; Lavender Saison, with heady floral notes; Bramble Blackberry Barleywine; Hot Pepper Ale; and Harvest

Cider, a blend of barleywine and apples. The Nutty Belgian, a Belgian Tripel, uses walnut syrup tapped from trees on the farm instead of traditional candy sugar.

Travel tip: From Kansas City, take US 69 South to 359th Street exit and turn left. Head four miles, turn right onto State Line Road, and turn left on Northwest 16002 Road. Continue on gravel road for 1.3 miles as it bends right and becomes Rural Route 1. GPS guidance is recommended.

Isinglass Estate Winery

16241 West 381st Street, LaCygne, KS 66040
913-226-2287
isinglassestate.com

"Isinglass Estate is a nearly six-hundred-acre piece of heaven," said Sarah Vore, who co-owns the property with her husband, Brandon. "We have thirty acres of vineyards, a full-production winery, a tasting room that opened in October 2016, guest house, cottages, stables with ten horses, and miles of wooded trails and lakes to explore."

The name Isinglass harkens back to the farm of Sarah's grandfather on Isinglass Road in Huntington, Connecticut. Sarah added, "Isinglass is the name of a horse who won the British equivalent of the US Triple Crown in the early twentieth century. Isinglass is also a fining agent used for many years to clarify white wines."

Around 2004, the property's previous owner steadily planted grapes each year. Currently, Isinglass grows Zinfandel, Riesling, Marquette, La Crescent, Brianna, Viognier, Frontenac, and Frontenac Gris grapes. Vineyard steward Alejandro Mendoza has worked the vineyard for more than ten years, since the first vine was planted. "He manages a team of additional staff to care for the vines, manage the horses, maintain the trails, operate the winery, and oversee the entire property," said Sarah. "His abundant talents are botanical, technical, and mechanical. He is the heart and soul of our estate."

The winery began wine development in late 2016. Look for single varieties and blends of reds and whites with its releases. "We have partnered with former Kansas City Chiefs wide receiver Eddie Kennison to take advantage of his incredible knowledge of wine, and his palate in our production facility," said Sarah. "We stock local foods, and items in our tasting room. We encourage a 'stay for the day because we are all old friends, anyway' atmosphere."

Team Isinglass consists of owners Brandon Vore and Sarah Vore (not pictured), vineyard steward Alejandro Mendoza (second from right), and vineyard workers. Courtesy of Isinglass Estate Winery.

Travel tip: From US 69 South, take the 359th Street exit. Turn right onto West 359th Street. Proceed 4.5 miles. Turn left onto Somerset Road, which becomes West 375th Street. Make a slight left onto Somerset Road. Turn right onto West 381st Street.

Jolly Fox Brewery

110 North Walnut, Pittsburg, KS 66762
620-875-6568
facebook.com/The-Jolly-Fox-Brewery

Joel Stewart, a twenty-year homebrewing veteran, opened Jolly Fox for business in 2017. The brewery has a tasting room and patio with rotating food trucks available on weeknights. Guests are invited to gather and spin tall tales and long-winded stories over a beer in a relaxed environment. Stewart brews Irish, Scottish, and English ales because "the calcium carbonate and minerals in Pittsburg's well water favors those beer styles."

Highlights: King Me Dark Scottish Ale; Zellekin Cream Ale, named after a pre-Prohibition brewery in Baxter Springs, Kansas; lemon-dill Foxxy IPA, with a solid malt base; and Lucky Streak Pale Ale, named for the local casino, with hints of Sauvignon Blanc notes from the hops. Stewart also brews saisons, pale ales, and IPAs. His sister business, Vixen Cellars, sells sparkling cider (sweet, dry, and dry-hopped) and fruit-infused mead.

Travel tip: From US 69 South, turn right onto West Atkinson Road. Keep left to continue on US 160 West/US 69 South. Turn left onto West 20th Street. Turn right onto North Walnut Street.

Vogel Family Vineyards

305 Hillcrest Drive #101, Galena, KS 66739
417-434-1900
vogelfamilyvineyards.com

Established in 2004, Vogel Family Vineyards is tucked into the southeast corner of Kansas due west of Joplin, Missouri. The vineyard is situated in the Reflection Valley region of the Ozark foothills. Fog from Shoal Creek shelters the vines from early spring frost. This microclimate enables winemaker Philip Vogel to grow grapes that don't normally thrive in the state, such as Cabernet Sauvignon, Petite Sirah, and Malbec. Vogel produces five full-bodied varietals, including Meritage, Cabernet Sauvignon, a Cabernet Sauvignon/Merlot blend, Chardonnay, and Riesling.

Highlights: Legato, made with Riesling grapes, produces aromas of amaretto and ginger, a crisp, refreshing edge of green apples and minerals, and lush, juicy flavors of pineapple, peaches, and lime. Cabernet Sauvignon exhibits a firm body with medium tannins and flavors of plum, berries, and currants preceded by notes of espresso and spicy oak.

CHAPTER 4

SOUTHEASTERN KANSAS, I-35 SOUTH

Beyond the outskirts of Olathe's suburbs, Interstate 35 extends past New Century, Gardner, and Edgerton. Ottawa is home to the county's Quilt Block Tour, with more than thirty-five quilt block patterns displayed on the sides of barns on farms and ranches, including Pome on the Range Orchard and Winery. The westward journey continues past El Dorado to Wichita, the most populated city in Kansas and home to several breweries, distilleries, and area wineries.

The Sioux word *Kansas* has been interpreted to mean "people of the south wind." By early June, hot dry winds blow across green and golden fields bleached by the sun. Highway patrol cars in the median shine like beetles and bask with the patience of turtles in sunlight, waiting to bolt fast as jackrabbits. In this arid climate, farmers, ranchers, winemakers, and others who work the land ply their trade in a hot breeze, if any, during summer. A chilled glass of wine, cocktail, or beer sourced from Kansas purveyors sounds all the more inviting.

Union Horse Distilling Company

11740 West 86th Terrace, Lenexa, KS 66214
913-492-3275
unionhorse.com

Founded in 2010, Union Horse was one of the first post-Prohibition distilleries to open in the Kansas City area. This family-owned and family-operated business takes a grain-to-bottle approach to small-batch craft distilling. Union Horse offers scheduled public tours ($17/person, advance purchase, ages twenty-one and up) for up to twenty-five people on select dates each month, listed on the website and social media. The two-hour tour begins in the luxurious Rider Room, where guests may order a cocktail before learning about the process of milling, mashing, fermentation, distillation, barreling, and bottling by hand. The distillery uses Missouri corn, Kansas wheat, and rye from the upper Midwest in its spirits. Spent grain is sent to a local dairy farm.

"We discuss the science of distilling on the tour," said cofounder Damian Garcia, "barrel aging, proof of the spirit, and how the change of the season, hot summer temperatures, and barrel affect maturation of the spirit. We use a sour-mash process, one of only a handful of craft distilleries to do so." Visitors will meet

Union Horse Distilling tours begin in the Rider Room, where a bartender prepares cocktails featuring spirits made by master distiller Patrick Garcia and head distiller Travis Vander Vegte. Courtesy of Union Horse Distilling.

Chester Copperpot, a five-hundred-gallon Vendome column pot still, is a stop on the distillery tour that includes a visit to the barrel-aging room. Courtesy of Union Horse Distilling.

Chester Copperpot, a five-hundred-gallon Vendome column pot still, view the expansive barrel-aging room, and return to the Rider Room for a taste of four award-winning spirits. Private tours may also be booked.

Union Horse was cofounded by four siblings: master distiller Patrick Garcia, general manager Eric Garcia, director of sales and marketing Damian Garcia, and director of special events Mary Garcia Gallagher. "We wanted to make something and build a generational business to leave a legacy," said Patrick. "I also worked in investments for ten years and got into whiskey. That's where I got the idea for distilling."

Blending each batch of whiskey is an art and science that requires an understanding of each barrel's contents and how they can be combined for optimal flavor and aroma. "From batch to batch, there are constants with some variance," said Patrick. "Each batch is like a different song on a recording from the same band. Each batch has a different rhythm and beat. We're a band trying to get people turned on to us and listen." Message heard, loud and clear.

Highlights: Head distiller Travis Vander Vegte works closely with Patrick to produce Union Horse's brands, including Reserve Straight Bourbon Whiskey, Reunion Straight Rye Whiskey, Long Shot White Whiskey, and Rider Vodka. *Wine Enthusiast* described the bourbon (92 rating) as a "good sipper" with "rich brown sugar and vanilla aroma. This whiskey is relatively lean and austere, featuring plenty of oak up front, leather mid-palate and finishing long with plenty of tingly spice." *Tasting Panel* magazine gave Reunion Straight Rye Whiskey another 92 rating, describing the spirit as "silky and long" and as having "[a] toasty, spicy nose; caramel, cinnamon, and aromatic oak." The spirits are also sold by retailers in Missouri, Kansas, Nebraska, Iowa, Oklahoma, New York, New Jersey, Connecticut, and California.

Stone Pillar Winery

11000 South Woodland Street, Olathe, KS 66061
913-839-2185
stonepillarvineyard.com

While on vacation at Niagara-on-the-Lake in Ontario, Canada, George and Brandi Hoff, cofounders of Stone Pillar Winery, saw lush grain fields near family-owned vineyards and wineries. The sight reminded them of the family farm in Kansas, owned and operated by five generations of the Hoff family, dating to pre–Civil War. Stone Pillar's first vines were planted on six acres in 2007, and the winery opened three years later. Additional grapes are sourced from a ten-acre farm in Atchison, Kansas.

Surrounded by Olathe's suburbs, the vineyard is a reminder of the land's heritage as a hundred-year-old former cattle pasture and turn-of-the-century pear orchard. The Hoff family practices sustainable agriculture. The winery features a tasting room, pavilion event space, and live music on the weekends along with food trucks on Friday evenings.

Highlights: Tastings include five tastes. Joceaux—a play on JoCo, short for Johnson County—is a barrel-aged semisweet red blend with hints of vanilla and oak. 2015 Carménère, aged in American oak, exhibits a dark cherry and rasp-

Stone Pillar Winery, based on a farm owned and operated by the Hoff family since before the Civil War, makes award-winning red, white, and fruit wines. Photo by the author.

berry aroma with a smooth, satiny finish. It's an ideal pairing with chocolate. Cayuga produces a light white wine with hints of apple and lemon followed by a crisp finish. Bestselling Hofftoberfest is a semisweet white with tropical overtones. Fruit wines include peach, blackberry, and peach mango.

Kansas City Wine Company

13875 South Gardner Road, Olathe, KS 66061
913-915-4297
kcwineco.com

Kirk Berggren, a former Air Force pilot who flies for FedEx, and his wife, Julie, bought a forty-acre farm, obtained a farm winery license in August 2014, and opened Kansas City Wine Company to the public the following June. Their daughter, Taylor Roesch, manages the winery's operations. Visitors may receive a wagging-tail welcome from yellow Labrador, Maggie, and chocolate Labrador, Charlie, en route to the tasting room and event space, The Barrel Room.

The winery's semicircular domed building stands out among nearby century-

Housed in a converted quonset hut, Kansas City Wine Company's four-legged ambassadors in-clude yellow Labrador, Maggie, and chocolate Labrador, Charlie. Photo by the author.

old hedge trees, grapevines, mature shade trees, and a four-acre fishing pond. The Berggrens converted a quonset hut—the corrugated metal building that houses The Barrel Room—by lining its exterior and interior with cedar. They added chandeliers, wine racks, a bar, and other fixtures. Weekends bring a steady parade of wine lovers eager to try the selection of a dozen wines.

The Berggrens also own the Kansas City Pumpkin Patch, previously located in Gardner, Kansas, and now situated on the south side of their Olathe farm. The seven-acre vineyard with three thousand grapevines is planted on the north side. Vintner Austin Wahaus tends to the vineyard and oversees the winemaking operation. The winery annually produces around twenty-five thousand bottles.

Some varieties grown at the vineyard include Saint Vincent, Seyval, Norton, Chambourcin, and Cayuga grapes. For its Riesling and Rougeon wines, the win-ery sources grapes from the Finger Lakes region of central New York. "When my daughter graduated from college, she wanted to do a farm winery," said Kirk. "We've spent a lot of time, money, and effort on these grapes. We planted two hundred Riesling vines in our vineyard in 2016. It will be two years before they produce. We also planted two hundred vines of Cayuga White."

Kirk Berggren (pictured) and his wife, Julie, established Kansas City Wine Company. Their daughter, Taylor Roesch, manages the winery's operations, including the busy tasting room. Photo by the author.

Highlights: Seyval Blanc is medium-bodied, dry, and tart. Semisweet Traminette, made from late-harvest grapes sourced from a Salina vineyard, introduces apricot-honey notes initially, followed by floral, spicy flavors. Riesling leans to the dry side, with fragrances of apple and spiced pear. Vignoles has a silky mouthfeel, with prominent honey and peach notes. Chambourcin's deep purple color is matched by intense grape-fig flavor and earthiness. Semisweet Sunflower Red, a popular blend, and Prairie Rose, a blush rosé made with Chambourcin and Concord, appeal to palates seeking sweetness that isn't one-dimensional.

White Tail Run Winery

2327 North 400 Road, Edgerton, KS 66021
913-893-6860
whitetailrunwinery.com

White Tail Run Winery represents Dan Fuller's drive to keep busy in retirement after working for the Olathe, Kansas, post office for thirty-one years. His wife,

White Tail Run Winery sources 60 percent of its grapes from Kansas and 40 percent from Missouri growers to produce its wines. Photo by the author.

Nancy, son Dusty, daughter-in-law Jennifer, and daughter Christy also operate the winery. Growing grapes led to making wine two years later. Dan used Seyval grapes for his first wine. After he entered the wine in an amateur competition and won a bronze medal, Dan and his family never looked back.

The five-acre vineyard grows Chambourcin, Seyval, Noiret, Cabernet Sauvignon, La Crosse, Traminette, and Vignoles grapes. Up to 60 percent of the winery's grapes are Kansas-grown, with the remainder sourced from Missouri growers. "La Crosse is a northern climate grape," said Dan. "We're one of the few wineries raising the grape this far south. It has a green apple-pear note with high acidity, slight sweetness, and crisp finish."

Production has steadily grown from 10,200 bottles in 2014 to an estimated 33,000 bottles in 2016. The winery self-distributes to more than a dozen area liquor stores in Lawrence, Ottawa, Wellsville, and Overland Park. White Tail Run also sells at the Overland Park Farmers' Market on weekends.

In the log cabin–style tasting room, tastings cost $5 per person. The fee is waived with the purchase of two bottles of wine. Sweet wines such as Blushing Buck, Seyval, and La Crosse sell best. Kansas cheese and summer sausage are also available for sale.

Highlights: Chambourcin, dry-oaked and aged in stainless steel, is made into dry, semisweet, sweet, and blush wines. Dry-oaked Chambourcin won a Jefferson Cup at the 2012 Jefferson Cup Invitational Wine Competition. The semisweet version earned two silver medals at the Florida State International Wine Competition. Crisp Seyval comes in dry, semisweet, and sweet styles. Daring Doe, a blend of Seyval and Traminette grapes, is a full-bodied dry white with floral aromas and balanced fruit tones. Sweet peach wine uses fruit from Gieringer's Orchard a mile down the road.

Travel tip: Head south on I-35. Take exit 205 to merge onto Homestead Lane. Follow Homestead Lane north to 199th Street. Turn left (west); proceed two miles to US 56. Turn left onto US 56 West/Morgan Street and proceed four miles. Turn right onto E 2300 Road, drive two miles, and turn right onto North 400 Road. The vineyard is one-third of a mile up the road. After visiting the winery, head east to Gieringer's Orchard (39675 West 183rd Street, Edgerton; gieringers orchard.com) and pick and purchase peaches, blackberries, strawberries, pumpkins, and other seasonal produce.

Red Crow Brewing Company

20561 South Lone Elm Road, Spring Hill, KS 66083
913-247-3641
redcrowbrew.com

Lone Elm Road is named for a specific tree. In the mid-nineteenth century, westbound travelers on the Oregon, California, and Santa Fe Trails stopped to rest at Round Grove Campground. Livestock grazed there by a grove of elm trees and watered at a nearby spring. Over time, campground visitors cut down the trees for firewood except for one elm tree. In 1844, the campground was renamed Lone Elm Campground. The tree remained a recognizable landmark to westbound pioneers. The road now leads to modern brewing pioneers Chris and Mistie Roberts and Mistie's parents, Joe and Loretta Fisher, who opened Red Crow as co-owners in October 2015.

As head brewer, Chris brews a tempting selection of session beers that are approachable and easy-drinking. The brewery shares space with The Bowery event space and Artistic Concrete Surfaces. The 3,200-square-foot brewery houses a taproom, seven-barrel brewhouse, cold room, office, laboratory, and storage. Cyclists on long-distance country rides regularly stop at the brewery. "We are a family-friendly brewery with a pet-friendly patio and outdoor area," said Mistie.

Families, beer lovers, and pets are welcome at Red Crow Brewing's taproom. A garage door opens in warm weather to a patio with lounge furniture and landscaped grounds. Photo by the author.

"We try to create a laid-back feeling that allows people new to craft beer and those already familiar with it to sample and discuss without judgment or criticism. I like the warm, welcoming image that we are creating and hope that we don't ever lose that."

Guests place food truck orders in the taproom, where the food is delivered. A food truck schedule is posted on the brewery's Facebook page.

Highlights: The brewery's beers are named after women in the Roberts and Fisher families. Isabelle, a Belgian blonde ale, is made with barley and wheat malt and seasoned with coriander for a fruity, spicy flavor that finishes dry. Elaine, a rye porter, uses rye and roasted malt to produce dark beer with peppery spice, roasted notes, and a velvety mouthfeel. Louise India Pale Ale blooms with floral and citrus flavor accented by hop aromas of passionfruit, mango, and white grape. Donna American Wheat's grapefruit and lemon flavor is grounded by a hint of bitterness.

Pome on the Range Orchard and Winery

2050 Idaho Road, Williamsburg, KS 66095
785-746-5492
pomeontherange.com

Pome on the Range sells fruit-based wines (no grape wines), apple cider, frozen apple slushies, fresh seasonal produce, and locally made preserves. Provisions include honey from Phifer Honey Farm in Perry, Kansas, and Ottawa-based Tree-house Berry Farm preserves.

Mike and Donnie Gerhardt planted Pome on the Range by hand in 1983. Today the twenty-five-acre apple and peach orchard is part of an eighty-acre property with another six acres of peaches parceled on a forty-acre parcel three miles south. The orchard also produces cherries, plums, pears, blackberries, pumpkins, asparagus, and other vegetables.

Mike Gerhardt (pictured) and Donnie Gerhardt started Pome on the Range as an orchard in 1983. The tasting room features the winery's apple wines blended with other fruits and also sells regional food products and fresh seasonal farm produce. Photo by the author.

Highlights: Popular apple-based wines blended with fruit include red raspberry, blackberry, Homewood Hooch, and apple-raisin wine. Semisweet and dry elderberry wine is made from Wyldewood Cellars Winery's elderberry concentrate blended with apple wine. Pome's wines are sold only at the tasting room.

Travel tip: Pome on the Range is six miles southwest of Ottawa. Take exit 176 on I-35 and head east onto Idaho Road, which becomes a gravel road a few hundred feet away. Turn right into the orchard and winery. For a local dining spot, continue on I-35 South to Williamsburg and visit Guy and Mae's Tavern (119 West William Street) and order the ribs.

Radius Brewing Company

610 Merchant Street, Emporia, KS 66801
620-208-4677
radiusbrewing.com

Emporia is known for Emporia State University, famous author and journalist William Allen White, and Radius Brewing Company. In April 2014, brewmaster Jeremy "JJ" Johns, chef Justin "Gus" Bays, and general manager Chad Swift first launched the brewpub in a building that dates back to the 1800s.

The brewery's name, Radius, "is sparked by the idea of sourcing local product when possible and giving back," says Swift. "Five cents from each beer goes back to local nonprofits and scholarship funds." Radius has donated thousands of dollars to local organizations and works closely with area businesses to be a hub in a growing downtown community.

Johns brews batches regularly on a three-barrel system to keep up with in-house demand. The enclosed brewhouse is in the center of the dining room. The kitchen prepares pizza and other dishes using local ingredients on a wood- and gas-fired brick oven in the open kitchen. As the oven blazes at more than six hundred degrees, the rotating platform ensures even cooking in mere minutes. Chef Bays creates a weekly "chef's menu" of dinner specials that use local and regional ingredients. Beyond regular tasty pub fare, the kitchen prepares dishes such as duck pâté, beef stroganoff, and pizza loaded with bacon, shaved pork loin, pork belly, onion, and mozzarella topped with porter barbecue sauce.

Highlights: William Allen Wheat, an American-style wheat beer, is named after Emporia native William Allen White, an editorial writer, journalist, poet, and author of several novels and nonfiction titles. His editorial "To an Anxious

Radius Brewing Company brews thirst-quenching beer, such as Rumor Has It IPA. The brewpub is also known for its wood-fired pizza and chef's dinner specials. Photo by the author.

Friend," a statement for free speech, earned him the 1923 Pulitzer Prize. Try the robust porter with chocolate, caramel, and coffee notes. Ryedius, an amber ale, is slightly malty and toasty with a crisp hoppy finish. Bestselling Rumor Has It IPA explodes with piney, hoppy notes. Warm weather seasonals like Peach Pi Weiss and Gose'n'Berry show the creative side of Johns's brewing skills. Check the website or display behind the bar for current tap selections.

Walnut River Brewing Company

111 West Locust Avenue, El Dorado, KS 67042
316-351-8086
walnutriverbrewing.com

Constructed between 1917 and 1920, the brick building that houses Walnut River Brewing Company has been a cradle for the hopes, dreams, and livelihood of numerous business owners and operations for nearly a century. Past residents included the People's Supply Company, Wm. Graham & Son Grocery, Mrs. Marie Troxell Creamery, S & H Bakery, and Century Plastics. Goldie Reidie operated

Walnut River Brewing's co-owners B. J. Hunt, Rick Goehring, and Travis Rohrberg. Behind them, an image of Graham & Son Grocery that once operated in the historic building. Photo by the author.

the popular but infamous Goldie's Place, a two-dollar brothel, for more than two decades. During Prohibition local law enforcement focused more on gambling and drinking than shenanigans at Goldie's. Reidie ran her business upstairs in the building while a succession of downstairs tenants sold supplies, groceries, and dairy. Once the bakery owner acquired the building in 1946, Goldie, her girls, and the town clientele were out of luck.

For modern-day pleasure seekers, the building is now home to Walnut River Brewing Company. Co-owners B. J. Hunt, brewer Rick Goehring, and microbiologist Travis Rohrberg make no guarantees on the company that guests may find in the taproom.

Foremost, Walnut River Brewing operates as a production brewery to supply beer for distribution in Kansas and Missouri. Hunt and Goehring weren't interested in a brewpub with a restaurant, so they opted for a tasting room next to the brewhouse. The brewery launched in July 2013 with a two-barrel system. Hunt said, "We needed to prove the concept to ourselves, the bank, and our wives before we ramped up." Now Walnut River Brewing's thirty-barrel system produces two thousand barrels in volume annually. The company began canning its beers for distribution in January 2016.

During the research phase prior to opening, Goehring researched forty-five water quality reports in the region and determined that El Dorado had the best water quality for a brewer's needs. Being close to the Walnut River and El Dorado reservoir near surrounding pastureland, rather than crop fields, meant that little chemical runoff sullied the purity of the water. "The mineral content in the water was also perfect for brewing most beer styles," said Goehring.

The Walnut River provided inspiration for the brewery's name. More importantly, the water source motivated Goehring to relocate from Wichita and build a dream brewery with his business partners. It just happens to be located in one of the most storied buildings in the city.

Highlights: Warbeard Irish Red, the mightiest seller, is deep ruby in color with a malty caramel sweetness and slightly dry finish. Highbeam IPA is a Pacific Northwest–style India pale ale with floral, citrusy hop aggressiveness that's still quaffable. Coffee Porter uses a locally roasted coffee brewed on-site to amp up the flavor and aroma without the acidity and bitterness of coffee. Falconer's Wheat is a hoppy wheat that balances breadiness with lemon notes. The taproom's seasonal and experimental releases rotate every two weeks. Homemade orange soda and root beer, and sandwiches, sliders, and pizza are available at the taproom.

Old Town Wichita

oldtownwichita.com

Wichita, the largest city in Kansas, has boomed over the past decade, with a diverse array of restaurants and breweries popping up in thriving districts. A handful of wineries dot the surrounding region in small towns. Based in the heart of downtown Wichita, Old Town is full of brick-lined streets and converted brick warehouses that date back to the 1800s. With more than a hundred businesses, hotels, and luxury living spaces, the district continues to be a hub of dining, drinking, shopping, and entertainment for the city's residents, travelers, and tourists. Several public parking lots are available near the walkways and attractions of Old Town.

Wheat State Distilling

1635 East 37th Street North, Suite 6, Wichita, KS 67219
316-831-7413
Distillery 244 Old Town
244 North Mosley Street, Wichita, KS 67202
316-201-1260
wheatstatedistilling.com

Wheat State Distilling founder and Wichita native David Bahre first opened a production facility (now closed to the public) that manufactures gin, vodka, whiskey, bourbon, and rum for distribution to retailers. Bahre studied grain science and milling at Kansas State University, where he learned to distill ethanol. He also began brewing beer at home. After completing a Master of Agribusiness degree, Bahre wanted to put his deep knowledge of grains to use by creating craft spirits as a product and built the original distillery. Bahre sources premium grain direct from farmers to create spirits at both distilleries. His mission: produce Kansas spirits from "farm to mill to still to bottle."

Each bottle's label bears a handwritten notation for the batch and

The custom-built pot still at Distillery 244, the showcase distillery and event space of Wheat State Distilling, is topped with a German-made copper helmet. Courtesy of Wheat State Distilling.

bottle number, an indication of Wheat State's attention to detail and pride in its craft. By entering the numbers on the Wheat State Distilling site, the field-to-bottle tracking system provides details on who distilled the spirit, the day of distillation, the spirit's distillation proof, the type and toast/char condition of the barrel used for aging, the aging period, the mash recipe, and the yeast strain used for fermentation. This detail enables consumers to better understand the process and factors involved in creating the small-batch craft spirit.

In 2016 Bahre opened Distillery 244, a distillery located in a 1930s-era building that once served as a Yellow Cab Company garage in Wichita's Old Town dining and entertainment district. This second venue is a 120-seat tasting room and lounge with a twenty-four-foot copper-topped bar, retail shop, and 580-seat event space. At this new location, guests may learn about the distillery's operations and enjoy handcrafted spirits and cocktails at the bar.

The still at Distillery 244 is the centerpiece of the new location. The pot still's helmet is made of five pieces of copper joined together by tig welding, a skill that requires a high degree of craftsmanship. "It's made in Eislingen, Germany," said Bahre. "Only four coppersmiths in the world can do this type of work." Distillery 244 is a must-visit destination to see Wichita's only distillery, tour the space, and enjoy a cocktail created with locally distilled spirits.

Highlights: Wheat vodka, made from a mash bill of 55 percent wheat with 45 percent corn, is creamy and rich with a wheat aroma and trace of vanilla. Bella Bahre's Bourbon is named after David Bahre's daughter. The spiced rum is aged seven months in a barrel and infused with ginger, cinnamon, vanilla, and clove. The rum is aged further in a freshly emptied bourbon barrel for nine months, producing a spirit with a heavy body and butterscotch notes. The distillery's citrus-forward gin is complemented by notes of cardamom and coriander with a light cinnamon finish. Bourbon Barrel Rested Gin, aged for four months, has light oak notes to enhance the other flavors.

River City Brewing Company

150 North Mosley Street, Wichita, KS 67202
316-263-2739
rivercitybrewingco.com

River City Brewing's building was once an abandoned warehouse, built in 1905 by Bennett Paint Company. Other past occupants included a tannery, grocery store, and Southwest Paper Company. The brewpub, founded in 1993 by Monte

Established in 1993, River City Brewing Company was among the first wave of craft brewpubs in Kansas. It continues to thrive in Wichita's Old Town district. Credit: Peter Thody.

Griffin, was a novel concept in Old Town, a district that only had two other restaurants and hadn't yet solidified its place as an entertainment destination.

The brewpub featured repurposed materials from other buildings and sites, including leaded glass windows from the Vickers Mansion in Wichita. The bar is constructed from wood sourced from Wichita's old Salvation Army building. Some of the other wood in the building was obtained from a house in Jackson County, Kansas, and material for the booths was acquired from homes in Kansas City's historic Quality Hill. A church in nearby Cheney was the former home of the pews and overhead lights used in the booths.

Griffin ran the 440-seat, 12,000-square-foot restaurant and brewery until 1997, when he sold his shares to business partner Bill Shea. Two years later, a group of businessmen took ownership. They recruited Chris Arnold, a Wichita native who ran a restaurant in Arkansas, to return home and operate the brewpub. Today, Arnold and fellow businessman Jeff Johnson own River City Brewing. Arnold educated himself about the brewing process and promoted server and homebrewer Dan Norton to the role of brewmaster. The brewpub's craft beer selection has become more sophisticated, with barrel-aged and seasonal beers.

Highlights: Flagship beers include Harvester Wheat and Rock Island Red, a crisp red-hued ale; Emerald City Stout; Old Town Brown; and Tornado Alley IPA. Ask about seasonal and specialty beers on tap. The brewpub serves a full range of sandwiches, burgers, salads, pizzas, steaks, five types of mac and cheese, and more.

Central Standard Brewing

156 South Greenwood Street, Wichita, KS 67211
316-260-8515
centralstandardbrewing.com

Brewing beer was "a passion that outgrew our garages," explained the cofounders of Central Standard Brewing, head brewer Ian Crane and Andy Boyd. Positive feedback from fans of their homebrewed beers stoked that passion. Crane and Boyd decided to scale up to professional brewing. Fellow head brewer and partner Nathan Jackel, who began brewing professionally in 2012 by learning from River City Brewing's head brewer Dan Norton, joined the Central Standard Brewing team. The trio opened the brewery in August 2015 across the street

Central Standard Brewing's taproom is a hip, colorful, and eclectic space with dynamic energy from its patrons and friendly staff. Photo by the author.

from Hyde Park near downtown Wichita. The founders' wives, Emily Boyd and Sumer Crane, are also co-owners.

The brewery and taproom includes a patio lined with tropical plants, picnic tables, and handy bicycle racks. Sunlight streams through glass windows on garage doors into the four-thousand-square-foot taproom. An eclectic mix of mismatched couches, tables, chairs, lamps, artwork, and plants creates a hip-casual vibe. The taproom looks like it could appear in a design-savvy lifestyle magazine, a look quite unlike other taprooms dotting the Midwest. "We wanted it to feel open and spacious, but also comfortable," said Andy. "The eclectic decor is mostly due to Sumer. She has an eye for vintage flair."

Working with a seven-barrel system in the brewhouse, the brewers go beyond basic styles to brew beers as memorable as characters from a Wes Anderson film. Their focus on yeast yields appealing aromas and flavors. "We use many different strains of Sach. yeast, Brett., Lacto., and Pedio., depending on the beer," said Ian, referring to various yeasts and bacteria used to ferment beer and produce flavor and aroma. "Yeast contributes just as much, if not more, flavor than malt and hops in most of our beer."

Central Standard's brewers work with a range of yeasts to produce the distinctive flavors and aromas of its beers, such as wild wit Cyclogenesis and Wally Rye Farmhouse Ale. Photo by the author.

Highlights: With limited distribution in Wichita, approximately 95 percent of Central Standard's beers are consumed on-site and rotate often on tap. Standard Issue, an oak-fermented tart grisette, earned a silver medal at the 2016 Great American Beer Festival in Denver. Hop Theory is tart and citrusy with prominent hops. Other beers include the floral wild wit dubbed Cyclogenesis, Wally Rye Farmhouse Ale, and Mango Reinhardt Double IPA. Red and white sangria are also available. The brewery sells 64-ounce growlers and 32-ounce crowlers. Meat and cheese boards, snack mix, and other light bites are available. Or, grab a bite from a local food truck usually stationed streetside. The rotation of trucks includes Flying Stove, Noble House Hawaiian, LoLo's Crepes, and Uno Mas Tacos.

Travel tip: Central Standard Brewing is a short walk to Hopping Gnome Brewing Company, another newer brewery in the city.

Hopping Gnome Brewing Company

1710 East Douglas Avenue, Wichita, KS 67214
316-708-3629
hoppinggnome.com

Look for the gnome hopping over a beer barrel on the sign above the brewery. It's a welcome sign to pop into the forty-five-seat taproom filled with gnome statues, craft beer, and social banter. Homebrewer Torrey Lattin, a 3D drafter and designer for MKEC Engineering, and his wife, Stacy Ward Lattin, own the curiously named craft brewery, Hopping Gnome. Miniature statues of gnomes, known in folklore for imbibing beer, line shelves throughout the taproom. *Hopping* refers to the hops used in brewing. Lattin brews on a five-barrel system in the brewhouse.

The small taproom is cozy, with the funky vibe of an artsy coffeehouse. Customers gather around the bar or cluster around tables to drink pints, chat, and play cards or board games. Free popcorn is available. Otherwise, guests may purchase food from local food trucks stationed either outside the brewery or at nearby Central Standard Brewing.

Highlights: The selection is small but representative of classic session beers such as bold, citrusy ICT IPA, Design District Coffee Stout, malty Sepia Amber Ale, and crisp Douglas Ave Pale Ale. Earl of ESB, an extra-special bitter style, is actually more malty than bitter. Lattin has received regional and national gold medals for the ESB. Hopping Gnome also offers one or two seasonal beers each

Hopping Gnome Brewing's forty-five-seat taproom is a cozy, funky space full of lively conversation, fresh beer, and, of course, an extensive collection of gnome statues. Photo by the author.

month. The brewery's graphics for the beer labels, T-shirts, and other items are fun, bold designs. They are reminders to craft beer geeks and newcomers that fresh local beer should be celebrated as something to enjoy without too much seriousness.

Wichita Brewing Company

West Side
8815 West 13th Street, Suite 100, Wichita, KS 67212
East Side
535 North Woodlawn Street, Wichita, KS 67208
316-440-2885
wichitabrew.com

Wichita Brewing Company is a craft brewpub founded by Jeremy Horn and Greg Gifford, with a menu offering a wide selection of craft beer, beer flights, beer cocktails, and beer shots as well as signature drinks and lots of copper decor.

Wichita Brewing Company's two brewpub locations have nineteen taps each for its year-round and seasonal beers, plus wood-fired pizza, calzones, and more in a family-friendly setting. Photo by the author.

Food includes pub-style appetizers such as garlic cheese bread, spinach artichoke dip, and stuffed mushrooms, salads, an extensive selection of wood-fired pizzas and calzones, sandwiches, pastas, and desserts.

Highlights: WBC Wheat is brewed with bitter orange and lemon peels for ample citrus presence. Crushed coriander added to the boil complements the subtle spice of the wheat malt in the beer. V6, so named because it is version six of the beer, is an American IPA with generous amounts of Cascade and Amarillo hops. What Winter? is a winter warmer ale with notes of caramel and balanced hops-malt character. At 8.5 percent ABV, Seal Team 6 Black IPA kicks butt as a robust ale with chocolate notes and assertive hops.

Third Place Brewing

630 East Douglas Avenue, Suite 150, Wichita, KS 67202
316-833-2873
facebook.com/ThirdPlaceBrewing

Tom Kryzer, a doctor, and Jason Algya, a Cessna pilot, opened their cozy microbrewery and taproom in mid-August 2016 on busy Douglas Avenue near Wichita's thriving Old Town district. The duo has homebrewed together since 2005. When they wore out their brewing system at home, they began to evaluate new equipment, developed plans, and ultimately decided to open a brewery.

Third Place Brewing's name draws from the anthropological idea that people seek a "third place" besides home and work. Kryzer said, "It's where you go to commune with others." The modest brewhouse has a 1.5-barrel system with four fermenters located in a back room a few feet away from the taproom. The operation enables them to offer up to eight beers on tap, including four core beers and several seasonals.

The taproom is an eclectic mix of furniture and materials, such as doors refashioned into tabletops and repurposed wood built into a bar countertop. A fireplace mantel is mounted against the wall behind the bar. The thrifty approach and resourcefulness lends the space a youthful, DIY feel—kind of like a couple of college buddies launching a tech company out of a dorm room or garage. That sense of collegiality and youthful energy works here, infusing the room and its collection of owners, bartenders, and beer-faithful customers with enthusiasm.

Highlights: Ali's Pale Ale, named after one of Kryzer's three daughters, is an easy-drinking session beer. Red Truck IPA gets its name from a 1973 Scout that Kryzer drove in high school and passed on to his daughter, who also drove it to high school. Black Toro Stout's sweetness comes from added lactose balanced by a hint of coffee and biscuit flavor. The stout was named "by a guy that did concrete work in Jason's yard," explained Kryzer with a smile. "He named it for us." Springboard Blonde, a light "gateway" beer, English Pale Ale, and Vanilla Porter are some of the other rotating beers on tap.

Travel tip: Third Place Brewing is an easy walk from Old Town. Grab a bite from local vendors such as Charlie's PizzaTaco food truck or nearby Garden of Eatin'.

Tom Kryzer (pictured) and Jason Algya opened Third Place Brewing as a collegial gathering spot near Wichita's Old Town. Ali's Pale Ale is named after one of Kryzer's three daughters. Photo by the author.

Aero Plains Brewing

117 North Handley Street, Wichita, KS 67203
316-448-2811
aeroplainsbrewing.com

Lance Minor, a homebrewer since 2007, Minor's nephew Ryan Waite, and business partner Brent Miller, an art gallery owner, opened Aero Plains Brewing in fall 2016 after a lengthy delay and an emergency that threatened Minor's life.

Minor served twenty-one years in the Marine Corps, including a longstanding role as a strategic mobility and force management planner. He also taught English at a university. He returned to his native Wichita in late 2012 with the intent to open a brewery with Waite and Miller. Minor briefly apprenticed at Black Market Brewing Company in Temecula, California. The team began the arduous process of raising funds and developing the business plan. Meanwhile, Minor worked as an instructional designer, project planner, and quality assurance manager at NexLearn, an e-learning design company. Suffice it to say, Minor had polished skills in planning and logistics that came in handy later.

In January 2014 Minor contracted the potentially fatal H1N1 flu virus that put his brewery dreams and life itself on hold. He spent seven weeks in a medically induced coma on a ventilator and lost forty pounds in the process. Minor made a miraculous recovery that involved weeks of additional time to heal and learn to walk again under his own power. His innate drive to survive was bolstered by Marine training and sheer will. Ultimately, Minor rebuilt his physical condition, worked with his partners to find funding, and completed construction of the 11,500-square-foot production brewery.

The ongoing quest to open a brewery was also inspired "by a sense of servitude" after meeting the director of operations at the Kansas Leadership Center. "Teaching was not challenging enough," Minor said of his earlier role. The daunting task of opening a large-scale brewery presented a challenge with purpose. "I wanted to be a business leader with a genuine concern for the community."

Production breweries are designed for large-volume brewing capacity so that beer can be readily sold in kegs and/or in packaging via a distributor to bars, restaurants, and retail accounts. While some production breweries operate an on-site taproom, these breweries differ in purpose and scale from restaurant-driven

Aero Plains Brewing is the latest chapter in brewer Lance Minor's amazing life story. The 11,500-square-foot production brewery includes a twenty-barrel brewhouse, taproom, art gallery, and outdoor patio. Photo by the author.

brewpubs. Aero Plains's production brewery includes a 20-barrel brewing system and 160-barrel fermentation capacity, quality assurance lab, spacious beer hall, and taproom with twenty taps, a lounge, and a gallery. An overhead door opens to the large front patio.

Highlights: Ruby-colored Bingo's IPA uses classic German and bold American hops that result in subtle spiciness, sweet citrus, and grapefruit aromas. The name of Dove Runner Red Wheat alludes to "soiled doves," or working ladies at a brothel in the heyday of Wichita's historic Delano district. To the delight of Chisholm Trail cattlemen and consternation of churchgoing townspeople, the "doves" once bathed on the banks of the Arkansas River. Dove Runner is made with more than 50 percent red wheat and roasted barley to yield a red color.

Delano

The historic Delano district is one of Wichita's oldest neighborhoods, at the end of the Chisholm Trail. Delano Bed and Breakfast (305 South Elizabeth Street; delanobedandbreakfast.com) is in a bungalow originally constructed in 1914 by automobile dealer pioneer Morris Schollenberger. In 1900 Schollenberger and his two brothers opened the first REO gasoline car dealership in Kansas.

Wyldewood Cellars Winery

951 East 119th Street, Peck, KS 67110
316-554-9463
wyldewoodcellars.com

Merry Bauman, her brother Dr. John Brewer, and his wife, Beth Brewer, co-founded Wyldewood Cellars Winery in 1995 as a way to "make the family farm profitable." John worked for eighteen years with high-tech firms before retiring to start the winery. Previously, he made wine as a hobby and shared bottles as gifts during his travels around the world. John, Beth, Merry, and the family needed to determine the future of its thousand-acre farm and ranch in the Flint Hills near Howard, Kansas. They didn't wish to continue the existing ranch operation. After doing market research, John found that "many people said they really loved grandmother's elderberry wine, but they could not get it anymore because grandmother passed away."

The tasting room at Wyldewood Cellars Winery is stocked with more than forty varieties of its elderberry, fruit, and grape wines, plus regional food products and gifts. Photo by the author.

The existing demand and lack of supply provided an opportunity. The family farm had fifty acres of elderberries that could supply raw ingredients and distinguish Wyldewood from regional wineries. Furthermore, the crop didn't overlap with the harvest of grapes that Wyldewood planted for winemaking. "There are no commercial growers of elderberry in the US. Our berries bloom in June and are harvested in August," said John. "Seventy percent of the national wine market is for sweet wines. With sugar, wines can be made from any fruit." Wyldewood's name is an alteration of Beth Brewer's maiden name, Wilder, as well as a reference to harvesting wild elderberries in the woods.

Wyldewood Cellars Winery has earned more than five hundred international awards and titles to date. Four generations of family members work at the winery, which produces grape and fruit wines made from blackberry, raspberry, and cherry. Wyldewood is best known for its six types of elderberry wines.

While the average yield for Kansas grapegrowers is two tons per acre, Wyldewood's yield falls between six and nine tons per acre. Wyldewood grows Concord, Traminette, and Chambourcin and supplements its inventory with California grapes for some wines. Most varieties of *Vitis vinifera*, abundant varieties used

Cofounder Dr. John Brewer says that wines from Wyldewood Cellars Winery have earned more than five hundred international awards and titles. Photo by the author.

for winemaking in California and other regions worldwide, don't typically prosper in the Midwest, although some growers have had success with them. According to John Brewer, these varieties cannot survive rapidly changing fall weather. Thus, regional wines are mostly made from native and hybrid grapes, and perhaps account for the popularity of sweeter fruit-based wines in Kansas and Missouri.

Brewer draws a clear distinction between the grapegrowing and winemaking sides of the industry. "Wineries are processing plants and vineyards are where you grow grapes," he said. "They are separate businesses. All wineries are agritourism businesses. Fifteen years ago, wineries were places that produced wine. Now they are entertainment venues that sell wine. You don't have to grow grapes to make wine. We're a processing plant. Our business model is commercial production like most California wineries and not the business model of a 'retirement hobby.'"

Highlights: Free tastings include up to five samples. Six types of award-winning elderberry wines range from sweet to dry. C3 Cato Creek Chambourcin, made from estate-grown red grapes, is made in a dry Cabernet style. Prairie Sunshine, a popular fruity wine that sells well especially for Christmas, is a semisweet blend similar to Riesling with a nose of green apple, candy, and tropical fruit. Sand Plum, made with the eponymous native American wild fruit, is sweet with a tart finish. The tasting room stocks more than three dozen wines, elderberry concentrate, jelly, and other goods.

Wheat State Wine Company

23622 Springhill Farm Drive, Winfield, KS 67156
620-229-9463
wheatstatewineco.com

The Walnut River twists and turns south from Winfield past the doorstep of Wheat State Wine Company on Springhill Farm, wooded fields, and lush farmland. Bound for Arkansas City, the river eventually joins the larger Arkansas River before the waters cross the Kansas-Oklahoma border. The scenic riverway has left behind rich soil deposits that fortify the land with minerals and nutrients. Not surprisingly, rows of Vidal Blanc, Saint Vincent, Chambourcin, Seyval Blanc, and Norton grow quite well here. More than 2,100 vines are planted on eight acres of hillsides and flat fields.

Owner Chris Tyler founded the winery in 2008 and planted the first three acres of grape vines that year. Springhill Farm, named after the large spring that comes out of the side of the hill, was originally homesteaded in 1876. Tyler said, "We still have the federal land grant paperwork that was signed by Ulysses Grant."

Tyler's uncle Tom, a wine collector, and his sister influenced his early interest in wine. When his family purchased Springhill Farm, the land reminded Tyler of hills in Sonoma's wine country and limestone hills in Burgundy, France. With the winery located at the base of the Flint Hills, Tyler said, "The limestone bluffs impart a certain mineral characteristic, especially to our Vidal Blanc wine, Dandy Horse."

Highlights: Tastings are free. Wheat State Wine's eight wines include bestselling 2014 Dandy Horse, a crisp dry Vidal Blanc with notes of grapefruit, lemon, lime peel, and fresh-cut grass. Tropical passionfruit, grapefruit, and pear aromas appear as well. The 2015 Redbud Rosé is a semisweet eighty-twenty blend of Vidal Blanc and Saint Vincent with notes of bubblegum, honeydew, and celery preceded by honeydew and bubblegum aromas. Ad Astra, a dessert wine made with Chambourcin and fortified with brandy, was named the 2012 Kansas Wine

En route to the tasting room and fine Kansas wines at Wheat State Wine Company on Springhill Farm, drivers pass by verdant woods and lush farmland along the Walnut River. Photo by the author.

of the Year by the Kansas Grape Growers and Winemakers Association. Perfect for a hot summer night, semisweet 2014 Dog Run Red suggests black currant, cranberry, and plum with a light hint of oak.

Travel tip: GPS assistance is recommended. From Wichita (one hour approximately), head south on I-135/KS 15/US 81. Take I-35 South/Kansas Turnpike toward Oklahoma City for 22.6 miles. Take exit 19 for US 160 toward Wellington/Winfield, turn left onto US 160 East, and continue 18 miles. Turn right onto County Road 4E/Country Club Road for 1.5 miles and then onto 71st Road for 1.5 miles. Turn right onto US 77 S. Turn left onto 212th Road and proceed 6 miles to your destination. No food is available, so pack a picnic basket before the drive. Informal tours are available with no set times.

Grace Hill Winery

6310 South Grace Hill Road, Whitewater, KS 67154
316-799-2511
gracehillwinery.com

Drs. David and Natalie Sollo founded Grace Hill Winery and opened the tasting room in 2008 after planting grapes in the vineyard over the previous five years. While the Sollos have active careers with medical practices, the couple's passion for tasting wine on their travels and membership in tasting clubs inspired the venture.

The Sollos acquired an abandoned farmstead west of Whitewater and north of Wichita and prepared the land before planting grapes. After launching the winery, they later opened a larger tasting room and event center. The nine-acre vineyard produced sixteen tons of grapes in 2015 with a 2016 projection of more than twenty-five tons.

Several of the colorful labels feature pets and animals from the farm. Local

Grace Hill Winery's colorful labels feature pets and animals from the farm. Even more lovable are the award-winning wines in the bottles. Photo by the author.

artists such as Janet Fisher and Kelly Remacle created artwork displayed on the labels. Tastings are free, but run $5/person for eight or more in a group. Advance reservations are requested. Dry, sweet, and mixed wine flights are available. Tours explore the vineyard, winery, barrel room, event center, and cellar.

Highlights: Named after the family's bulldog, Chloe's Cuvee is an off-dry blend of Vignoles and Seyval aged nine months in a stainless steel tank. Peckerhead Red, a red blend of three grapes, and Dodging Tornados, made with Chambourcin, are bestsellers. The 2013 Barrel Reserve Red, made with Chambourcin and Noiret, was aged two years in American oak barrels and is dark plum in color with black currant and cherry flavors. F5, a port-style dessert wine that pairs with rich chocolate, is blended from five grape varieties. Fruit Bomb, a blend of apple and raspberry wine, makes a perfectly punchy sangria.

Travel tip: From downtown Wichita, take I-135 North 15 miles to exit 25 for Whitewater/El Dorado. Turn right at KS 196 and go east on KS 196 for 7 miles to Grace Hill Road. Turn north (left) at Grace Hill Road. The vineyard and winery are on the right, a half mile north of KS 196.

Hank is Wiser Brewery

213 North Main Street, Cheney, KS 67025
316-542-0113
hankiswiserbrewery.com

Hank Sanford's interest in beer has been a lifelong hobby. He worked for twenty-two years for a Wichita manufacturer and traveled regularly for his sales job. Along the way, he collected brewery memorabilia, visited more than four hundred breweries across the country, and homebrewed for fifteen years. By his estimate, Sanford also tasted more than five thousand beers.

April 1, 2005, marked the day that Sanford served his first beer as the owner of Hank is Wiser Brewery. The brewery's grand opening began mere hours after he took early retirement from his sales career. Sanford, his wife, Jane, and their son Steve, the full-time brewer, started a new chapter in the family's life as operators of a barbecue restaurant and local microbrewery.

The building has its own history of note. Constructed from brick, iron, and stone for $8,000 in 1898, the Collins & Joslyn Building was the first two-story structure in downtown Cheney. Past occupants included the Cheney drugstore

Hank Sanford (right), his wife, Jane, and their son Steve combine mouthwatering barbecue and handcrafted beer at Hank is Wiser Brewery, a snapshot of small-town America. Photo by the author.

Hank is Wiser Brewery was once the Armstrong ice cream parlor, Cheney drugstore and apothecary, and other businesses. The back bar is a nod to the building's past as a vital part of downtown Cheney, Kansas. Photo by the author.

and apothecary, Armstrong ice cream parlor, general store, Masonic lodge, telephone company, seamstress shop, and bar and grill. Sanford and his son bought the building in 2004 and remodeled it.

Tender, aromatic barbecue and fresh small-batch beer draw regulars. The array of brewery advertisements and memorabilia displayed throughout the taproom is a trip through yesteryear. Stop in for ribs, brisket, and beer, and perhaps some eight-ball in the billiard room.

Highlights: Hank is Wiser typically serves four house beers and two guest taps. The taproom also has rotating seasonals, a full liquor bar, and more than fifty different bottled beers, including rare Samuel Adams Utopias from different years, sold by the ounce. House beers Cherry Pale Ale and Blueberry Pale Ale, both made with extract; Wiseman Wheat; Krippled Kangaroo IPA; and Wedlock Pale Ale are popular sellers. Mocha Man Coffee Imperial Stout is aged with ancho, chipotle, and Hatch chilies and brewed with cacao nibs and coffee to produce robust flavor.

MISSOURI

CHAPTER 5

GREATER KANSAS CITY

Prohibition along the Kansas-Missouri State Line

Before Prohibition became the law of the land in 1920, Kansas City, Missouri, was awash in saloons that served beer and spirits made by local breweries and distilleries. Regional politics and social movements in the 1800s played a significant role in shaping how the alcohol manufacturing industry diminished in Kansas and flourished in Missouri. Unsurprisingly, people in the area came to Kansas City, Missouri, to drink whiskey, beer, and other booze.

Throughout the mid- to late 1800s, the alcohol-intolerant temperance movement in Kansas gained momentum. Carrie Nation and others led a moral fight against alcohol consumption. The morally conservative social attitude bled into the state's politics and laws. Kansas was the first state in the nation to enact alcohol prohibition. Kansas voters approved an amendment to the state constitution in 1880 that prohibited the manufacture and sale of intoxicating liquors statewide, effective January 1, 1881. Five years before national Prohibition, Kansas also passed "bone dry" laws in February 1917 "prohibiting the importation or manufacture or possession of intoxicating liquors for any purpose except in use in churches."

This unfriendly climate led distillers, brewers, and winemakers to open businesses in Missouri, where the laws on manufacturing and consumption of al-

111

cohol were more permissive than in Kansas. Saloons and taverns opened and prospered along State Line Road near 9th Street in Kansas City's West Bottoms. At one point twenty-two of twenty-four businesses operating between State Line Road and Genessee Street—dubbed "the wettest block in the world"—were alcohol-based establishments. Thirsty Kansans crossed the state line and nearby railroad tracks to join Missourians in these saloons after finishing work shifts. Even during national Prohibition from 1920 to 1933, Kansas City's powerful mayor, "Boss" Tom Pendergast, and his corrupt political machine encouraged police to overlook vice. Illegal booze flowed through the city's jazz clubs and businesses.

The Eighteenth Amendment was repealed on December 5, 1933, and beer, wine, and spirits were again legal to buy, sell, and consume. However, it took decades for a new wave of distilleries to open and reintroduce locally made spirits. Today, locals and out-of-town visitors alike may visit several area distillers that produce high-quality vodka, gin, and whiskey. Breweries and new wineries have also opened and flourished throughout greater Kansas City, Missouri.

EAST AND WEST BOTTOMS, CROSSROADS, DOWNTOWN

J. Rieger & Co.

2700 Guinotte Avenue, Kansas City, MO 64120
816-807-3867
jriegerco.com

Jacob Rieger first opened a distillery in 1887 near the Livestock Exchange in the West Bottoms and shuttered its doors in December 1919, one month before the onset of Prohibition. At one time the iconic brand offered more than one hundred alcoholic products and served a quarter million unique customers by mail-order delivery services. Ninety-five years after Prohibition, J. Rieger & Co. revived and opened a new distillery in the East Bottoms near the site of the historic Heim Brewery.

Co-owned by Jacob's great-great-great grandson Andy Rieger and cofounder Ryan Maybee, the distillery draws on family roots intertwined with the spirit of Kansas City's heyday. The depth of knowledge, applied craftsmanship, and savvy acumen of its founders—along with that of head distiller Nathan Perry—have

Ryan Maybee (left) and Andy Rieger cofounded J. Rieger & Co. distillery in 2014 and revived the Rieger brand. Andy's great-great-great grandfather Jacob first opened a distillery in 1887 in Kansas City's West Bottoms. Credit: Samantha Levi Photography.

propelled J. Rieger & Co. into a modern era of innovative craft distilling that hasn't forsaken its roots. Its Kansas City Whiskey honors the original brand by using a blend of corn, malt, and straight rye whiskeys, all aged at least four years. Further, the distillery has added fifteen-year-old Oloroso sherry from the Williams & Humbert Bodega in Jerez, Spain, to its whiskey. This step revives a practice common in the 1800s—blending sherry with whiskey—that results in a new classic with a hint of sweetness. A woodsy, burnt-sugar aroma leads to flavors of sandalwood, rose petals, ripe peaches, and light caramel.

The original recipe for Midwestern Dry Gin was developed by master distiller Tom Nichol, formerly of Tanqueray. The gin's London dry style has a botanical base of juniper, coriander, angelica, licorice root, and orange peel that results in notes of pine resin, sweet orange, and star anise. The gin and whiskey both earned "excellent" ratings in the Ultimate Spirits Challenge, regarded as the industry standard for spirits evaluation.

Midwestern Premium Vodka is distilled from potato, wheat, and corn for smooth balance. Left For Dead is a series of limited-release beer-based spirits resulting from a partnership with Boulevard Brewing Company. J. Rieger & Co. also developed Caffè Amaro, their take on the classic Italian bittersweet liqueur amaro, made with orange, vanilla, gentian, and cardamom. The amaro is then

Andy Rieger, master distiller Tom Nichol, and J. Rieger head distiller Nathan Perry. Nichol developed the original recipe for J. Rieger & Co.'s Midwestern Dry Gin. Credit: Samantha Levi Photography.

blended with a single-origin coffee toddy, or coffee concentrate, from Thou May-est Coffee Roasters and sweetened for balance and to amplify coffee notes. The liqueur is consumed as an after-dinner *digestivo* or mixed in cocktails.

The distillery's spirits have gained an audience in the Paris of the Plains and beyond. J. Rieger & Co. is sold in stores in Missouri, Kansas, and more than a dozen states and in DC. In Kansas City, the spirits are a staple at many restaurants and bars, including The Rieger and underground speakeasy Manifesto (1924 Main Street).

Highlights: The two-hour tour covers the distillery's history with visits to the 750-gallon copper still and barrel room. It includes samples, plus goods from neighboring butcher shop Local Pig and boutique shop Urban Provisions. Visit the distillery website for dates and to book a tour.

Amigoni Urban Winery

1505 Genessee Street #100, Kansas City, MO 64102
913-890-3289
amigoni.com

Michael and Kerry Amigoni opened Kansas City's first urban-based winery in 2007. The winery is based in the former *Daily Drovers Telegram* newspaper building, an old printing shop and industrial warehouse in the Stockyards District of the historic West Bottoms. The building has been transformed into a sleek tasting room with a mezzanine on the second floor and ample natural light. The adjacent barrel room with a bar serves as the event space.

Amigoni's ten-acre farm in Centerview, Missouri, has a six-acre vineyard with an unusual selection of grapevines. *Vitis vinifera*, the vine species that produces the vast majority of grapes used in wines around the world, is not typically grown commercially in the Midwest—the plants usually don't survive the temperature changes or prosper as the seasons shift. However, Amigoni has been able to plant, grow, and produce wine from its Cabernet Franc, Chardonnay, Cabernet

View from the second-floor mezzanine of Amigoni Urban Winery's tasting room based in the former Daily Drovers Telegram *newspaper building. Photo by the author.*

Sauvignon, Viognier, Mourvèdre, Petit Verdot, and Malbec vines. This grape selection distinguishes Amigoni's wines from other wineries throughout Missouri and Kansas that focus on native and hybrid varieties. The winery also works with a grapegrower in northern California that supplies grapes from the West Coast. Amigoni uses these grapes to experiment with different varieties and expand the production of its blends.

The vineyard's terroir plays a key role in grape production. The limestone and shale bedrock base lies about five feet below the surface, allowing ample space for the vine's roots to sink deep into the soil. The surface layer of the terraced land is black, firm, silty-clay loam rich with minerals and nutrients. Air circulation and black limestone also factor into growth and development of the grape's character, leading to complex flavors and aromas from the grape juice used to make wine.

Tastings include samples of five wines. Private tastings and tours are available by appointment. Barrel tasting tour packages, where wines are sampled straight from the barrel, and blending classes are also available.

Highlights: The 2015 Urban Bianco, a fifty-fifty blend of Viognier and Sauvignon Blanc, has lush tropical fruit and a hint of citrus on the finish. 2015 Sauvignon Blanc is crisp and dry with citrus on the nose, notes of grapefruit and a hint of pineapple on the finish. The 2015 Viognier, a medal of merit winner at the 2015 Jefferson Cup Invitational, is full-bodied with a violet aroma, notes of stone fruit and honey, and smooth acidity. The 2014 Cabernet Sauvignon, a medal of excellence winner at the 2015 Jefferson Cup, is medium-bodied with bright flavors and aromas of cherry and raspberry and a medium tannin structure. Cabernet Franc, Amigoni's first grape planted and first vintage that launched the winery, has won multiple awards. Its 2013 vintage is earthy with hints of berries and tobacco on the nose, prominent fruit and pepper accents, and pronounced tannin and oak notes from eighteen months of aging.

Travel tip: Access the vineyard via the 12th Street Bridge to the West Bottoms, turning left (south) on Genessee Street. Also, visit Stockyards Brewing located within walking distance on Genessee Street. Local restaurants on Genessee Street include Genessee Royale Bistro, Voltaire, and Lucky Boys, a dive bar with tasty grub.

Stockyards Brewing Company

1600 Genessee Street #100, Kansas City, MO 64102
816-895-8880
stockyardsbrewing.com

Stockyards Brewing Company, established in 2015, draws its name from the historic Stockyards District, where rugged ranchers once ended cattle drives in Kansas City's West Bottoms. The brewery occupies the original home of legendary steakhouse The Golden Ox (1949–2014) on the first floor of the Livestock Exchange Building. Brewery owner Greg Bland has preserved the western aesthetic and embedded history of the space while updating the building.

Behind a sixty-five-year-old meat locker door, the brewhouse holds a state-of-the-art fifteen-barrel, three-vessel system where head brewer Micah Weichert plies his craft. The taproom retains hallmarks of the Golden Ox era. A spacious bar, brass fixtures and taps, original circular booths and western print carpeting, stained glass windows, and iconic statues and photographs channel the heyday and character of the stockyards and Kansas City itself. A hallway offers a view

Stockyards Brewing occupies the original home of legendary steakhouse The Golden Ox and retains its western look and feel in the taproom. Photo by the author.

of photographs from yesteryear and a view of the brewhouse on the way to an event space in back.

Highlights: Golden Alt is cold fermented with ale yeast to yield a light, easy-drinking beer. Telltale notes of banana and clove confirm that West Hef is an unfiltered hefeweizen, or German-style wheat beer. Saison, a wheat and rye farmhouse ale with Belgian yeast, opens up the palate with notes of orange peel, lemon peel, and crushed black pepper. Brunch Stout is a classic session stout with coffee and chocolate notes. West Bottoms IPA draws elements from Midwest and West Coast IPAs through its selection of hops for tropical fruit flavor, aromatic hop notes, and use of malts to strike a balance between sweetness and bitterness.

Travel tip: Stockyards Brewing also has wine and local coldbrew coffee on tap, plus classic cocktails made with premium spirits. Light assorted bar snacks are available. For heartier fare, visit Lucky Boys dive bar across the street for poutine, a hot chicken sandwich, burger, or veggie burger. Voltaire is another, more upscale dining option.

Tom's Town Distilling Company

1701 Main Street, Kansas City, MO 64108
816-541-2400
toms-town.com

Founders David Epstein and Steve Revare named their distillery and cocktail lounge Tom's Town after "Boss" Tom Pendergast, the former corrupt political boss of Kansas City. During his reign, jazz sizzled and booze flowed in the Paris of the Plains, despite the restrictions of Prohibition. Epstein and Revare later discovered they had family connections to Pendergast and Kansas City's storied past. Namely, the Pendergast machine ruined David's grandfather's bootlegging business, while Steve's great-great-uncle, Maurice Milligan, brought Pendergast down on tax evasion charges in 1939.

Tom's Town is a production distillery and a swanky lounge, where its spirits are sold by the bottle, straight up, or in cocktails. The lounge recaptures Gatsby-era glamor, the optimism of the art deco era, and the freewheeling spirit that roared in the heyday of Kansas City's past. Distiller Rob Vossmeyer oversees production of the distillery, which is viewable from the lounge. A full complement of cocktails and stylish plates of upscale foods are available. Tours

Tom's Town Distilling, located along the KC Streetcar line, recaptures cocktail culture during the reign of former Kansas City mayor "Boss" Tom Pendergast as well as the city's free-spirited days despite Prohibition. Courtesy of Tom's Town Distilling.

($10/person, up to fifteen people) may be reserved online. Dates and times vary each month.

Highlights: Pendergast's Royal Gold Bourbon borrows a brand maneuver from Boss Tom himself. Pendergast procured fine bourbon from Kentucky and Tennessee, bottled it, trademarked the brand name, and sold Royal Gold at a premium. Similarly, Tom's Town revives Pendergast's Royal Gold Bourbon brand by "finishing" bourbon more than four years old in hand-selected fourteen-year-old port casks as part of its "curated" whiskeys. Named after Pendergast's shady city manager Henry McElroy, McElroy's Corruption Gin is a spicy New Western–style gin. To create the gin's profile from scratch, Vossmeyer used fourteen botanicals, such as lemongrass, long pepper, grains of paradise, kaffir lime leaf, orris root, coriander, and cubeb pepper, to complement the essential characteristics of juniper. Eli's StrongArm Vodka, distilled sixteen times, is a firm nod to the strong-arm tactics of Pendergast's bodyguard and political gatekeeper Elijah Matheus. Notably, McElroy's Corruption Gin took home a silver medal and Eli's StrongArm Vodka took home gold at the 2016 American Craft Spirits Association.

Travel tip: Tom's Town Distilling is a few walkable blocks from the Power & Light District and two KC Streetcar stops at Kauffman Center (16th and Main) and Crossroads (19th and Main).

Lifted Spirits Distillery

1734 Cherry Street, Kansas City, MO 64108
816-866-1734
liftedspiritskc.com

Lifted Spirits Distillery occupies a completely renovated two-story red brick building, formerly an 1880s horse stable and salvage warehouse, in the East Crossroads Arts District. Decades ago, the second floor once held hay bales that were dropped through trapdoors in the floor to stables below. Kyle Claypool, Darren Unruh, and head distiller Michael Stuckey opened the distillery in late 2016. This rustic spirit house now features a tasting room, infusion bar, second-floor event space called The Hayloft, barrel room, and production area for distilling.

"Transparency and authenticity are a huge part of our DNA," said Claypool. "We want people to come in and see, smell, taste, and share our passion for spirits and how they're made. That means free tours daily, events that get into the processes, traditions, and history of specific spirits, and drinks that really highlight those spirits and their traditions."

The first floor houses a twenty-plate, thousand-liter column still, grain mill, Missouri white oak barrels for aging, fermenters, mash tun, and other equipment. The still is split into three columns, so whiskey, vodka, and gin can be produced on a single still. From the second-floor Hayloft, visitors may view the still and observe the distilling process.

"Our starting lineup is made from a specific strain of red winter wheat grown by a farmer outside of Wellsville, Kansas," said Claypool. "The vodka is dangerously smooth. Our Bright Gin (which is the first of several gin recipes) is crisp and accessible, while still maintaining layers of flavor and complexity. Bartenders have referred to it as a 'conversion gin,' something that the gin newcomer will enjoy just as much as die-hard gin fans will."

Lifted Spirits Distillery designed its twenty-plate still to be split into three columns so that whiskey, vodka, and gin can be produced on a single still. Photo by the author.

Highlights: The distillery produces vodka, Bright Gin, white whiskey, hopped white whiskey, and absinthe verte. Lifted Spirits uses red winter wheat, rye, and millet sourced from a Kansas family farm to create spirits with midwestern character. The bar serves classic cocktails, signature drinks, local beer, and wine from KC Wineworks.

KC Wineworks

1829 McGee Street, Kansas City, MO 64108
816-256-4608
kcwineworks.com

KC Wineworks, based in a 1920s-era building, is a full-production winery and tasting room in the heart of the Crossroads Arts District. Owners James and Lindsay Lowery transformed the 5,500-square-foot urban space into a sleek

KC Wineworks, which opened its urban winery and stylish tasting room in spring 2016, earned its first gold medal at the 2016 Missouri Wine Competition for its 2014 Chambourcin. Photo by the author.

tasting room, lounge, barrel room, and event space. Behind the scenes, the winery houses a laboratory and production area, where the grape crush, filtration, aging, bottling, and storage take place.

The tasting room features a curved bar with notched spaces that resembles a gear, symbolizing the cyclical nature of winemaking. It also creates inviting nooks for guests to gather and sample wine. The room's modern furnishings and spacious setting offer a relaxed contemporary feel in an urban environment.

KC Wineworks sources grapes from its four-acre Silver Leaf Vineyard, part of the family's 160-acre property in Macon, Missouri, north of Columbia. The land has been in James Lowery's family since the 1870s. Planting began in 2002 and includes varieties such as Vignoles, Chardonel, Traminette, and Vidal. Maréchal Foch, a French hybrid grape named after French WWI marshal Ferdinand Foch; Noiret; Chambourcin; and Norton are the three red varieties. The winery also sources grapes from other Missouri vineyards.

Highlights: Barrel aging teases out flavors of cherries, red currants, and a hint of cranberries balanced with vanilla and spice aromas in the Chambourcin.

Fermented in stainless steel to retain bright flavors and crispness, Chardonel's melon and pear flavors play off acidity and subtle minerality. Chardonel Reserve, fermented in new American oak barrels, is richer than its sister wine, with oak notes complementing melon and delivering a creamy finish. Crossroads Red blends Chambourcin and Noiret. Blackberries and currants with spice and oak are evident. A portion of the wine was aged in American oak barrels to provide balance. Pineapple and melon flavors dance around crisp acidity and a smooth citrus finish in the blended Crossroads White. Norton Nouveau uses the Missouri state grape in a Beaujolais Nouveau style, resulting in dry cherry and floral notes with this light-bodied red. Crossroads Apfel is a superb cider for those who prefer a light apple aroma and subtle sweetness followed by a dry finish.

Torn Label Brewing Company

1708 Campbell Street, Kansas City, MO 64108
816-656-5459
tornlabel.com

Torn Label, a fifteen-barrel brewhouse and production brewery operated by brewers and cofounders Rafi Chaudry and Travis Moore, is on the east end of the Crossroads Arts District. The intimate taproom was designed by local artist Peter Warren, known for incorporating repurposed wood into his work. The tasting room and deck are popular spots on weekends, First Friday art walks, and special-release beer events.

The brewery balances an approachability of classic styles with a penchant for experimentation to create bold beers with character not found elsewhere. Chaudry and Moore develop American craft beers with the spirit of innovation, anchored in English, German, and Belgian brewing tradition and fundamentals of brewing.

Highlights: Brewery tours ($10) on Sundays at 12:15 p.m. (first come, first serve) include three beer samples plus a Torn Label pint glass and stickers. Beer is available by the glass or flights. On Thursdays the brewery taps its Rough Draught series of taproom-only beers. Outside food is welcome. Year-rounders include Monk & Honey, a Belgian-inspired ale with local honey and a touch of spice; House Brew, a coffee wheat stout brewed with Sumatran toddy from Crossroads neighbor Thou Mayest Coffee Roasters; and crisp Alpha Pale Ale. Ask the servers about limited-release and seasonal beers on tap, such as West Coast–style Hang 'Em High IPA, tart Tonguelash hoppy wheat, and hefty Old

Bartenders at Torn Label Brewing's cozy urban taproom guide customers through the tap list. The taproom was designed by Kansas City artist Peter Warren, known for his use of wood and natural materials. Photo by the author.

Believer Russian Imperial Stout with big, bold roasted malts and silky body. The brewery's beers are served on tap throughout Kansas City. Alpha Pale, House Brew, and Monk & Honey are packaged in six-pack cans, and several of its beers in 22-ounce bottles are available at area liquor stores.

Travel tip: Located on the south side of the white Studio Inc. building. Enter through the gate under the bottle on the southeast corner. Head up the deck stairs and enter the doorway into the taproom.

Double Shift Brewing Company

412 East 18th Street, Kansas City, MO 64108
doubleshiftbrewing.com

Double Shift Brewing draws its name from founder Aaron Ogilvie, who works dual shifts as a Leawood Fire Department firefighter and brewery owner. The brewery's taproom is a lively, casual setting, where a garage door is raised on

Double Shift Brewing is a popular stop for brewery bus tours, neighborhood guests, and First Friday visitors to the Crossroads Arts District. Guests may bring in food from nearby restaurants and food trucks. Photo by the author.

the side of the building on warm-weather days. Beer drinkers gather at the bar and communal tables to socialize and play board games. Current beer selections are listed on a chalkboard behind the bar. Brewer Bryan Stewart oversees daily operations in the small-batch, five-barrel brewhouse.

Highlights: Core beers rotate on tap and include River Pirate Oatmeal Stout, Don't Call Me Radio IPA, 80s Saison-tage, Run-Around Rye, and the 18th Street Pale Ale experimental series. The tap list rotates regularly to include seasonal and special-release beers. Briar & Bramble English Pub Ale is light, malty, and sweet. Don't Call Me Radio IPA veers toward dank, hoppy flavor and tropical aromas. River Pirate Oatmeal Stout offers characteristic coffee and chocolate aroma from roasted malt with prominent hops.

Brewery Row

Double Shift Brewing and next-door neighbor Border Brewing are regular stops on two Kansas City–based brewery tours, Barley Bus (barleybus.com) and KC Beer Tour (kcbeertour.com). Brewery Emperial is within walking distance, as is Grinders, a craft beer bar with pizza and grinders. Torn Label Brewing is a few blocks to the east.

Border Brewing Company

406 East 18th Street, Kansas City, MO 64108
888-320-5199
borderbrewco.com

Border Brewing's cozy forty-two-seat taproom is a popular stop for urban residents, downtown workers, and craft beer fans on the brewery trail. Founders Eric and Tracy Martens own and operate the brewery and taproom. The brewhouse is visible behind a fenced-in area, where Eric makes small-batch beers. Local artwork adds an eclectic look and ties into the Crossroad's arts roots.

These easy-drinking session beers are true to style with subtle variations as a reflection of the brewer's craft. Border sponsors a quarterly "Brew for You" contest, in which patrons may vote online for which limited-release beer will be brewed next and served on tap. The contest creates interactivity and offers patrons a voice in the selection.

Highlights: Backyard Blonde Ale is light and crisp with citrus notes. Patio Pale Ale loads up on American Cascade and Simcoe hops, boosting its citrusy hop profile offset by malt. American-style Rooftop Red Ale has a deep amber-red color and sweet, slightly nutty malt backbone. Rye IPA uses rye malt for a bready malt flavor and notes of earth, pine, and peppery rye on the hoppy finish. Campfire Porter, aged on toasted American white oak, has a subtle oak finish to complement roasted malt notes. Served on nitro, Pub Dweller ESB and Chocolate Milk Stout are creamy dark beers to savor. Available in a bottle, Firepit Porter Imperial is dark and malty with a higher alcohol content and robust chocolate, coffee, and oak notes, and finishes with a velvet touch.

Border Brewing's taproom, located on busy East 18th Street, is an ideal spot for people watching, viewing sports, and socializing over a pint. Photo by the author.

Brewery Emperial

1829 Oak Street, Kansas City, MO 64108
816-945-9625
breweryemperial.com

Brewery Emperial partners Keith and Julie Thompson, Ted and Jackie Habiger, and Rich and Shannon Kasyjanski opened this East Crossroads brewery and restaurant in late 2016. The partners and friends have decades of experience in the brewery and restaurant industry at venues including McCoy's Public House, 75th Street Brewery (since closed), The Foundry, and Room 39. They united to create a brewery that focuses on the modern presentation of classic ales and lagers paired with a wood-fired grill experience.

The brewery's name is an homage to historic Imperial Brewery, formerly located three miles away in the Westside neighborhood, which rose to prominence until Prohibition. The name also emphasizes that the business focus is a brewery,

Bring an appetite for beer and food to Brewery Emperial. Brewmaster Keith Thompson makes easy-drinking session beers. Chef Ted Habiger and his kitchen team prepare savory meat, fish, and vegetables over a wood-fired grill. Photo by the author.

first and foremost. Brewery Emperial also strives to produce quality food and beer that is majestic and worthy of royalty. It's a fitting aspiration in a city of champions.

Highlights: Inside Brewery Emperial, Keith oversees production of a fifteen-barrel system acquired from Hitachino Nest, a Japanese brewery. The brewery produces session beers with respect for the hallmarks of each style, such as a pre-Prohibition-style pilsner, lager, nut brown ale, Biscuit, Kölsch, porter, and other beers that pair well with grilled foods. Ted, a veteran chef, created the restaurant's menu and concept with a range of meat, vegetables, and other dishes prepared in a custom-made hearth over a wood-fired grill. The open kitchen is visible from the bar. In addition to indoor seating, outdoor patio seating is available in the beer garden. Local graffiti artist Scribe's animal-based characters appear in select locations on the brewery's walls, a nod to the urban feel and roots of the Crossroads Arts District.

Boulevard Brewing Company

Tours & Rec Center and Beer Hall
2534 Madison Avenue, Kansas City, MO 64108
816-474-7095
boulevard.com

Boulevard Brewing, established in 1989 by John McDonald, has grown to be Kansas City's largest brewery and a major craft beer destination for local residents and tourists worldwide. The brewery, Tours & Rec Center, and Beer Hall are located in the Westside neighborhood minutes from downtown Kansas City. The Tours & Rec Center and Beer Hall, both adjacent to the brewery in a separate building, opened in summer 2016 in response to increasing annual traffic for tours that outgrew the brewery's capacity.

The Tours & Rec Center operates as a welcome center to greet visitors and as a launch point for tours. The center also has informative, educational exhibits

Boulevard Brewing's Beer Hall, Tours & Rec Center, and gift shop is a must-visit destination for craft beer lovers. It's also a family-friendly place to grab a beer and a bite to eat, learn about brewing, and tour Kansas City's largest brewery. Photo by the author.

Keith Kennedy is one of the entertaining and informative tour guides at Boulevard Brewing. On the tour, Kennedy shares the history of the first tank that brewery founder John McDonald used in Cellar 1. Photo by the author.

about brewing and the history of the brewery on display. The first-floor gift shop sells a wide range of merchandise, work by local artists and businesses, and packaged Boulevard beer. Free guided walking tours take small groups through various areas of the brewery, where guests learn about Boulevard's history, brewing process, and philosophy. The tour concludes in the tasting room, where guests may sample a variety of Boulevard beers.

The second floor is home to the ten-thousand-square-foot Beer Hall, a grand room dedicated to the social experience of craft beer. The main taproom bar features twenty-four beers on tap with rotating selections, indoor seating at communal tables, a photo booth, an expansive deck, and other attractions. The Beer Hall also serves a range of light snacks, meat and cheese boards, and food to complement its beers.

Visit the website for FAQs and detailed information about tours, the Tours & Rec Center, and holiday schedule.

As part of Boulevard's Visitor Center, the Beer Hall has ample space for guests to dine on house-made snacks, choose from twenty-four beers on tap, play games, visit the photo booth, and socialize. Educational exhibits and the gift shop are on the first floor. Photo by the author.

CENTRAL—WESTPORT, WALDO, AND BROOKSIDE

Green Room Burgers and Beer

4010 Pennsylvania Avenue, Suite D, Kansas City, MO 64111
816-216-7682
greenroomkc.com

Green Room Burgers and Beer, a made-from-scratch burger joint with the feel of a small-town diner, located in Westport, is also home to a one-barrel nano-brewery. Owned by Michael and Cindy Ptacek, the brewhouse may be "toured" in a minute by walking past a window that offers a view of a small room with

The name says it all. Stop in at Green Room Burgers and Beer. Dig into a tasty old-fashioned burger with fries. Wash it down with a house ale or beer from the taplist. Photo by the author.

brewhouse equipment. The burgers and beer, however, are worth taking far more than a minute to explore and enjoy.

Michael and two assistant brewers share brewing duties. Green Room typically offers English pub-style beers that involve less conditioning as well as several craft beers from other breweries. A rotating beer selection is also served directly from a cask.

Highlights: Papa Louie's is a dark, mild cask ale named after Ptacek's paternal grandfather. Old Country Promise, a French saison, is another favorite on rotation. Bird Lives, a double IPA brewed and served every August 29, is a tribute to Kansas City jazz legend Charlie "Bird" Parker.

McCoy's Public House

4057 Pennsylvania Avenue, Kansas City, MO 64111
816-960-0866
mccoyskc.com

Located at the intersection of Pennsylvania Street and Westport Road, McCoy's Public House sits at the epicenter of the Westport dining and entertainment district. Named after Westport founder John C. McCoy, the brewpub is a natural destination to dine, drink craft beer made on-site, and enjoy the upbeat atmosphere indoors and on the patio.

Established in 1997, McCoy's is the oldest operating brewpub in the city and remains at the forefront of a dynamic local craft brewing community. McCoy's and its sister businesses (Beer Kitchen, The Foundry, and Char Bar) in Westport provide multiple watering hole options for craft beer made locally, across the United States, and overseas. The restaurant group also hosts the Westport Beer

Established in 1997, McCoy's Public House is Kansas City's oldest operating brewpub. The brewery-restaurant is named after Westport founder John Calvin McCoy. Photo by the author.

Festival each June and the Strong Ale Fest each November (beerkc.com) and participates in KC Craft Beer Week in November.

The brewpub's in-the-round bar creates a natural gathering spot for customers to huddle, order beer and food, socialize, or catch up on televised news and sports. McCoy's offers ample indoor seating, plus a hallway connecting to next-door craft beer taproom The Foundry. A spacious outdoor patio with a bar is prime real estate year-round for dining, imbibing, and people watching.

Brewers Morgan Fetters and Emily Yeager run a tight ship in the brewhouse to keep a steady supply of core beers, seasonals, and rotating favorites on tap. The kitchen is known for brewpub classics, such as its half-pound burgers, award-winning mac and cheese, pizza, and comfort food entrées. Weekend brunch with chicken and waffles and beermosas are a regular draw.

Highlights: Check the website or chalkboard above the bar for current selections. Staples include Hogpound Brown Ale, Newcom's IPA, unfiltered wheat, oatmeal stout, and ginger shandy. The brewery has dozens of styles in its repertoire to keep choices interesting. McCoy's earned a gold medal for Ursa Minor, an imperial brown ale, at the 2015 Great American Beer Festival in the strong beer category. This popular beer is in high demand during winter, while supplies last.

Kansas City Bier Company

310 West 79th Street, Kansas City, MO 64114
816-214-8691
kcbier.com

Brewery founder Steve Holle created Kansas City Bier Company in 2014 to produce and offer German-style craft beer. He saw opportunity where other local and national breweries were focused on English, Belgian, and American styles of craft beer. Holle's insight and pursuit connected with craft beer fans and beer drinkers overall. Brewer Karlton Graham produces Kansas City Bier's selection of German-style beers made fresh and true to style with authentic ingredients from Germany.

The production brewery expanded in 2016 to keep up with demand for its beers in more than 425 locations throughout greater Kansas City. The brewery also added a bottling line to sell packaged beer to area retailers. The brewery's German beer hall–style tasting room and beer garden serves traditional German sausages, cheeses, and breads that complement its German beer styles served

Kansas City Bier Company's biergarten provides a natural destination to spend a pleasant mid-western evening outdoors with a bier. The brewery and taproom is conveniently located next to the Trolley Track Trail, creating additional incentive to go for a stroll. Photo by the author.

in appropriate glassware. Live musicians perform traditional German music on weekends for a festive atmosphere.

Highlights: Dunkel, a malty brown Munich lager dark in color with a light body, is the brewery's best-selling beer. Helles, a golden Munich lager; hefeweizen; Weizenbock, a strong German wheat; pilsner; and Doppel Alt are a few of the rotating selections on tap. Der Bauer—meaning "the farmhouse"—is a German interpretation of a Belgian saison or farmhouse ale with floral notes. Oktoberfest's Festbier rolls out during the fall season. Small Batch Tuesdays feature a weekly specialty beer. Growlers are available.

BKS Artisan Ales

633 East 63rd Street #120, Kansas City, MO 64110
bksartisanales.com

Brian and Mary Rooney will open BKS Artisan Ales, a nanobrewery with a two-barrel brewhouse system in the Brookside East neighborhood, in early fall 2017. The 2,000-square-foot brewery and taproom is housed in a renovated 8,800-square-foot retail/office building renovated by developers Butch Rigby and Byron Pendleton.

The opportunity to open a nanobrewery in a more residential area arose due to the "nanobrew ordinance," notes Brian. In May 2016, Kansas City's city council voted to approve an ordinance change. The ordinance now allows tiny breweries to operate in neighborhood strip malls and storefronts. The Rooneys worked closely with Councilman Scott Taylor to get the ordinance changed to allow the brewery in the neighborhood.

Brian, a homebrewer for seven years, has regularly entered his beers into local and national homebrew competitions over the past five years and has won several awards.

Highlights: BKS Artisan Ales features farmhouse-style ales, Northeast-style hoppy ales, English mild ale, stouts, and a barrel program that includes spirit-barrel-aged stouts and barrel-aged sours.

SOUTH

Crane Brewing Company

6515 Railroad Street, Raytown, MO 64133
816-743-4132
cranebrewing.com

Crane Brewing, founded in 2014 as Raytown's first brewery, is a 17,500-square-foot production brewery and taproom. Known for its distinctive saison, lambic, and Berliner weiss styles, the taproom is a can't-miss destination for craft beer fans. Tours include an overview of the brewery and brewing process, with stops at the fifteen-barrel brewhouse, fermentation vessels and aging tanks, and bar-

Crane Brewing's beautiful taproom features a bar made from aged honey locust slabs, tables made from 110-year-old barn wood, and beer flight paddles made from a barrel that cofounder Michael Crane once used to age beer in his basement as a homebrewer.

rel room, where some beers are aged before release. The taproom offers special releases on occasion and hosts events.

Cofounders and homebrewers Michael Crane and Christopher Meyer assembled the crack team of brewers, Steve Hood and Randy Strange, to scale up the brewery and manage brewing operations. Crane Brewing is capable of producing up to three thousand barrels of beer annually. Its beers are bottled for distribution throughout Missouri, eastern Kansas, Nebraska, and Oklahoma, and their beers are sold on tap in numerous Kansas City–area bars and restaurants.

Highlights: Saison, a farmhouse-style ale, has toasty malt, fruity yeast, and a floral nose. Farmhouse IPA is big and bold with ample aromatic hops. Seasonals include Gooseberry Gose, Orange Gose, and Grapefruit Gose. Gose, a German beer style, has a crisp, slightly salty finish. The latter two are made with fresh zest for a refreshing citrus kick. Crane is also known for its flavored Berliner weiss, a tart wheat style, available seasonally in apricot, kumquat, tea (made with local Hugo Tea berry rooibos), and beet.

Travel tip: Crane Brewing is accessible from I-70, I-435, and Highway 350/Blue Parkway. On Raytown Road, take a sharp turn south onto Railroad Street and proceed to the lot and the white building.

Beer Festival Fun

Festival of the Lost Township, sponsored by Crane Brewing, is held each fall in Raytown (festivalofthelosttownship.org). Brewery festival season in Kansas City typically runs April through November. For a complete list of beer festivals, rare tappings, and other events, visit the KC Beer Scouts blog, kcbeerscouts.com.

Martin City Brewing Company

500 East 135th Street, Kansas City, MO 64145
816-268-2222
martincitybrewingcompany.com

Founded by Matt Moore and Chancie Adams in 2011, Martin City Brewing Company offers numerous reasons to visit the Taproom and Pizza Restaurant at the brewery and next-door pub. The brewery produces flavor-forward craft beer influenced by Belgian styles and expressed through the traditional brewing techniques and creativity of head brewer Nick Vaughn. The beers on tap span a wide range of styles with character that stand out from standard presentations of wheat, IPA, pale ale, and stout.

The brewery's kitchen prepares some of the city's best wood-fired oven pizza as well as starters, salads, and sandwiches. Along with indoor seating, the patio with fire pits is a popular spot during pleasant weather. The patio, sandwiched between the brewery and taproom/restaurant, features a regular slate of live music.

Next door to the brewery, The Pub has a rotating selection of craft beers from top regional and national breweries, including a couple of MCBC's beers. The Pub's kitchen prepares a mix of classic brewpub favorites, including wings, nachos, burgers, and sandwiches. Other specialties include tenderloin sliders, fried

The team behind Martin City Brewing: (left to right) brewer Grant Bergmann, owner Matt Moore, owner Chancie Adams, and head brewer Nick Vaughn. Photo by the author.

goat cheese salad, its famed mac and cheese, and daily entrée specials. Tours are available by appointment. The brewery and The Martin (13440 Holmes Road; themartineventspace.com), located down the street, offer unique options for event space.

Highlights: Belgian-style Abbey Ale has aromas of semisweet malt, cherry, and pear from the house Belgian yeast strain, followed by cherry and chocolate flavor. Refreshing Belgian Blond's blend of rye malt and Saaz hops infuses the beer with spicy notes, while dry hopping contributes floral and spice aromas. Hard Way American-style IPA's toasted malt flavor guest stars with citrus flavors and aroma produced by triple hopping. City Saison's straw-colored hue and foamy head are true to farmhouse style with robust spice, fruity, floral notes, and a crisp dry finish. Barrel-aged Big Boy Imperial Stout is bold and unapologetic

Head brewer Nick Vaughn of Martin City Brewing Company makes Belgian-influenced beers and variations on classic styles in the true sense of craft. The taproom list includes year-round, seasonal, and special releases that awaken the senses and satisfy thirst. Photo by the author.

with chocolate notes. Operation Yoga Pants, a gluten-free beer brew with millet and buckwheat, eases into peachy aroma and flavor. Ask the servers about beers available in cans, bottles, growlers, and crowlers.

CHAPTER 6

KANSAS CITY

NORTHLAND AND NORTHERN MISSOURI

North Kansas City is a separate municipality within the Kansas City metropolitan area north of the Missouri River, collectively known as the Northland. The Northland is home to numerous breweries, wineries, and distilleries in the city or a short drive away through scenic countryside in Weston and other areas.

The Big Rip Brewing Company

216 East 9th Avenue, North Kansas City, MO 64116
816-866-0747
bigripbrewing.com

The Big Rip's name refers to a scientific theory about the origin of the universe. Rather than the Big Bang, the Big Rip theory proposes that the universe is expanding. Eventually, the universe will defy gravity, disband celestial structures, and end. Meanwhile, this cozy brewery and taproom serves up a wide variety of beers.

Before founding The Big Rip, Josh Collins and Kipp Feldt, respectively, made wine and beer at home. They joined forces to open the brewery in May 2013. The taproom has a relaxed feel, with current beers on tap listed on a chalkboard behind the bar. Televisions stream classic horror and sci-fi films, a nod toward the

Order a beer on tap at The Big Rip, relax and enjoy classic horror and sci-fi films on television, peek into the adjacent brewery, or slip outside to the beer patio. Velvet Elvis above the door knows if you've left the building. Credit: William Hess Photography, courtesy of The Big Rip Brewing Company.

owners' love of the genres. The beers are named after characters and references from films and television shows.

The four-barrel brewhouse is visible through a taproom window. Guests gather inside and outside in a courtyard with picnic tables and yard games. The brewery has an event room for meetings and private parties. Annual events include March Snake Saturday festivities, the brewery's anniversary party in June, a Fourth of July party with outdoor movies and fireworks viewing, and Ripper Halloween Party.

Highlights: Popular beers include Aisle 12 West Coast IPA, flagship Hathor's Sweet Brown Ale, creamy 237 Milk Stout, Zelda's Vanilla Cream, and Hefe the Killer, a hefeweizen. Fruit-based gluten-free beers, such as blackberry and raspberry; cocktails; and homemade nonalcoholic root beer and sarsaparilla are also available. A portion of each beer sale is donated to charity. Since inception, The Big Rip has donated thousands of dollars to local charities and helped others raise money through private events and other donations.

Cinder Block Brewery

110 East 18th Avenue, North Kansas City, MO 64116
816-298-6555
cinderblockbrewery.com

Bryce Schaffter, who cofounded Cinder Block Brewery with his wife, Ashley, and fellow homebrewer John Baikie met Bryan "Bucky" Buckingham at the 2013 Great Nebraska Beer Fest. Buckingham, a twenty-year veteran in the beer business, joined Cinder Block as brewmaster and director of brewing operations.

The taproom attracts a steady following of local residents and craft beer fans who socialize, watch sports, and gather outdoors to play yard games and lounge. Geek trivia on Tuesday evenings draws a regular competitive crowd. With twenty taps, Cinder Block offers six year-round beers, up to eight seasonal beers, French apple cider and English cherry cider, and special releases. Racks of brandy, bourbon, and wine barrels are dedicated to the barrel-aged beer program. Specific styles of beer are aged for up to eighteen months before being released as limited editions.

Cinder Block Brewery's spacious taproom connects to an event space next door and a patio with lounge furniture. Cellar Man Kitchen food truck also operates at the brewery. Photo by the author.

Highlights: Flagship beers include crisp, light Northtown Native; Block IPA, brewed with six different hop varieties; Prime Extra Pale Ale; Pavers Porter; and Belgian Weathered Wit. Seasonal and limited releases include barrel-aged Black Squirrel Russian Imperial Stout, Belgian strong ale winter warmer Cinder Noel, English brown ale Coffee Hop'd, and KC Weiss, a tart Berliner weiss. In addition to growler sales, several of Cinder Block's beers are sold in four-pack cans at the bar. Cellar Man Kitchen food truck prepares beer-friendly, hearty pub fare.

North Kansas City Craft Beer Crawl

Plan a craft brewery crawl with stops at Cinder Block Brewery, Calibration Brewery, Colony Handcrafted Ales, and The Big Rip Brewing Company. These breweries are located within blocks of each other. In addition, Restless Spirits Distillery is across the street from Cinder Block. Other nearby craft beer destinations include Grain to Glass, a taproom and homebrew supply shop, Tapcade NKC, and Screenland Armour, a movie theater with premium craft beer selection and arcade games.

Restless Spirits Distilling Company

109 East 18th Avenue, North Kansas City, MO 64116
816-492-6868
restlessspiritsdistilling.com

Restless Spirits's building is hard to miss. The facade displays a larger-than-life Paul Bunyan–like character hauling a sledgehammer with a whiskey barrel as its massive head. This "stone breaker" is emblematic of the hundreds of Irish immigrants who carved out Kansas City's first streets from limestone bluffs in the River Market and downtown in the early and mid-nineteenth century.

Michael Shannon, president, and Benay Shannon, vice president and head distiller, cofounded the distillery. They drew on the Irish heritage of the Shannon family and the city's working-class Irish community. Michael is fifth-generation Irish born in Kansas City. Accordingly, Restless Spirits's blend of Irish and American heritage forms the character, backbone, and style of its gin, vodka, and whiskey.

The mighty "stone breaker" wielding a whiskey barrel on the end of his hammer taps into the history of Kansas City's Irish workers who carved out and built the city's first streets. The character also makes it hard to miss Restless Spirits Distilling. Photo by the author.

Tours explore the distillery's five-hundred-gallon Vendome pot still, tasting room, mash tun, fermenters, laboratory, event space, barrel room, and shipping. Apparel and bottles of spirits are available for sale in the tasting room. When visiting, ask about the Pendergast-era reference that is made by the rabbit featured on bottle labels and the distillery's logo.

Highlights: Builder's Botanical Gin, striking for its aromatic lavender and rosemary bouquet, won silver at the 2016 San Diego Spirits Festival International Spirits Competition. Duffy's Run Vodka is bold and smooth with a hint of sweetness. The name Duffy's honors the fifty-seven Irish men who died while doing railroad work on Duffy's Cut, a stretch of railroad twenty miles northwest of Philadelphia. Irish laborers died there more than 175 years ago from cholera and, research suggests, violence. Irish-American Stone Breaker malt whiskey is twice-distilled in-house and blended with imported four-year-old Irish whiskey to develop its character and body. Sons of Erin Irish Whiskey is a collaboration with Great Northern Distillery of Dundalk, county Louth. Restless Spirits sources this sweet, light, four-year-old whiskey straight from the Land of Erin, the nickname of Ireland.

The five-hundred-gallon Vendome copper pot still at Restless Spirits Distilling is a beauty. Tours explore the distilling operation, barrel room, and tasting room for samples of Irish American spirits. Photo by the author.

Calibration Brewery

119 Armour Road, North Kansas City, MO 64116
816-994-8277
calibrationbrewery.com

Calibration Brewery founder Glen Stinson, a former homebrewer, transformed a former automobile repair shop and dealership into a brewery with a seven-barrel brewhouse. The large taproom features a bar and tabletops made from reclaimed wood, a fireplace, and cozy lounge furniture. Outside, guests may enjoy a beer on the patio or in the game area.

Chef Adam Clay's menu includes classics such as a Chicago-style hot dog, chili-and-cheese hot dog, and bacon and beer cheese dog. Other diverse foods include chicken wings (hot, mild, garlic, teriyaki, Parmesan), black bean hummus and pita basket, and an open-faced avocado sandwich.

Calibration Brewery, one of four breweries in North Kansas City, makes a convenient stop on a mini brewery tour to drink a beer in the spacious taproom or on the outdoor patio. Photo by the author.

Highlights: Carry On Milk Stout has roasted chocolate notes and a creamy finish. Prominent banana and clove bloom in Some Kind of Wonderful Hefeweizen. Mildly hoppy Scare Myself IPA has floral and pine aromas. Malty Compared to What Scottish Ale conjures dark fruit-spice flavors and All Day All Night Coconut Brown Ale is subtly nutty.

Colony KC and Colony Handcrafted Ales

312 Armour Road, North Kansas City, MO 64116
816-800-4699
colonykc.com

Zach Henderson and Drew Cobb originally established their coffee shop and craft beer taproom to serve coffee and espresso, plus craft beer from other breweries. They later opened Colony Handcrafted Ales, a two-barrel nanobrewery, in

Cofounders Zach Henderson (right) and Drew Cobb (not pictured) launched Colony Hand-crafted Ale inside their coffee shop and taproom, Colony KC. Brewer Rodney Beagle (left) produces distinctive ales, regional IPAs, and other styles. Photo by the author. Image first published in Flatland.

the shop based on popular demand—customers kept asking which beers on tap were made by Colony. Subsequently, Henderson and Cobb hired veteran home-brewer and taproom bartender Rodney Beagle to become head brewer.

The shop has a relaxed atmosphere, communal-meets-industrial feel, and casual-comfort design aesthetic. Colony serves twelve rotating selections of beers—its own and some from featured local and regional breweries. Along with more than eighty packaged craft beers in stock, the bar prepares coffee and espresso made from locally roasted beans. Light eats include fresh baked goods from Scratch Bakery and local food trucks.

Highlights: Fuller, a caramel latte porter, is a tasty staple. Beagle specializes in fruit-forward ales and cream ales, such as "It's a Cream Dream." Cocktails include classics and crafted creations using locally distilled spirits from S. D. Strong and Tom's Town distilleries.

S.D. Strong Distilling Company

8500 Northwest River Park Drive, #136A,
Parkville, MO 64152
sdstrongdistilling.com

Established in 2012 by Steve Strong, S.D. Strong Distilling produces its name-sake full-bodied vodka, Straight Rye Whiskey, and Pillar 136 Gin. The gin's name refers to Pillar 136, one of many such structures that provide support in Parkville's commercial underground caves. The distillery is located underneath the Park University campus.

Local artist Valerie Jahraus painted the artwork on display in the distillery and featured on the spirit's labels. The dashing, mustachioed strongman is inspired by Jahraus's great-uncle Charles Wesley Copeland, a famous artist who produced hundreds of magazine illustrations and paperback novel covers over his career.

Highlights: In 2017 the distillery released an oak barrel–aged straight bourbon. The Straight Rye Whiskey, available only at the distillery, has characteris-

Distiller Steve Strong produces his award-winning spirits from an underground cave in Parkville. S.D. Strong hosts "house" concerts and occasional tours at the distillery located at Pillar 136 in the commercial man-made caves. Image courtesy of S.D. Strong Distilling.

tic peppery notes from the grain. S.D. Strong Vodka earned silver at the 2016 Washington Cup, a one-of-a-kind competition exclusively for American-made spirits and liqueurs. Pillar 136 Gin took top honors at the 2015 and 2016 Washington Cup competition and earned bronze at the prestigious 2015 San Francisco World Spirits Competition. The gin's distinctive bouquet and citrus taste is derived from hand-zested blood orange, lemon, and lime combined with other botanicals.

Travel tip: Take MO 9 North toward Parkville. Before you reach the city, the entrance to Park University is on the right. Turn right and follow the bend to the cave entrance. Turn on your vehicle lights and proceed slowly toward 136A.

Rock & Run Brewery and Pub

114 East Kansas Street, Liberty, MO 64068
816-415-2337
Rock & Run Brewery and Tap Room
115 West Washington Street, Kearney, MO 64060
816-635-2492
rockandrunbrewery.com

Rock & Run Brewery taps into rock-and-roll, running, and a relentless spirit in a dynamic way. Owners Gene DeClue, a brewmaster and founder of rock band Cherry Bomb, and Dan Hatcher, a long-distance runner and entrepreneur with a twenty-five-year career in construction management, opened this Northland brewery in December 2013. The original 3,200-square-foot brewery with a one-barrel brewhouse and pub was in a building (110 East Kansas Street) more than a century old and a block away from Liberty's historic square.

DeClue and Hatcher had nearly completed plans to expand operations into a space in the Bedinger Building, but after a wall collapsed in early May 2016 and forced a temporary closing, they shifted gears, acquired the former The Bell restaurant and bar space (114 East Kansas Street) next door, and reopened. Now Rock & Run's brewery, pub, and restaurant operates out of both spaces under their banner. The acquisition included an eighty-seat patio and a prime corner spot at a major intersection. The brewer also upgraded its brewhouse to a three-barrel system that will increase its production capacity. The food menu is driven by wood-fired pizzas, soups, salads, burgers, pastas, and sandwiches. The pub is a popular destination for locals and craft beer geeks to dine and drink.

Rock & Run Brewery and Pub in downtown Liberty draws guests for its craft beer, wood-fired pizza, and upscale casual brewpub menu. Craft beer fans also flock to their Kearney-based production brewery and taproom for year-round and special beer releases. Photo by the author.

In 2016 DeClue and Hatcher acquired a building in Kearney ten minutes away from their flagship location. They built a twenty-barrel brewhouse and pilot brewing system to expand capacity for their core beers, seasonals, and limited releases. Plans for the future include adding a canning line. This location features a taproom with brewery-only beers available, and there are plans for a beer garden.

Highlights: Core beers include light ale Liberty Squared, unfiltered Farmhouse Funk dry-hopped with Sorachi Ace hops, 5k IPA, Ryely Porter, and Saminator, a quadruple IPA fermented a second time with sake yeast and honey, named after DeClue's youngest daughter, Samantha. The brewery offers many rotating seasonal beers in varying styles and flavors, such as Apricot Beach Blonde Ale and Rocktoberfest Märzen. A digital board lists the house and guest brewery beers on tap, featuring a selection geared toward hardcore craft beer fans.

Belvoir Winery

1325 Odd Fellows Road, Liberty, MO 64068
816-200-1811
belvoirwinery.com

Belvoir Winery, a wedding and reception event space and nine-bedroom inn, is located at the former Odd Fellows Home, which dates back to the 1900s. Jesse Leimkuehler, whose family owns the winery, manages renovation and business operations. The property's architecture and the fraternal order have a fascinating history, detailed on the winery's website. The winery's grounds encompass the Odd Fellows Home, Old Folks Home Building, a former hospital, school, cemetery, and four acres of vineyard. The winery's haunted reputation was featured on SyFy's *Ghost Hunters* in February of 2013. The Travel Channel's *Ghost Adventures* team also filmed an episode on-site.

Belvoir Winery is housed in the former Odd Fellows Home on an expansive estate. Surrounded by four acres of vineyard, the tasting room, inn, and event space is supposedly haunted. Credit: Kim Horgan Photography.

Belvoir's tasting room is open seven days a week. Leimkuehler shares notes during free tastings about the winery's on-site production, bottling at Les Bourgeois Winery, and wines.

Highlights: Norton's violet and spicy earth aromas are complemented by peppery notes and rich berry flavors. Casanova, a blend of Missouri-grown Chambourcin and Saint Vincent with California Syrah, delivers juicy berry flavor, a medium body, and soft finish. Chardonel's pear and apple aromas accompany a lightly oaked, full-bodied dry white with a crisp finish. Plumeria, a blend of Seyval, Traminette, and Vignoles grapes, begins with a rich, floral nose, offers subtle sweetness, and has a crisp finish.

Fence Stile Vineyards and Winery

31010 West 124th Street, Excelsior Springs, MO 64024
816-500-6465
fencestile.com

The charm offensive begins with the drive to Fence Stile Vineyards and Winery, accessible from several major highways. Local roadways to the winery curl past serene wooded lanes that are especially colorful in autumn.

Shriti and William Plimpton established Fence Stile in 2006 and opened it to the public in 2009. The winery's drive leads past six acres of established vineyard planted in 2007. Varietals include Seyval Blanc, Vidal Blanc, Vignoles, Chambourcin, Concord, and Noiret. Crimson Cabernet, a hybrid of Norton and Cabernet Sauvignon, and Cabernet Doré, a white grape hybrid, were newly planted in 2016 on four additional acres. The winery is home to an expansive tasting room, manmade underground wine caves, cellar garden, love locks wall, private wine tasting room, outdoor patios, fire pit, and other attractions.

William died in 2015. Shriti, who lives and works in Kansas City with her son Amrish, continues to manage operations as proprietor and host in the tasting room.

Tours on Saturdays offer walks through the vineyard, crush pad, winery tasting room, and caves. Guests learn how wine is produced on-site. Fence Stile offers a wine club with many benefits, an adopt-a-vine sponsorship program, and an exclusive Cellar 57 club. Named in honor of William's memory, the club signifies 57 as a reoccurring number: born in 1957, William passed away at age 57; the club only has 57 members; the goal is to build 57 wine lockers (each holds 57 wine bottles) in the cave; and club members receive 5 bottles of red and 7

After sampling wine at Fence Stile's tasting room, guests relax by the fireplace, gather by the fire pit on Fridays, lounge on the patio, or stroll in the vineyard, depending on the season. The scenic winery is a charming destination to take others and make friends over a glass of wine. Photo by the author.

bottles of white with their initial membership. Wine-In, which features outdoor movies on the patio; Fire Pit Fridays; and patio concerts are popular social events near a cozy fire on cool evenings.

Highlights: Tastings include five pours. Several wine labels feature painted artwork by Shriti's sister Mayuri. Amrish's artwork is displayed on the label of port-style wine Deliciar. More than a dozen wines are available, including Seyval, an oaked white that presents vanilla on the nose and citrus on the finish. Becca Blend, named after the family's golden retriever-poodle mix, is bronze in color with a floral nose, hints of citrus and honey, and crisp finish. Reserve Chambourcin, a dry red, asserts itself with fruit-forward flavor, cherry and violets on the nose, and subtle oak. Popular Firepit Red, a full-bodied Norton-Chambourcin blend, balances cherry with smoky oak. Ishq, a sweet dessert wine made in the style of Sauternes, is named after a word that means "love" in a dozen pan-Arabic and Persian languages. Crown Valley in Saint Genevieve, Missouri, produces Fence Stile's sparkling wines using the *champenoise* method.

Travel tip: Light bread, crackers, cheese, sausage, olives, and other snacks are available. The outdoor grounds are an inviting space for a picnic. See the website for detailed directions.

Of the Earth Farm Distillery

38391 West 176th Street, Rayville, MO 64084
660-232-1096
oftheearthfarm.com

Farmer and distiller Jim Pierce is a regular fixture at the Saturday farmers' market in Kansas City's City Market (5th and Grand), where he offers samples of his fruit-based spirits and explains their provenance. Jim and Sarah Burnett Pierce

Jim and Sarah Burnett Pierce, who operate Of the Earth Farm Distillery, bring their fresh produce and fruit-based spirits to the City Market in Kansas City on weekends and sell direct to shoppers. Photo by the author.

operate Of the Earth distillery using a copper pot still from Portugal on their forty-acre farm an hour north of Kansas City.

With no tasting room or retail space on the farm, Jim brings apple brandy and other spirits to market. That's quite a deal for produce shoppers at the market, who can chat with the distiller and sample spirits at a tasting booth in the open-air venue. The farm also grows and sells seasonal produce such as chestnuts, Asian pears, pluots, and other fruits, and sells charcuterie.

Highlights: Apple brandy, made with a blend of apples from the Pierces' orchard, has a gentle heat with soothing apple. Blackberries are sourced from the Mule Barn Berry Patch in Lathrop for the blackberry liqueur, full of fresh berry flavor. Ray County Rye Eau de Vie uses rye for its peppery character. The French term *eau de vie de fruit*, or *eau de vie* for short, refers to a clear, colorless fruit brandy not made from grapes. *Eau de vie de vin* refers to what is commonly called brandy in the United States. Of the Earth's grappa uses pomace, the solid remains of grapes after the crush, from Baltimore Bend Winery.

Van Till Family Farm Winery

13986 State Highway C, Rayville, MO 64084
816-776-2720
vantillfarms.com

The Van Till Family Farm Winery is beautiful and fun to visit year-round. The drive through rolling hills and verdant countryside is especially nice during the spring bloom and autumn season. Native Californians and industrious fourth-generation farmers Cliff and Debbie Van Till moved to Rayville, Missouri, to farm and connect with the community. They approach sustainable farming as stewards of the land. Their value-added farm operation includes a winery, wine garden patio, and event space as a destination venue. Van Till is also a popular corporate weekday meeting venue.

The Van Tills focus on pairing their wines with farm-fresh foods. Wood-fired pizza is served with full table service with china, glassware, silverware, and cloth napkins. Pizza is available April through October on Friday and Saturday, 12–9 p.m., and November through March on Friday, 5–8 p.m. and Saturday, 12–8 p.m. Call to confirm service during winter.

Highlights: Van Till Family Farm Winery is a corporate sponsor of the Dream Factory of Greater Kansas City. Daydream, a Norton-Chambourcin blend that is full-bodied and dry with a hint of oak, was blended specifically for Dream Factory. A portion of proceeds benefits the nonprofit. The 2015 Missouri Norton is provocative with rich fruit, spicy earth notes, and light tannins. Aged in French and Missouri oak, Chambourcin finishes with light tannins and cherry. Red Tractor is a semidry red blend made for watching sunsets. Farm Shed Red, also semidry, is fruit-forward with a touch of citrus and ideal for pairing with pizza and pasta. The semisweet Vignoles stands out with fragrant pineapple and pear notes. Traminette leans sweet with a bouquet of honeysuckle and a touch of apricot. Ranch Red, a sweet Concord blend, bursts with raspberry and cherry flavors. Ever-popular Sweet White introduces itself with honeydew and tropical fruit. The winery also offers fruit wine and dessert wines.

Ladoga Ridge Winery

100 East Pope Lane, Smithville, MO 64089
816-866-4077
ladogaridgewinery.com

Ladoga silt loam, a soil found in the northern tip of Missouri, and four other soil types make up the slopes and ridges of Ladoga Ridge Winery, located one mile north of downtown Smithville. Rolling vineyards are spread across this deep, well-drained soil. The winery's Tuscan-inspired tasting room houses a bar and gift shop with a patio in the back that overlooks grapevines, gentle slopes, and pastoral countryside.

Galen and Leinda Haddock began planting the vineyard in spring 2010 and opened two years afterward. "We originally planted two thousand plants on four acres, ninety blackberry plants, and some fruit trees," said Leinda. "We lost half the vineyard and fruit trees in 2012. We replanted lost vines except one acre and now have three acres of vineyard." Galen, a former railroad carman for twenty-five years, manages the vineyard and makes the wine. Leinda manages office operations, the tasting room, events, and much more. The couple built a new life on land they could nurture as a sanctuary, place of celebration, and business to pass on to their children and grandchildren.

Breathtaking sunsets are a backdrop to flowers and trees that radiate a spectrum of color, especially in autumn. Entertainers perform live music during a fall series of Fireside Fridays. Year-round picnics, weekend getaways, and the annual B Cause breast cancer event offer additional excuses to relax, reflect, and escape the demands of daily life. Tastings include three complimentary samples, or eight samples for $5. Logo wine glasses are $2. Call ahead for large groups

Galen and Leinda Haddock built Ladoga Ridge Winery on lush land that serves as a breathtaking backdrop for picnics, live music, and sharing a wine bottle or two. Image courtesy of Ladoga Ridge Winery.

of ten or more. Art by local watercolor artist Judy Blankenship and Leinda's scenic photographs grace the wine labels.

Highlights: Strawberry Rhubarb, a sweet-tart rhubarb wine with natural berry juice added, is the best seller. Fruit wines include watermelon, peach, blueberry, and blackberry. Whites include Sully's, a semidry white blend mostly made from Vignoles, named after Leinda's German maiden name of Sullenger. Galen's Red is a dry Chambourcin aged two years and eight months in American oak, with smoky oak presence and pepper and cherry notes. Toad-a-Lope, a semisweet Concord-Chambourcin blend with the flavor of grape jelly and spice, is named after a group that once lived in the 1900s on lands now covered by Smithville Lake. B Cause, a rosé made with Catawba grapes, is named in honor of family and friends who have died from breast cancer. A portion of sales are donated to local organizations.

Travel tip: From Highway 169, take Highway DD (Main Street) east to the four-way stop. Turn north onto Bridge Street. In two blocks, turn east onto Highway F and proceed for one mile. Near a bend to the right on the highway, head straight left onto Pope Lane and follow it to the entrance.

Holladay Distillery

1 McCormick Lane, Weston, MO 64098
816-640-3056
holladaydistillery.com

Kentucky businessman Ben Holladay and his brother Major David Holladay opened Holladay Distillery in 1856, near a limestone spring that produced fresh mineral-rich water ideal for distilling. Over time, the distillery changed ownership several times and became known as McCormick Distilling Company. McCormick remains the country's oldest distillery west of the Mississippi still operating in its original location.

McCormick revived Holladay Distillery in 2016 and opened a welcome center that includes a tasting room, a timeline of the distillery, historical bottles and memorabilia, and a gift shop. The facility now distills and ages bourbon on-site for the first time in thirty years. The hand-dug cistern, approximately fifteen feet

An employee at Holladay Distillery inspects samples of the mash from Batch 34. Tour visitors observe the mash in progress firsthand in the steamy stillhouse. Photo by the author.

The Holladay Distillery guided walking tour includes a trip to Barrel Warehouse C, where barrels of bourbon age on sturdy racks. Photo by the author.

wide and thirty-five feet deep, contains more than forty-five thousand gallons of limestone spring water. Visitors may tour the distillery, see and taste bourbon being made, and view the limestone and spring on the property.

Highlights: Tours include spirit tastings and a visit to the Ancient Cave, an in-ground building dating back to 1839 that was used for aging spirits before their shipment by wagon train or stagecoach. The walking tour includes views of the original structure, which was once used as a meat-packing facility before its conversion to a stillhouse, the limestone spring and cistern, Barrel Warehouse C, and the one-column, seventeen-plate copper still used to produce bourbon. Tours ($10/person) include tastings for guests of legal drinking age.

Travel tip: Spirits are available for purchase at the welcome center. For a larger selection, the company also operates the McCormick Country Store on Main Street in Weston, Missouri.

Vox Vineyards

**19310 Northwest Farley Hampton Road #3,
Kansas City, MO 64153
816-354-4903
TerraVox Tasting Room at Green Dirt Farm Creamery
1099 Welt Street, Weston, MO 64098
816-386-2156
voxvineyards.com**

Rows of American heritage grapes line rolling hills covered in rich deposits of loess. Vines feed on layers of soil that were once covered by ancient glacial caps. Jerry Eisterhold and his wife, Kate Garland, founded Vox Vineyards here in 1996, built a home on an eighty-six-acre property in unincorporated Platte County, and created the TerraVox label—the name means "voice of the earth."

Eisterhold, a former agronomist who now runs a design firm for interactive museum exhibits, has made wine since he was a kid. He grew up in Osage County

Owner Jerry Eisterhold of Vox Vineyards stands before rows of obscure American heritage grapevine varieties gathered from across the United States, planted, and cultivated to develop truly unique North American wines. Photo by the author.

on the Gasconade River in the winemaking country southeast of Jefferson City. Several years ago, Eisterhold sought to establish a vineyard at his Kansas City home.

Eisterhold chose not to use solely common native varieties and French hybrids suitable for Missouri's climate and soil. He has spent twenty years tracking and obtaining American heritage grapes. Less well-known American varieties such as Cloeta, Hidalgo, and Wetumka have been brought from across the United States as cuttings, unavailable from nurseries anywhere.

Eisterhold grew interested in these heritage grapes after reading viticulturist Thomas Volney Munson's 1909 book *Foundations of American Grape Culture*. In the late 1800s, Munson identified thirty-one separate genera of grapes. All but four are indigenous to middle America. American heritage grapes have their origins in one of those twenty-seven grape species. Munson was the most significant of several fellow midwesterners (many of them native Germans living in Missouri) to collect and document native American grape species and breed new varieties from them.

In the twenty-first century, Eisterhold, renowned educator and technologist Clark Smith, and vintner Moss Bittner have undertaken a task similar to Munson's exploration of native American species. They have planted more than 4,300 grapevines of some sixty domestic heritage grape varieties. With time and evaluation, they seek to narrow stock to around two dozen grapevines that will produce superior-quality, distinctive wines.

As Vox Vineyards continues to refine its growing methods and winemaking production, Eisterhold wants the story of heritage grapes to be heard. "It's the theme of TerraVox," he said, "to rediscover and uncover the deep significant history of Missouri. The wine has a missionary role to bring out the heritage of the area as the 'voice of the land.'"

Highlights: The 2014 Cloeta, a jet-black grape, produces a wine with rich body, soft tannins, and an aroma of plums, chocolate, and coffee. 2014 Wetumka, a white wine with the aroma of elderberry flowers, is slightly acidic with a touch of candied-fruit sweetness to balance the sugars. The 2013 Munson Report's complex character and deep structure comes alive with bright acidity and balanced sweetness. The 2014 Traminette, from a Gewürztraminer hybrid that may be made dry or sweet, flexes spice and floral aromas that end with some residual sweetness. The 2015 Saignée is a rosé-style wine produced by an early pressing of dark 2015 Norton and then aged in oak for six months.

Vox Vineyards's tasting room is housed inside neighboring Green Dirt Farm Creamery in Weston. Guests may sample and purchase wine, order a light meal featuring local cheeses and breads, purchase Green Dirt's award-winning cheeses, and picnic on the grounds. Photo by the author.

Travel tip: Vox Vineyards's TerraVox wines are available at the tasting room in Green Dirt Farm's Creamery in Weston. After sampling wines, with expert insight from tasting room manager Winifred Wright, visit the creamery's cheese counter to order cheese, sandwiches, and other foods for noshing indoors or having a picnic outside. The winery also hosts many scheduled events at the appointment-only winery and vineyard, where they have limited quantities of their wines. The Vox wine club ensures access to these rare wines.

Weston Brewing Company

500 Welt Street, Weston, MO 64098
816-640-5235
westonirish.com

Weston Brewing Company, first established in 1842, is also home to Irish-themed American Bowman Restaurant and O'Malley's Pub, where visitors may enjoy fresh beer in these venues near Main Street in downtown Weston. Current owners Corey Weinfurt and Michael Coakley purchased the brewery in May 2005. It is the second-oldest west of the Hudson River and one of the oldest lagering breweries in the United States. Its location near Pedee Creek and Bear Creek was ideal for nineteenth-century brewers to cut and haul ice from the waterways. Ice was packed around solid oak lagering tanks in underground cellars, keeping the lager cool as it conditioned for six weeks before being served.

The brewery tour and website recount more detailed history about the various owners. The one-hour tour includes a walk through the twenty-five-barrel brewhouse, a descent into several historic underground cellars, the secret fourth

Brewer Michael Coakley, who co-owns Weston Brewing Company with Corey Weinfurt, leads a brewery tour that includes a visit to underground cellars and O'Malley's Pub, plus a beer tasting. Photo by the author.

cellar, and beer tasting underground in O'Malley's Pub. This highly recommended tour is one of the area's more in-depth explorations of a historic brewery that goes well beyond the fundamentals of brewing. The tour price is $5 for guests over 14. RSVP by phone is encouraged but not required.

Weston Brewing also hosts its annual Irish Festival in October, a three-day, family-friendly event that draws thousands for live music, dancing, food, beer, and more as announced on the website.

Highlights: Royal Lager, an easy-drinking American lager, is similar to light beer brewed by major domestic breweries. Bestselling O'Malley's Cream Ale is a light golden ale with a hint of sweetness. Drop Kick Ale is a classic English-style amber ale with a smooth balance between malt and hops and a crisp finish. O'Malley's Stout, a dry Irish stout, is smooth and silky with coffee notes and rich, dark malt.

Travel tip: Dine on Irish pub fare at American Bowman, next to the brewery. O'Malley's Pub has a full schedule of live music each month. Tour Weston's antique and retail shops, explore Green Dirt Farm Creamery for fresh cheeses and Vox Vineyard wine sampling, and visit Holladay Distillery at McCormick Distilling Company's campus.

Pirtle Winery

502 Spring Street, Weston, MO 64098
816-640-5728
pirtlewinery.com

Established in 1978 by Elbert and Patricia Pirtle, Pirtle Winery is one of the region's oldest wineries. Elbert and Patricia's sons Ross and Scott currently own and operate this family business in a former Lutheran Evangelical church built in 1867 by German immigrants. A vine-covered wine garden with a wine bar and deck offers ample seating at the main building. The tasting room and gift shop are on the second floor. Wines are produced and bottled in a brick production building across the street.

Scott Pirtle and winemaker Chaz Judy produce Pirtle's award-winning wines. Pirtle offers red, white, rosé, and port wines, plus fruit wines and several meads, both still and effervescent. Mellow Red won best of class at the 2016 Indy International Wine Competition. Also, Mellow Red and Effervescent Mead took double gold, Effervescent Apple and Vignoles won gold, four wines brought home

Co-owner Scott Pirtle and winemaker Chaz Judy in the tasting room of Pirtle Winery, one of the oldest, most awarded regional wineries and meaderies. Photo by the author.

silver, and the honey mead won bronze. Earlier in 2016, Effervescent Mead won best of class in the sparkling category at the Missouri Governor's Cup and at the 2015 Indy International Wine Competition. Tastings are free. Contact the winery for group tastings and pricing.

Highlights: Citrine, made from Riesling grapes, is a dry or *trocken*-style white with aromas of pear and mineral notes. Bestselling Mellow Red is a sweet Norton-based wine that's been around since the winery opened. Dry Missouri Norton is aged in American oak and French oak for six months each to add depth of flavor. Made with Saint Vincent grapes, Weston Bend Red is a spicy dry red with black pepper and raspberry notes. Fruit wines include apple, aronia berry, blueberry, cherry, and Effervescent Apple, made with Honeycrisp apples, similar to hard cider with light carbonation. Pirtle is also known for its award-winning meads made from California orange blossom honey. Its mead is the official wine of the Kansas City Renaissance Festival.

Weston Wine Company

540 Main Street, Weston, MO 64098
816-386-2345
westonwinecompany.com

Owned by Jowler Creek Winery founders Jason and Colleen Gerke, Weston Wine Company's bright purple building stands out among Main Street's shops. Purple, the color of royalty, is also a tipoff that this wine experience has a royal theme. Tastings ($7) include samples of eight wines. The winery has also created "tasting experiences" that pair six wines and cupcakes ($14/person), six wines and cheeses ($14/person), and other options for events and special occasions. One-week advance reservations are requested. A logo wine glass is included for each guest. From the wraparound patio, drink wine and watch others stroll along Main Street.

Get the royal treatment at this posh purple tasting room. Indulge in tasting experiences that pair six wines and cupcakes, or simply relax on the outdoor deck with a bottle and watch passersby on busy Main Street in Weston. Photo by the author.

Highlights: The seven wines are named after diamond cuts—King Brilliant, Radiant, Princess, etc. The wine selection includes dry, semisweet (cherry notes), and sweet red; dry, semisweet (citrus, peach aroma), and sweet (tropical fruit, white flower aromas), and rosé.

Jowler Creek Vineyard and Winery

16905 Jowler Creek Road, Platte City, MO 64079
816-858-5528
jowlercreek.com

Jowler Creek is a sustainable winery that uses solar power, Olde English Babydoll sheep to control weeds through managed, rotational grazing, and chickens to aid with pest management in its six-acre vineyard. The grapegrowing and winemaking skills of founders Jason and Colleen Gerke have resulted in the production of nine award-winning wines.

Jason was born and raised on a fifth-generation family-owned cattle and row crop farm in central Missouri. Colleen studied viticulture and enology in college

Jowler Creek is a scenic and sustainable winery that hosts many tastings, wine-food pairings, and other wine and music events at its tasting room, event space, and patio. Photo by the author.

in California and began making her own wines. The couple met, married, settled in Kansas City, and began making wine in their basement as a hobby. When they bought a home in Platte City, they also planted 250 Norton grapevines in spring 2004. They began producing wine by autumn the following year. The Gerkes added Vignoles and Traminette and expanded the vineyard to more than three thousand vines in subsequent years. Jowler Creek's wines have accumulated awards from the Jefferson Cup Invitational, Midwest Wine Competition, Missouri Wine Competition, and other competitions.

Highlights: Norton, a dry, full-bodied red with bold cherry notes and oaky characteristics, is made from Jowler Creek's own grapes. Chambourcin is earthy and spicy with cherry notes and soft tannins. Semisweet Traminette delivers pear, green apple, and citrus flavors with a touch of spiciness on the finish. Vignoles is light and crisp with flavors of peach, strawberry, apricot, pineapple, and honey. Nort is a dessert-style wine of blended Norton grapes with the aroma of blackberries, plums, and chocolates. It's a suitable sipper for cool nights.

Riverwood Winery

Tasting Room
22200 MO 45, Rushville, MO 64484
Estate Vineyards (by reservation only)
33655 Iatan Road, Weston, MO 64098
816-579-9797
riverwoodwinery.com

Riverwood Winery sits in the midst of prime territory for hiking and birding near Weston Bend State Park, Little Bean Marsh Natural Area, and other outdoor areas. The vineyard is situated on a farm in scenic Missouri River Bluffs north of the Snow Creek ski area. Cynthiana/Norton, Maréchal Foch, Cayuga White, Frontenac, Traminette, Vidal Blanc, and Saint Vincent have been planted in the seven-acre vineyard over successive years since 2008. The winery purchases some grape varieties, such as Chardonel and Chambourcin, from other growers.

The tasting room and gift shop are in a 1950s-era renovated school building, designed by noted architect Joseph Radotinsky. The building also served as a VFW meeting hall and antique mall. Riverwood Winery co-owners David Naatz and Ginah Mortensen bought the building in 2005, converted it into a winery, and opened for business two years later.

The winery offers full tastings of all its wines, including dessert-style wines and wine slushie or hot spiced wine. A partial tasting includes a choice of seven wines. The winery can also arrange group tastings, private seated tastings with or without food pairings, and flights of bourbon, Irish whiskey, and single-malt Scotch. The whiskey bar offers more than a hundred selections. Food options include cheese and charcuterie boards, olives and crackers, bread and cheese, and other savory bites, plus gourmet food items in the gift shop.

Highlights: Chardonnay is fermented and aged at Riverwood Winery. Half of the wine is aged in Missouri white oak barrels and the remainder is aged in stainless steel to yield a crisp wine with subtle oakiness. Fermented in stainless steel, Riesling delivers crispness with aromas of apples, apricots, peaches, and pears. Still cider, made with local Jonathan and Golden Delicious apples from Sibley Orchards, also comes in a barrel-aged version. The Asian pear wine, sweet with hints of butterscotch, caramel, and a spicy finish, is a distinctive blend of Shinseiki and Twentieth Century varieties of Asian pears from the orchard. Sweet Tempered Red, made with Cabernet Sauvignon, comes alive with fruity raspberry aromas and jammy flavors.

Tipple Hill Winery

10501 Southeast US Highway 36, Easton, MO 64443
816-294-7968
tipplehillwinery.com

Bill and Roxyann Schreiber founded Tipple Hill Winery, the first winery in Buchanan County, just east of Saint Joseph, Missouri. The winemakers planted the vineyard in 2010 with Chambourcin, Vignoles, and Concord grapes and completed the first harvest four years later. They initially released two wines: a dry red Chambourcin wine and semisweet Antique Harvesters wine, a Chambourcin-Concord blend. They now carry nearly a dozen wines made with their grapes and imported varieties, plus fruit wines. Fruit wines are named after family members.

Tastings are free. The tasting room accommodates up to seventy people and features live entertainment and events for indoor and outdoor settings.

Highlights: Black Cherry Sensation blends Pinot Noir with black cherry and red berries. Bridget's Raspberry Beckoning highlights Pinot Noir enhanced by sun-ripened raspberries. A portion of the sales of Breathe Easy White Zinfandel is donated to the Cystic Fibrosis Foundation in honor of Bridget. Other grape wines include Chambourcin, Sauvignon Blanc, and Riesling.

Laura's Peach Longing is one of the half dozen red and white fruit wines, plus nearly a dozen varietals of grape wine, available at this tasting room located five miles from Saint Joseph. Photo by the author.

Windy Wine Company and Twin Dragon Brewery

9478 Southwest State Highway J, Osborn, MO 64474
816-675-2002
windywine.com

Dating back to 1986, the Missouri Century Farm program was established by the University of Missouri to recognize farms and ranches that had been in the same family for one hundred years or more. Windy Wine Company and its neighbor Tipple Hill Winery are both Missouri Century Farms.

Years ago, Becky Keesaman asked her husband, Kraig, a homebrewer who also wrestles professionally as "The Vintage" Kraig Keesaman, if he could make her some wine. He made a Burgundy-style wine from a kit, leading to a hobby of winemaking. Gradually, Kraig learned the craft by working at a local winery and studying enology at the University of Missouri. Since then the couple has planted six acres of grapes, including Vignoles, Delaware, Concord, and Chambourcin and has begun commercially producing wine. The taproom has a neighborly feel. Local summer sausage and cheeses from KK Farms are sold in the shop.

At the 2015 Finger Lakes International Wine Competition, Good News Red earned silver while Raspberry and Peanut Butter & Jelly took bronze. Competing in the invitational Missouri Governor's Cup 2015, Raspberry brought home best of class fruit wine and a gold; Pony Express Red, Silver Brock, Blushing Mallard, and Good News White earned silver; and bronze went to Tyrannosaurus Red, Pony Express White, Apple, Campfire Mead, Good News Red, and Peanut Butter & Jelly.

Kraig, his brother Kasey (who is a deputy sheriff), and assistant Tim Hanttoula make beer under the name Twin Dragon Brewery. The brewery sells year-round and seasonal beers on tap and growlers to go. Beers include Rye Kwan Do, a light sweet ale made with rye instead of wheat, Oktoberfest Amber Ale, and creamy White Belt Ale.

Highlights: Pony Express Red is made with Missouri Chambourcin grapes and aged with French oak. Sangria-inspired and sweet, Good News Red is made with grapes, strawberries, raspberries, and added natural citrus flavors. Good News White is a white Niagara with lemon and orange accents.

Grindstone Valley Winery

595 Clinton Street, Osborn, MO 64474
816-675-2525
grindstonevalleywinery.com

Bill Arthur opened the white door of the building, stepped outside, and mounted a US flag in a flagstand by the front steps of Grindstone Valley Winery's tasting room. A brass plate on the brick wall lists the building's former occupants: *Farmer's Bank of Osborn 1909–1933, Lincoln-Anderson Post 169 American Legion 1950–Forever.* The bank was shuttered by the Roosevelt administration during the Great Depression. More than eight decades later, the building has been refurbished with gleaming wooden floors, pristine white walls, room for live music and painting classes, and a wine bar in the tasting room. A spacious wood deck and fire pit in the back is an invitation to settle in, sip on wine, and absorb this small Missouri town's charm.

Inside, rows of photographs and memorabilia are displayed on the walls. Ar-

Grindstone Valley Winery's home was formerly the Farmer's Bank of Osborn, 1909–1933, and Lincoln-Anderson Post 169 American Legion. Inside, stories of a Midwest community and bottles of remarkable wines await. Photo by the author.

thur offered an impromptu history tour of relatives and others from the community. These men and women served in the Civil War, World Wars I and II, Vietnam, Afghanistan, Iraq, and other conflicts. As Arthur recounted their names and military service, it was evident how powerful, personal, and important these sacrificed lives are to him and a community in the heart of our country.

Arthur—co-owner of the winery, Marine veteran, and newspaper writer—told stories about wine, friends in the community, and history. He was quick to joke with an old friend or delve into the finer points of grape varieties and production methods.

Arthur farmed many acres from 1975 to 2006, and still raises cattle two miles away from the tasting room. When his son and daughter pursued careers in medicine instead of farming, Arthur shifted his energy in 2009 to planting and growing grapes in the vineyard. Like farming, tending to the vineyard gave Arthur time to think in solitude. He ponders the Gospel of Thomas and other topics, takes photographs of the landscape, and appreciates the innate beauty of nature. He's also passionate about the wines made at Grindstone, named after a creek in the area that runs through his property.

Bill Arthur, co-owner of Grindstone Valley Winery, speaks with reverence about the photos of American servicemen and -women in the tasting room. He's also a jovial sort who enjoys cracking wise with guests and regulars. Photo by the author.

Arthur's son-in-law and vintner Jeff Harbison makes red, white, and dessert wines that line the bar in the tasting room. The wine is made in a processing building on the farm at one of the vineyards and is labeled in the basement of the winery. Vignoles, Alpenglow, Geneva Red, Traminette, and other varieties are grown at Grindstone. Norton grapes are sourced from Albonée Vineyards in Independence, Missouri.

Highlights: Semisweet 2015 Vignoles, a silver medalist in the Finger Lakes International Wine Competition, has a pineapple aroma with notes of apricot. Norton's dry tannin and delicate oak is softened with berry flavor. Heritage Red, a semidry Norton, is oaked in both American and French oak. Grindstone Black Cherry is made with Geneva Red and a touch of natural flavoring. Bestselling Lincoln Red is a sweet Concord jam that is all fun and no pretense.

Travel tip: Head east on US 36 (from I-29) or west on US 36 (from I-35). Turn south on Highway M and continue south past churches. Look for the brick building on the right before the post office. Local attractions include a barbecue restaurant, antique shops, and Home Inn Hamilton, a bed and breakfast in Hamilton (homeinnhamilton.com).

Levi Garrison and Sons Country Brewery

105 West Bird Street, Hamilton, MO 64644
816-668-9421
ninjamoosebrewery.com

Housed in an old brick telephone company building, Levi Garrison and Sons Country Brewery (formerly known as Ninja Moose Brewery) is located between the J. C. Penney Museum and the Missouri Star Quilt Company. Scott Falke founded the company in July 2014 and began serving beer to customers four months later. Not many towns with a population of nearly 1,800 residents have their own brewery.

Bartender Levi Dunham and the brewery are both named after brewery founder Scott Falke's great-grandfather Levi Garrison. The brewery is part of the heart of downtown Hamilton and a must-visit destination in the area. Photo by the author.

In the mid-1990s, Falke's father began homebrewing and Falke soon picked up the hobby. While working on a PhD in biochemistry, he began learning more about brewing and honing his skills as a homebrewer. Meanwhile, he worked as a biochemist and microbiologist, served in the US Army Reserve (and still does), and spent two years in Afghanistan. While overseas, Falke devised plans for a fictitious brewery. To keep costs down, he decided that once he was back in the States he would build this brewery himself. Falke regularly mentioned these plans to his wife—he had planned the brewery in his head for a decade. She asked him if he was going to keep talking about it or actually open a brewery. With that challenge, Falke soon began filing paperwork, opened a bank account, and launched the business the following year.

The brewery's original name alludes to a moment when Falke misread "Nina Moose Lake" on a map during a canoe and fishing trip with his dad, cousin, and uncle. While filing paperwork for the business a year later, the name "Ninja Moose" popped back into his head. The new name is a reference to Falke's great-grandfather Levi Garrison, who owned a sorghum company.

Falke gutted, refurbished, and expanded the building that houses the brewery, a treasured watering hole for town residents. The taproom has a casual pub feel where customers hang out, drink, and swap stories. Falke, Levi Dunham, and Joey Samrany brew within sight of the taproom.

Conveniently, food may be ordered at the taproom from local restaurants that deliver to the bar. J's Burger Dive makes a Double Hornet patty melt loaded with pepper jack cheese and jalapeños. Locals recommend the pork loin sandwich at Hank & Tank's BBQ.

Highlights: Beer flights are available. Mug Club members and investors drink from hefty mugs made by Sunset Hills Stoneware. The tap selection generally features ten year-rounders and two seasonals. American Amber's malty caramel notes are balanced with hops. Rockwell Porter perfectly expresses the chocolate and coffee notes of its roasted character. Floral aromas arise from the Farmhouse Ale. Deacon's Oatmeal Cream Stout is dry and creamy with a light body. Apple Pie Hard Cider, spiced with cinnamon, tastes like a slice of pie.

Travel tip: The nearby J. C. Penney Museum, located in the same building as the Hamilton Public Library, honors James Cash Penney, the department store founder and executive who grew up in Hamilton. Avid quilters know that Missouri Star Quilt Company is a must-stop destination.

Black Silo Winery

4030 East 10th Street, Trenton, MO 64683
660-357-2208
blacksilowinery.com

Opened in 2013 by Jennifer Hottes and Duane Urich, Black Silo Winery is located in the rolling hills of northern Missouri. Urich grew up in the area and his family resides in Laredo, twenty miles from Trenton. After buying the property in December 2009, Hottes and Urich began planting vines the following year. Since 2010, they have planted Chambourcin, Vignoles, Landot Noir, Crimson Cabernet, Cabernet Doré, Traminette, Concord, and Elvira vines in the 8.5-acre vineyard. Black Silo sometimes sources grapes from other vineyards, depending on the season.

Hottes and Urich repainted the red block silo in the middle of the property. As Black Silo, they created a brand name and landmark (with sharp logo design by Bauerhaus Design) that is now easily recognizable on sight and distinguishable from other regional wineries. The winery's tasting room is in a refurbished dairy barn that retains its rustic feel with modern updates. Production takes place in another building to the east. "We tried very hard to restore and keep the dairy barn, since so many people in the area remembered the place for what it was," said Hottes. Black Silo is also an event venue for weddings, rehearsals, reunions, parties, and other occasions.

The couple works with a winemaker and consultant on the vineyard and wine production. Hottes runs daily operations at the winery. Between the two of them, they have studied enology and viticulture as steps toward learning the craft.

Highlights: Seasonal fruit wine Just Peachy and 2 Lane, a sweet, crisp white with an apricot aroma, are crowd favorites. Jesse James is a dry earthy red with cherry notes.

CHAPTER 7

WESTERN AND CENTRAL MISSOURI, I-70 EAST

LEE'S SUMMIT, COLUMBIA, JEFFERSON CITY

Smoke Brewing Company

209 Southeast Main Street, Lee's Summit, MO 64063
816-525-2337
facebook.com/Smokebrew

Smoke and beer make sense at this brewpub, established in 2017 and housed in a hundred-year-old building. Cofounders Josh Edwards and his father, Jeff, both homebuilders by trade, have a decade's worth of homebrewing experience. They also own a competition barbecue team dubbed Building Smoke BBQ. The team name inspired the name of the brewery, which serves beer and competition barbecue on-site.

Lanni Edwards, Josh's wife, runs front-of-house operations at the taproom. Renee Edwards, who is married to Jeff, markets the business. Brewmaster Bert Lightle, an experienced homebrewer, studied advanced brewing theory at the renowned Siebel Institute of Technology. Lightle's involvement with Lee's Summit's beer culture and a local homebrewing club and his status as an Iraq War veteran were key factors in his hiring. Jeff Edwards is a Marine and Vietnam veteran.

Highlights: The twelve-tap taproom features a half dozen core beers as well as several seasonal, special-release, and collaboration beers. "We are not just an IPA and hop-forward brewery," says Josh. "We have a lot of great hop-forward beers and will definitely be able to satisfy the hop heads, but we also believe that craft beer is about choice. We will push the limits of several styles."

Stonehaus Farms Vineyard and Winery

24607 Northeast Colbern Road, Lee's Summit, MO 64086
816-554-8800
stonehausfarms.com

Established in 1996 by Ken and Carol Euritt, Stonehaus Farms has expanded and shifted its wine production since the Euritts' son Brett and his wife, Jacque, took over operations at the award-winning winery about a decade ago. Origi-

Stonehaus Farms Winery offers multiple award-winning wines and a friendly experience as a popular stop on the Kansas City Wine Trail. Photo by the author.

nally, the winery was focused on sweet fruit wines that remain perennially popular throughout Missouri and Kansas. Brett diversified into grape wines ranging from sweet to dry.

Grapes grown in the vineyard include Norton (Cynthiana), Vignoles, and Chambourcin. Grapes are also procured from other Missouri growers, and the wines are produced and bottled on-site. The tasting room features a spacious bar and lively, knowledgeable servers behind the counter, in a space with European winery decor and atmosphere.

Highlights: Vivant, a hybrid grape that originated in Ontario, Canada, in the early eighties, resembles a light Chardonnay or Chardonel. Stonehaus uses the grape to make a dry white with the kind of buttery profile that appeals to many white-wine drinkers. Aged in French oak, Vivant finishes crisp and smooth. Cynthiana exhibits tart black cherry flavor with spice on the finish. Semisweet Vidal Blanc has apricot and tangerine flavors while award-winning Vignoles offers citrus, apricot, pear, and pineapple notes.

Travel tip: While in the area, drop by Jazzy B's (1803 Northeast Colbern Road) for a "jazzy" take on barbecue and fusion comfort food.

Odessa Country Winery

2466 McNeel Road, Odessa, MO 64076
816-633-7843
odessacountrywinery.com

Deep in the heart of central Missouri countryside and back roads, Joe Laxson and Janice Putnam established the quaint Odessa Country Winery and tasting room in 2006. A four-acre vineyard and fruit orchard surround the building that contains the modest tasting room and production space. Apples, pears, and peaches grown on-site and from local farms find their way into sweet fruit wines popular with locals and Midwest travelers.

Highlights: Moore's Diamond, a hardy grape variety from upstate New York and grown at the Odessa vineyard, is used to make sweet, golden-colored Diamond. Butterfly Kisses is a blend of Cayuga White infused with cranberry. Happy Chef is a Concord-Norton blend, Front Porch Red blends Norton with blackberry, and Trophy Buck is a straight, fruit-forward, unoaked Norton. The winery also makes elderberry wine, often consumed as a nightcap by winery regulars.

Joe Laxson and Janice Putnam of Odessa Country Winery produce sweet wines that please midwestern palates. The couple is a treat to socialize with as they entertain local residents and travelers at their cozy country venue. Photo by the author.

Travel tip: From Odessa, take I-70 to Highway 131 and head south. Turn right onto Highway OO and proceed four miles. Turn right onto Newton Road, go one mile, and turn left onto McNeel. From Highway 50, turn north onto Highway 131. Turn left onto Newtown Road, go four miles, and then turn left onto McNeel.

Arcadian Moon Vineyard and Winery

19203 Old US 40, Higginsville, MO 64037
660-584-6661
arcadianmoon.com

"Nature's peace will flow into you as sunshine flows into trees. The winds will blow their own freshness into you, and the storms their energy, while cares will drop off like autumn leaves," wrote John Muir, author of *Our National Parks*, naturalist, and environmental philosopher. As you view the seventy-five-acre

The lake, pastoral wooded land, and farm fields surrounding Arcadian Moon's tasting room and outdoor patio provide a serene setting to relax in nature. Live music, laughter, and wine helps, too. Photo by the author.

paradise bejeweled with four lakes at Arcadian Moon, Muir's words may come to mind. Nature's beauty is not solely protected in parks, of course. It is wild and domesticated, ultimately beyond human control, yet certainly shaped and affected by it.

Remarkably, this peaceful (and festive, at times) winery and brewery is located a few minutes from the nation's busiest interstate. Established in August 2013 by Brandon and Mary Fahrmeier and partners who share a love of wine and beer, Arcadian Moon was created with respect for expansive country views and uninterrupted skies above.

Formerly, the property was home to a catfish farm and farmhouse. The homestead kitchen became the tasting room. An adjacent wood deck and pathway leads down the slope to one lake. The Lakeside Live Series on the deck showcases live musicians on weekends. Two outbuildings were converted to event space and production space for brewing and winemaking.

Head winemaker Brandon Fahrmeier and assistant Kim Musket craft Arcadian Moon's red, white, and dessert wines. They source grapes from Fahrmeier

Family Vineyards in Lexington and make most of the wine for that location. Grapes are also sourced from three Missouri vineyards and one Arkansas grower. Their Explorer Series highlights wines made from grapes brought in from California, Oregon, Washington, Ohio, and New York. Wine styles at Arcadia and the Lexington winery taste entirely different based on the grapes and blends used. It's all the more reason to visit both wineries and compare.

Arcadia Moon's head brewer Bill Crook makes nearly a dozen beer styles on-site. Future brewhouse plans include area distribution, after switching from a two-barrel to a twenty-plus-barrel system.

Highlights: Overall, Arcadia's wines have dynamic, distinct flavor profiles. Best-selling Luna, a sweet, balanced red, is a playdate with cherry, peach, and light citrus. Peach and pear notes are evident in Portia, a dry white blend of Traminette, Seyval, and Vignoles. Astraea, made from 2012 Vignoles, sweetly delivers apple and honey with a touch of apricot and cinnamon on the finish. Bellatrix, a 2013 Vignoles creation, begins with peach and honeysuckle and parts with nutmeg. Capella, made with 2014 Norton, unites cherry, rose petals, raspberry, and toasted oak. Also made with 2014 Norton, Rigel presents a smooth shift between complex layers of black currant, plum, hints of earth and leather, and light oak.

Nickel Draw Irish Ale is classically malty with a sweet finish. The 2000 PSI IPA hits hard with bitter hoppiness compared to the more sessionable, piney notes of Grand Circuit IPA. Exposition Hard Ginger Ale has a sweet bent offset by gingery spice. The beer names represent notable people, events, and details of Lafayette County.

Travel tip: The property offers a lakeside suite for rent and has RV hookups. Arcadian Moon is one mile west of the I-70 and MO 13 junction. The winery also offers food prepared by a chef on-site—starters, cheese plates, salads, rustic wood-fired Italian pizzas, and sandwiches.

Montserrat Vineyards

104 Northeast 641, Knob Noster, MO 65336
660-747-9463
facebook.com/Montserrat-Vineyards

Records show that land ownership of the Montserrat farm and vineyard, part of the former town of Montserrat, dates to 1842. The property changed hands

Raw, persistent wildness runs through the vines of Montserrat Vineyards, a locale for dramatic sunsets and outdoor picnics as grapes bide their time until harvest. Photo by the author.

many times over the next 140 years. In 1994 Phillip and Kelly Weinberger acquired the site then known as Blueberry Hill Farm, a "you-pick" operation that grew blueberries, blackberries, asparagus, and three acres of Vidal, Seyval, Catawba, and other grape varieties. In 1997 the Weinbergers removed the berries and produce, planted more grapes, and licensed and bonded the winery. With the addition of Norton and Traminette, the vineyard expanded to five acres. Today, the rejuvenating vineyard grows Norton and Traminette grapes, sources grapes from other vineyards, and cellars and bottles its wine in Rocheport. The winery hosts live music and events throughout the year.

Highlights: The modest, slightly weathered tasting room offers a small selection. Mont Blanc's Vignoles produces a floral nose with apple and honeysuckle notes. Tramonto—a name meaning "beautiful sunset"—is a semidry red made from Saint Vincent and Cayuga that is fruit-forward and has an ultra-vivid purple tint. Damifino, or "damn if I know," is the most popular option, and is Concord-based and blended with Chambourcin, Catawba, and Saint Vincent, resulting in raspberry and cherry aromas.

Travel tip: From US 50 heading east, carefully exit and head south on Northeast 651. GPS guidance will help point out where to turn in order to make a slow, safe exit. Continue on Northeast 651 across the train tracks to Northeast 641.

Bushwhacker Bend Winery

515 First Street, Glasgow, MO 65254
660-338-2100
bushwhackerbend.com

Bushwhacker Bend Winery is a charming winery in the heart of downtown Glasgow on the bank of the Missouri River at the sharp curve of Bushwhacker Bend. Owners Susan and Gene Marksbury, self-taught winemakers, opened the winery, tasting room, and gift shop in the fall of 2011, revitalizing an 1800s-era building that had been in disuse since the eighties. The Marksburys buy grapes from Schrader Vineyard in Boonville, about twenty miles south near I-70. They crush, destem, and ferment the grapes in the winery's production area downstairs.

During the Civil War, the town was the site of a battle, conflicts, and encampments by Confederate and Union soldiers. At one point, townspeople felt the

Bushwhacker Bend's deck offers an unparalleled view of the Missouri River below. The tasting room and wine shop is a charming place to pull off the road and visit. Image courtesy of Bushwhacker Bend.

wrath of Bloody Bill Anderson and his murderous gang of ransackers. Peaceful and calm now, the town features several restaurants on the main strip, such as River Bend Cafe and Muddy Mo Pizzaria, located by the winery. Bushwhacker Bend's deck offers a scenic view of the river below.

Highlights: Iron Horse Red, a blend of Saint Vincent and Norton, is a popular chilled wine with abundant berry flavor. Wheelhouse White, a Vignoles-Traminette blend, begins with floral aromas, introduces crisp apple flavor, and closes with a hint of pineapple. Dry reds include oaky Norton with black cherry flavor and Chambourcin, aged in Missouri oak, with sage and black cherry flavor. Wines such as Rivers Edge White, with pear-apricot notes, and floral, fruity River Rat Rosé are popular for those with preferences for sweetness.

Les Bourgeois Winery and Vineyards and Rocheport Distilling Company

Tasting Room
12847 West Highway BB, Rocheport,
MO 65279
573-698-2716
missouriwine.com

In 1974 Curtis and Martha Bourgeois purchased a fifteen-acre property along a blufftop overlooking the Missouri River near Rocheport. They planted a vineyard near their home and began a decade-long hobby of growing grapes and making wine from their grapes. In 1985, the Bourgeois family harvested a significant crop that prompted them to launch Les Bourgeois Vineyards. More than thirty years later, Les Bourgeois is one of Missouri's largest wineries. Many regional wineries also work directly with Les Bourgeois as a key resource for production and winemaking knowledge.

"We're an open book with what we do," said Drew Lemberger, partner and vice president of retail operations. "We help others get established. We have a vested interest in them getting started. There's lots of potential in central Kansas to develop wine and provide education. Being part of that growth also benefits us."

The winery includes a tasting room and gift shop with separate buildings for production, the Blufftop Bistro, and the A-Frame building, a separate wine

Certainly visit Les Bourgeois Vineyards's tasting room and gift shop just off I-70. Then continue to the A-Frame down the road, buy a bottle or glass of wine, and behold the ever-changing seasonal view of the Missouri River Valley from the terraced deck. Photo by the author.

bar and blufftop seating area with an unparalleled view of the Missouri River Valley. The spacious tasting room is a quick stop off the interstate to taste, explore, and learn about Les Bourgeois wines. The gift shop has an extensive selection of accessories, gift baskets, and wines. Tours ($5/person) are available on Saturday and Sunday at 1 p.m., 2 p.m., and 3 p.m., and include a guided tour of the winemaking facilities and a tasting of six wines. VIP and group tours are available with advance reservation.

Afterward, drive a mile north along West Highway BB to the A-Frame and Blufftop Bistro. The bistro is an award-winning, full-service restaurant open for lunch and dinner. The menu includes house-smoked meats, seafood, pasta, starters, salads, steak, and more, using regional ingredients. Pick up a bottle or two and picnic foods at the A-Frame wine garden, drift over to the terraced patio, and take in the river view.

Les Bourgeois also launched Rocheport Distilling Company, a small-batch distillery that produces rum, white rum, and dark rum.

Highlights: Ever-popular sweet wines include Concord with ripe Concord grape flavor, Riverboat Red's blend with aromatic raspberry and cherry, the honeysuckle bouquet with hints of honeydew and tropical fruit of blended Riverboat White, and silky port Rocheport with ripe berry flavor from Norton. Semisweet Vignoles debuts with a floral nose, brings a hint of sweetness, and finishes crisp. Dry wines include Jeunette Rouge, a medium-bodied Chambourcin blend with fruity character; Norton, with a violet bouquet and spicy earth tones; and Solay, a white blend with intense tropical overtones. Ask about the Collector's Series and Limited Edition wines.

Travel tip: The tasting room and gift shop is immediately off the exit north of I-70. The Bistro and A-Frame are a mile further north. Listed on the National Register of Historic Places since 1976, Rocheport attracts cyclists and hikers that traverse the nearby 225-mile Katy Trail. The historic town (rocheport.com) is near many regional attractions and is fifteen miles west of Columbia.

DogMaster Distillery

210 Saint James Street, Columbia, MO 65201
573-777-6768
dogmasterdistillery.com

DogMaster Distillery produces small-batch New American spirits in the North Village Arts District of downtown Columbia. Located near galleries, art studios, a music hall, retail shops, and a yoga studio, the distillery adds its own flair to the neighborhood. The distillery, tasting room, and bar are in a three-thousand-square-foot building, where spirits are produced and craft cocktails are prepared in a low-key setting. Music is played at low volume to facilitate conversation and interaction, a far cry from college bars elsewhere in town. At the tasting room bar, customers may order DogMaster's spirits, handmade cocktails such as a maple bourbon sour with bourbon, cinnamon syrup, and maple syrup, and classic drinks.

Owners Van Hawxby and Lisa Driskel-Hawxby, along with Dan and Stephanie Betliner, opened DogMaster in July 2014. The business name alludes to an old college nickname used by Hawxby and his buddies. As DogMaster's distiller, Hawxby creates bourbon, whiskey, vodka, and rum on a four-plate hybrid still in a nine-hundred-square-foot production area. Seth Fox, a seventh-generation distiller and founder of High Plains Distillery in Atchison, Kansas, designed DogMaster's still.

DogMaster is the culmination of Hawxby's vision to start a company that manufactured a consumable product and earned the loyalty of local customers. He wanted a business that could grow organically. While in Portland, Oregon, he learned about its distilling industry and interned at various distilleries. When he and Lisa moved to Missouri, he developed a business plan to launch the distillery in Columbia. Hawxby touts the distillery's hyperlocal sources—the distillery

Distiller Van Hawxby of DogMaster Distillery is part of the American revival of small-batch craft spirits. The in-house bar and lounge make it convenient to drink Hawxby's bourbon, vodka, rum, and gin near the source of production. Photo by the author.

uses Missouri grain and water to produce spirits, and Missouri oak barrels for aging are sourced from a cooperage in Higbee, Missouri.

Highlights: The bourbon is smooth with a rounded mouthfeel, gentle heat, vanilla and caramel notes, and cinnamon on the finish. The vodka is smooth and creamy with a mellow, clean finish. The rum, made with brown sugar instead of molasses, is aged in a whiskey barrel, picking up butterscotch notes with a vanilla aroma and smooth finish. The distillery released its gin in spring 2017.

Broadway Brewery

816 East Broadway, Columbia, MO 65201
573-443-5054
broadwaybrewery.com

Established in 2009, Broadway Brewery is located below street level in downtown Columbia. To reach it, take the stairs down past the zen garden. The brew-

Life gets steamy in the brewhouse at Broadway Brewing. Head brewer Shawn Oberle hoists a cold Eleven Point IPA between brews. Cooling off is easier in the artsy pub with a pint. Photo by the author.

pub has a slight English pub feel offset by vibrant paintings and photographs that add color and energy to the space. The seven-barrel system and brewhouse, encased in glass, is located behind the bar. Head brewer Shawn Oberle focuses on producing easy-drinking, approachable styles and low-alcohol session beers. Tours are available by request.

The brewery also has a thirty-barrel brewhouse system housed thirty miles west at Les Bourgeois Vineyards in Rocheport, Missouri, to handle large-volume production. The brewery's beers are distributed throughout Missouri's major cities and its central region. The brewpub serves lunch, dinner, Sunday brunch, a kids' menu, and a late-night menu. The made-from-scratch kitchen uses local ingredients as available, with a farm-to-table approach.

Highlights: Beers rotate regularly on the taps. Bestselling Eleven Point IPA, named after a Missouri river, with a piney-floral hop aroma, and Honey Wheat, made with local Bonne Femme honey, are popular staples. Shortwave Stout, a dark beer with mild body and roasted malts, uses locally roasted Peruvian coffee and coldbrewed toddy from neighboring Shortwave Coffee. Broadway Brewing partners with Les Bourgeois to produce Blue Heron Cider, an excellent dry cider with floral notes, using a blend of four organic Missouri apples. Bottled beer and wine are also available.

Columbia Brewery Crawl

For a mini taproom crawl, Broadway Brewing is located near Flat Branch Pub and Brewing and Logboat Brewing Company. Grab a bite to eat at Broadway or Flat Branch before continuing to DogMaster Distillery to sample fine spirits and cocktails for a change of pace. Located on the outskirts of Columbia, Bur Oak Brewing's taproom is a destination worth the drive for an evening visit on Friday or Saturday. Use a designated driver, as applicable.

Flat Branch Pub and Brewing

115 South 5th Street, Columbia, MO 65201
573-499-0400
flatbranch.com

Open since 1994, Flat Branch Pub and Brewing is a treasured fixture in Columbia's local restaurant and brewing scene. The first wave of microbrewing and brewpubs arrived in the Midwest during the nineties. Founder Tom Smith's pub and brewery was at the forefront of the trend. Flat Branch, Columbia's first brewery since 1841, was named after a nearby creek that provided freshwater for the city's first settlers. As craft brewing enjoys a renaissance two decades later, Flat Branch is a mainstay in Columbia's thriving brewery community. The pub occupies a 1927 brick warehouse that has a curved, barrel-trussed roof and was once a Hudson car dealership.

Brewer Kyle Butusov mans the 8.5-barrel brewhouse system, which produces 1,200 barrels annually. The brewery's American Hefeweizen and Oil Change Stout won silver medals at the 2010 Great American Beer Festival. The pub's food doesn't take a backseat to the beer. Flat Branch is a popular destination for lunch and dinner. The made-from-scratch kitchen equipped with a bakery and smoker serves spicy spinach dip, homemade beer bread, green chili chicken fingers, pizza, smoked brisket, seafood, burgers, salads, and more.

Green Chili Ale is a cult fave at Flat Branch Brewing. Fifty pounds of Anaheim chili peppers and two pounds of serrano chili peppers are used to make the mildly spiced ale. Photo by the author.

Highlights: Fifty pounds of Anaheim chili peppers and two pounds of serrano chili peppers are added to a top-loading fermenter used to make Green Chili Ale, a cult favorite that tastes and smells like chilies with faint spice. Bestselling Honey Wheat uses twenty-five pounds of honey in the brew for slight sweetness. Katy Trail Pale Ale is a classic American ale with an amber color, malt-hop balance, and citrus aroma. Great Pumpkin Ale, released on Halloween, is a seasonal favorite that has customers lining up out the door for a growler. Popular summer seasonal fruit beers include Blueberry Wheat Ale, which is fruit-forward with initial sweetness and dry finish. The bar has two Angram pumps used to dispense ESB and Irish Red in a traditional English style that is less carbonated and chilled than American beer.

Bur Oak Brewing Company

8250 Trade Center Drive, Columbia, MO 65201
573-814-2178
buroakbeer.com

Bur Oak Brewing, located east of downtown Columbia, operates as a production brewery with a taproom open on Friday and Saturday evenings. The brewery is named after a 350-year-old bur oak tree in McBaine, Missouri, a town southwest of Columbia on the Katy Trail. The ninety-foot-tall, ninety-three-inch-diameter tree has endured floods, lightning, and vandalism and already existed when the Lewis and Clark expedition passed nearby to the south on the Missouri River. The tree is fitting inspiration for a brewery that aims to grow and endure for years to come.

Brewery president and founder Craig Stichter was drawn to the allure of brewing craft beer while in Tampa, Florida, where he worked as a mechanical designer by day and was a student by night. New World Brewery was located across from his office. When Stichter and his wife, Janine, lived in Mount Pleasant, Michigan, she bought him a homebrewing kit for Christmas, which further encouraged his interest in brewing.

Fast-forward to Columbia, Missouri, where the couple now lives and Bur Oak Brewing was born. Head brewer Kraig Bridgeford, a homebrewer, brought industry experience from his work at two California breweries, Butte Creek Brewing and Lost Coast Brewery. Brewer Phil Fuemmeler, also a homebrewer, rounds out the team.

The brewery's approach is to make craft beer that honors traditional style with simple, clean, and bold flavor. The thirty-seat taproom features exclusive taproom-only beers. A wood wall displays a lasercut stainless steel depiction of the namesake bur oak tree.

Highlights: Boone County Brown, a ruby-brown porter, is loaded with caramel flavor and notes of dark chocolate and roasted coffee. Big Tree IPA's hops reach the upper end of bitterness (90 IBUs) as a well-balanced double India pale ale. Trail Bender is a seasonal made with three malts and US Hallertau hops for crisp, refreshing flavor. The vanilla and caramel flavors of fall seasonal Clyde's Caramel Cream Ale, a tribute to hardworking brewery cat Clyde, is a refreshing alternative to pumpkin beers. Dark Star Black Kölsch is dark ale with light body. Bur Oak's smooth Stout Heart, named after a giant Ent tree being that is protector of all things good, is also an ode to the famed bur oak tree. The brewery's canned beers are available throughout Missouri.

Logboat Brewing Company

504 Fay Street, Columbia, MO 65201
573-397-6786
logboatbrewing.com

Logboat Brewing draws its name from the history and spirit of the native peoples of the Missouri River and surrounding lands, people who navigated waterways on logboats, wooden dugout canoes. A logboat is positioned in the corner of Logboat Park, a grassy area with picnic tables and open space for outdoor imbibing, games, and relaxation.

The production brewery and taproom are housed in the former space of Diggs Packing Company, a meat packaging plant. The taproom's wood interior and exterior front facade create a rustic feel. Kansas City–based Elmwood Reclaimed Timber constructed the taproom's bar and tabletops using beams of Missouri heart pine reclaimed from a Horace Mann schoolhouse in Kansas City. Barn

Logboat Brewing's taproom has the look and feel of a rugged cabin that happens to have a production brewery in the back. Enjoy the great outdoors at Logboat Park, and toss a Frisbee or picnic while only a few steps from the taproom bar. Photo by the author.

wood siding is used throughout the building, as a touchstone of the history of places in Missouri now assembled in a cozy gathering space.

Highlights: Shiphead Ginger Wheat uses Peruvian ginger, coriander, and lemon zest for citrus tang and subtle kick. Mahogany-colored Mamoot Ale is a light ale with notes of jam, coffee, and chocolate that inspire thoughts of beer for breakfast. Snapper IPA uses four hop varieties to create a bouquet with piney notes and flavors of peach and pear. Limited-release Delta Series beers include Jerk Alert Double IPA and Haller-Tang Pale Ale, a beer with fruit-forward aroma and peppery hop notes, inspired by German lagers and American pale ales.

Serenity Valley Winery

1888 County Road 342, Fulton, MO 65251
573-642-6958
serenitywinerymo.com

Serenity Valley Winery, a boutique winery and tasting room, overlooks Serene Lake, a setting to sip on wine and behold dazzling sunsets and tranquil natural surroundings. Vintner Lee Ruppert and Regina Ruppert, proprietors, run the winery and event venue. Lee has twenty years of experience as a winemaker and viticulturist. These Old World–style wines use *Vitis vinifera* grapes not grown in Missouri but familiar to wine drinkers around the world.

Highlights: Fiery Opal, a semisweet Shiraz with cranberry, and Lil' Bit of Heaven Gamay, respectively, won gold and silver at the 2013 Finger Lakes International Wine Competition. Other wines include a Sauvignon Blanc, Gewürztraminer, Cabernet Sauvignon/Merlot blend, Barolo, Malbec, and numerous sweet and semisweet grape wines blended with fruits, such as Perfect Pair, a pear Riesling; and Jammin' Berry's Meritage with blackberry.

Prison Brews

305 Ash Street, Jefferson City, MO 65101
513-635-0678
prisonbrews.com

What better place for beer lovers to do time, or spend it, than at a prison-themed brewpub? Owned by Deb Brown, Prison Brews adopts its look and feel from its

Whether passing through or visiting Jefferson City, Prison Brews is a family-friendly place to do some time with fresh beer and wood-fired pizza. The bar is literally enclosed behind jailhouse bars, and booths are designated as "jail cells." Photo by the author.

proximity to the old Missouri State Penitentiary in the east side of Jefferson City. The bar is encased in floor-to-ceiling jailhouse bars. Pub booths in the main dining area are labeled as cells. Clearly, Prison Brews exhibits a sense of humor and local pride. The brewery occupies the former 1940s-era Landwehr Dairy. The building dates back to 1895 and once housed blacksmith and wagon-making operations.

Rod Dothage, brewer since the 2008 inception of the brewpub, makes straightforward craft beer with clean flavor and solid styles. He eschews barrel aging, sours, and highly hopped beers, focusing on tried-and-true crowd pleasers.

Prison Brews pulls in lunch and dinner crowds for hand-tossed pizza, beer bread and cheese, sandwiches, burgers, and hearty plates of filet, fish and chips, and peel-and-eat shrimp. Relax outdoors with a pint on the patio and play bocce while killing time on the "yard."

Highlights: Try Gone A-Rye Pale Ale with rye malts for a spicy, citrus hop finish, Maximum Sentence IPA amber ale brewed with cinnamon, ginger, nutmeg, cloves, and real pumpkin, popular I Ain't Your Honey Wheat, and Prison Town Brown, an English-style brown ale with a creamy tan head.

Canterbury Hill Winery and Restaurant

1707 South Summit Drive, Holts Summit, MO 65043
573-896-9966
canterburyhill.com

Poised on a blufftop that overlooks a wooded valley and Missouri River bottomlands, Canterbury Hill Winery and Restaurant is a short drive north of Jefferson City. The venue offers breathtaking views, wine, and full-service dining with an elegant dining room and spacious outdoor patio. The venue's royalty theme extends to the overall decor and wine names. Flights are dubbed King Tower, Queen Tower, and Prince Tower, with varying selections.

The menu runs the gamut from pasta to burgers, steaks to seafood, prime rib, and more. This scenic spot is a popular location for weddings and events.

The spacious outdoor patio at Canterbury Hill Winery and Restaurant, located on a steep blufftop, offers an unobstructed view of the Missouri River bottomlands and wooded hills. Photo by the author.

Highlights: The winery features Norton, Chambourcin, Vignoles, and blends with nonnative Missouri grapes. Noble Norton is made solely from the state grape. Excalibur, a red blend, has black currant and cherry flavor. Canterbury's Tale is a sweet red with Concord's jammy nose and blackberry jam flavor. MaLady Pink, a rosé made with Catawba and Cayuga White, offers sweetness accented with strawberry and rhubarb. White wines include dry Medieval Mist, sweet King's Choice with honey-pineapple notes, and sweet Blue Mist's aromas of baked apple and pear. Bottled beer, draft beer, cocktails, wine slushies, and California wines are also available.

CHAPTER 8

WESTERN AND CENTRAL MISSOURI, US 24 EAST

Mallinson Vineyard and Hall

3029 North River Boulevard, Sugar Creek, MO 64050
816-896-5744
mallinsonhall.com

Located north of Independence near the Big Blue Bend of the Missouri River, Mallinson Vineyard and Hall is set up for weddings, live music, and events throughout the year. The winery has indoor and outdoor settings, including a patio and tasting room. The winery has fresh pizza available on Fridays and Saturdays.

Highlights: Wines available are sweet white Citrine, semidry Savor the Mist, sweet rosé Enticement, semidry red Deception, and dry reds Vanishing Oak and Norton.

Albonée Country Inn and Vineyards

2200 Crenshaw Road, Independence, MO 64057
816-220-2820
alboneecountryinn.com

Al and Bonnie Renner (Al + Bonnie = Albonée) own and operate this charming country inn, vineyard, and winery on a beautifully landscaped twenty-four-acre property minutes away from Kansas City. The hillside country estate overlooking the Little Blue Valley is a relaxing retreat for tasting wine, picnicking on the deck or in the gazebo, or having a weekend getaway at their bed-and-breakfast.

The Renners developed the business after being inspired by trips to bed-and-breakfast inns in Europe and Missouri wineries. They planted Norton grapes in 2000, secured a license to operate in 2007, and opened the winery and tasting room two years later. They later added varieties such as Vignoles, Seyval Blanc,

Drive through the Little Blue Valley past wooded glades and fields to reach this European country–style retreat, Albonée Country Inn and Vineyards. Owners Al and Bonnie Renner are warm hosts who produce impressive Missouri wines, including notable dry varietals. Photo by the author.

Chambourcin, and Catawba to the nine-acre vineyard and also expanded the original production facility.

Mostly self-taught, the Renners learned some pointers from Holy-Field Winery and by talking to other winemakers, attending conferences, and reading. Now, Albonée Vineyards sells excess grapes to other wineries. Its Vignoles won silver and its Seyval Blanc earned bronze at the 2016 Missouri State Wine Competition.

Highlights: Norton, aged three years in American oak barrels, is full-bodied and rich with a hint of sweetness on the finish. Aged in stainless steel tanks, semidry Seyval Blanc's crisp pear flavor is followed by light spice. Vignoles's sweetness gives way to peach and apricot aromas. Catawba, a native American grape, is made into a sweet rosé best enjoyed chilled on a hot summer day. Jubilee, a blended red, delivers aromas of cherry and chocolate.

Travel tip: Albonée Vineyards is part of the Kansas City Wine Trail. The winery, near Little Blue Parkway and East Truman Road, is minutes away from Highways 291, 78, and 7, and I-70. The winery is east of the Harry S. Truman Library and Museum and local restaurants in historic Independence Square and is north of the Burr Oak Woods Nature Center.

La Bella Vineyards and Winery

11644 Flournoy School Road, Wellington, MO 64097
816-240-2404
labellawinery.com

Before La Bella Vineyards and Winery existed, the property was known as New Oak Vineyards, which operated from 1997 to 2010. The Soendker family (mother Cindy and brothers Ryan and Cory) acquired the Italian-inspired winery, vineyard, and event venue. The vineyard's rolling hills are lined with rows of Vidal, Vignoles, Seyval, Traminette, Chambourcin, Saint Vincent, and Norton grapes. After harvest, grapes are processed on-site.

La Bella's scenic grounds feature a ten-acre lake with gorgeous views of surrounding woodland; a tasting room, gift shop, and deck; and an event space for banquets, receptions, weddings, and other occasions.

Highlights: Norton presents vanilla tones and dark berry flavors. Gypsy Blossom blush is made with Chambourcin, Saint Vincent, and Vidal. Renegade

La Bella, an Italian-themed winery, is located in the midst of stunning woodland, hills, a ten-acre lake, and vineyards. The view alone is worth the drive, particularly in fall. Photo by the author.

Red, a Chambourcin, Saint Vincent, Concord, and Catawba blend with cherry-raspberry flavors, is best enjoyed chilled. Off-dry white Bella Shepherd is named after the winery's dogs.

Travel tip: From US 24, head south on Highway 131 to Highway FF. Head east on FF to Flournoy School Road and turn left (north). The winery is five hundred yards off of Highway FF and Flournoy School Road. GPS directions are not always accurate—call ahead for directions as needed.

Fahrmeier Family Vineyards and Winery

9364 Mitchell Trail, Lexington, MO 64067
816-888-9490
fahrmeierfamilyvineyards.com

The parents of Ron Fahrmeier purchased the Fahrmeier Family Vineyards and Winery property in the 1940s and operated a grain and livestock farm that sold pork to Kansas City's historic stockyards until its decline. The farm was too small for row crops. Instead, Ron, his wife, Joan, and their sons, Brandon, a former hobby winemaker, and Bret, who manages the produce operation, transitioned the business to a thirteen-acre sustainable vineyard, winery, and produce farm, powered in part by solar energy to reduce its carbon footprint. The vineyard produces fifty to seventy tons of grapes annually, provided the growing season and harvest go well. Varieties include Vignoles, Chambourcin, and Seyval.

Late operating hours on Friday and Saturday distinguish the tasting room, which is in a renovated cow barn, from other area wineries. The extended hours, live music, and events make Fahrmeier Winery a day-and-night destination for wine tourists and locals. Guests may order Mexican and Italian food from local restaurants for delivery to the winery.

Highlights: A full tasting includes thirteen wines, or a single wine tasting is $1 each. River Bluffs White, a blend of Vignoles, Vidal, and Traminette, is a sweet, fragrant wine with a hint of spice on the finish. Vignoles releases a pineapple bouquet with notes of strawberry, peach, kiwi, and citrus. Earthy Chambourcin is light and aromatic, suitably paired with grilled meats. Full-flavored Norton is aged in American, French, and Hungarian oak barrels and yields bold fruit, spice, and oak notes. Sweet Tempered Tart blends Chambourcin from three years to produce an offbeat, lightly sweet red with cherry and red notes and earthy aromas of tobacco and leather.

Travel tip: Fahrmeier's Country Cottage is the farm's original three-bedroom house, built in 1956 by Ron's parents and since updated, which is available to rent for a weekend getaway. From US 24 heading east, turn right onto Howe Road and then right onto Mitchell Trail. From I-70, take exit 37A and follow East Old Highway 40. Turn left onto MO 131 North and proceed 8.4 miles. Turn right on US 24 eastbound, go two miles, and turn right on Howe then right again onto Mitchell Trail.

Terre Beau Winery and Vineyard

100 South Lynn Road, Dover, MO 64022
660-259-3010
terrebeauwinery.com

Terre Beau's tasting room occupies a 150-year-old chapel built in 1858 for frontier settlers and pioneers headed west. Located ten miles east of Lexington, Do-

A lover of the Rat Pack era of Frank Sinatra and Dean Martin, John Tulipana of Terre Beau Vineyard continues a tradition of Italian winemaking that dates back to his grandfather. If you catch him at the tasting room or patio, Tulipana is known for telling rich, entertaining stories. Photo by the author.

ver was once a thriving river town on the old Santa Fe historic trail. Winery owner and vintner John Tulipana spoke with the bishop in the area, bought the parish, which had closed in 1993, and developed the winery with his brother Michael. Grapes are grown on the family farm. Terre Beau began selling wine in 2005, carrying on a tradition of winemaking that dates back to the Tulipana brothers' grandfather.

The small tasting room is an ode to Dean Martin and the Rat Pack, with music of the era playing in the background. A vine-covered patio outside, next to the church, provides a relaxing setting in which to drink wine.

Highlights: Tastings include samples of six wines. The selection includes Norton aged eighteen months in stainless steel with oak chips, Chambourcin, Chardonel, and semidry Gewürtztraminer Sari Lee's Smile, with the taste of peach and pineapple. Giovanni, a Norton blend, is named for the Tulipanas' father while Thelma's Delight is a tribute to their mother. Lafayette Red blends Chambourcin, Norton, and Chardonel.

Baltimore Bend Winery

27150 Highway 24, Waverly, MO 64096
660-493-0258
baltimorebend.com

Baltimore Bend's tasting room and gift shop is a popular stop for regional travelers. Named after a sunken boat on the Missouri River, the award-winning winery established the first vineyard in Lafayette County.

Baltimore Bend grows Chambourcin, Norton, Vignoles, Seyval, Chardonel, and Valvin Muscat. The first vines were planted in 1997 in rich farmland soil down the highway from the tasting room. Family members and partners in the business include farmer-grower Richard Livingston, wife Kathleen Livingston, daughter and vintner Sarah Schmidt, and son Scott Livingston.

Highlights: Tastings include eight wine samples. The 2012 Norton Reserve, released in April 2016 as a full-bodied red aged in French oak, was made from

Baltimore Bend Winery is owned and operated by Richard Livingston, Kathleen Livingston, daughter and vintner Sarah Schmidt, and Scott Livingston (not pictured). The tasting room is a convenient stop on Highway 24. Image courtesy of Baltimore Bend Winery.

grapes that hung on the vine longer to produce lower acids and higher sugars. Aged in American oak barrels, 2012 Chambourcin won a silver medal in the 2015 Jefferson Cup Invitational. Dry white 2014 Chardonel was barrel-fermented as a *sur lie*–style wine, a technique in which wine is aged a bit longer on the lees, a sediment of yeast, to further extract flavor before aging on French oak for eight months. Concord-based Arrowhead Red, apple-based Jubilee, and Just Peachy are some of the sweeter wines.

CHAPTER 9

CENTRAL AND SOUTHERN MISSOURI
OZARKS, SPRINGFIELD, BRANSON

Numerous businesses making wine, beer, spirits, and mead have sprung up in central and southwestern Missouri cities and towns. Several have been mainstays in their community as they upheld time-honored traditions. As travelers journey down highways and interstates toward the state's lakes and destinations such as Branson, these family-owned businesses along US 65, I-44, Highway 50, Highway 7, and other routes are worth investigating.

Red Fox Winery and Vineyard

1422 Northwest 800 Road, Urich, MO 64788
816-918-8161
redfoxwinery.com

Red Fox harvests grapes from vineyards in Urich and Ballard. Each has a distinct climate, soil elevation, and land profile. The Ballard vineyard's slopes and hills help circulate cooling air through the vines. Urich's higher elevation and warmer temperatures aid in boosting sugar levels and acids. Hot Missouri summer sunshine and cool nights in spring and fall aid development of tannins, flavonoids, and other characteristics in red wines while boosting aroma in white wines.

Highlights: Full-bodied Norton is aged in heavily toasted American oak that adds a hint of spice and gentle tannins for balance. Chambourcin leads with currant and cherry and finishes dry. Truman Red, sweet and juicy with prominent cherry and raspberry, is ideal in sangria or as a porch sipper. Crisp Vidal Blanc shines with citrus and green apple. The scent of rose introduces Traminette, a semidry white with a hint of sweetness. Semidry Vignoles brings a tropical party of pineapple, melon, and nectarine while balancing sweetness and acidity. Sweet Truman White is playful with tropical notes and floral aroma. The winery also offers rosé and fruit wines.

Travel tip: The winery is off Highway 7 on the outskirts of Urich. Hungry travelers may wish to stop and dine on starters (eggplant bruschetta, caprese, buffalo wings), burgers, sandwiches, or riblets for lunch, or hearty steaks, kabobs, ribs, or grilled salmon for dinner.

DeLaney Vineyard and Winery

1200 South Main Street, Nevada, MO 64772
417-667-5651
facebook.com/DeLaneyVineyardandWinery

Larry DeLaney and his wife, Sam, started their quaint family-run vineyard and winery after Larry and his brother-in-law paid several visits to wineries in Hermann, Missouri. Four generations of family, eighteen people in all, have worked at DeLaney Winery. Larry, a self-taught hobby winemaker, began making wine for family and friends. As demand and his volume of grapes grew, Larry increased wine production. He limits batches to four to six cases' worth at a time, and is only licensed to produce five hundred gallons per year.

He began planting grapes around 2001 and began sales to the public two years later. The vineyards include three acres of mixed varieties—including Concord, Traminette, Elvira, Baco Noir, Niagara, and Saint Vincent; a patch of experimental varieties behind the cottage; and six acres of Norton grapes are nearby.

The winery operates out of a cottage that houses a tasting room, gift shop, deck, and small event space for a dozen or so people. Guests may relax on the deck, enjoy live music on weekends, and share a bottle of wine.

Highlights: Sweet blackberry wine sells best and quickly. Apple and pear are two other sweet fruit wines available. Several wines are named after the De-

Winemaker Larry DeLaney with his wife, Sam, and one of their grandsons on the front deck of the winery's homespun tasting room. Photo by the author.

Laneys' grandchildren, such as Kaden's Kind, a dry red Baco Noir; light-bodied Chambourcin Layton's Liking; and semisweet red Liam's Liquid.

Travel tip: While in Nevada, grab a burger and shake at local diner White Grill (200 North Commercial Street).

Keltoi Vineyard

17705 County Road 260, Oronogo, MO 64855
417-642-6190
keltoivineyard.com

Erv and LeeAnn Langan established Keltoi Vineyard in 1997 after purchasing forty-three acres of land that includes their home, row crops, and five acres of pecan trees. They cleared forest, planted grapes, built the cottage, and made other

The Cottage, Keltoi Vineyard's Irish-themed tasting room, is an easy day trip to southwest Missouri. Guests waste little time pulling off the country road to park and find a spot on the patio or grounds to enjoy wine. Photo by the author.

improvements. In 2006 Erv built The Cottage, an Irish-themed tasting room, retail wine shop, and event space.

More than ten years later, the shop still does brisk business. During warm weather, guests take newly purchased bottles of wine and socialize on the patio connected to The Cottage.

LeeAnn works full-time as a program analyst, while Erv is retired from Missouri State University and the US Army. "I grew up on a farm in northeastern Kansas. My dad ran a construction company. I worked for both," said Erv. He leaned back with a glass of red wine and laughed. "Here I am in the autumn of my life, farming and doing construction."

Erv manages grapegrowing when he's not building projects at the winery. In addition to four acres of grapes planted on the hilly southeast side of the property, Keltoi has a three-acre vineyard on the north side. Keltoi grows Saint Vincent, Baco Noir, Villard Noir, Maréchal Foch, Cayuga White, Seyval, Vidal,

Owner Erv Langan and head winemaker Andrew Pennington of Keltoi Vineyard share a jovial moment between helping tasting room customers on a busy weekend. Photo by the author.

and Norton grapes. Grapes are also sourced from the nearby four-acre vineyard of Keltoi's head winemaker Andrew Pennington.

"It takes five years at least to grow the vines and produce wine," said Erv. "Until then, young white grape wine tastes grassy and young red wines taste like dirt. You need time for the roots to dig into the soil."

Pennington, who has studied chemistry, leads production. He applied his homebrewing skills to the craft of making wine, producing a range of wines with something to appeal to different tastes. Eventually, Pennington plans to open his own winery.

The winery's name, a reference to Celts and Erv's Irish heritage, reinforces the jovial Irish pub-style atmosphere of the tasting room and patio. A fireplace and cozy furniture create an inviting environment. Winery dog Cayuga (pronounced Cay-ga) is a friendly greeter.

Highlights: Norton is the biggest seller. Other reds include bold Nine Ladies, Saint Vincent, Carleo's semidry blend of Baco Noir and Villard Noir grapes, and crisp Chambourcin-based Red Shamrock. Irish-themed names continue with the white wines, such as semisweet, crisp Irish Moondrops, semidry Alainn, and sweet Irish Raindrops, a customer favorite. Fruit wines (apple, pear) and blushes are also available.

Travel tip: Keltoi is slightly more than two hours away from Kansas City due south, and a short hop from Pittsburg, Kansas, and Joplin, Missouri. From Kansas City, head south on US 71 to M Highway and turn right. Proceed 10 miles, cross Highway 43, and go 2 miles to County Road 260. Turn right, head north for 0.7 mile, and the vineyard is on the left. Jolly Fox Brewery in Pittsburg, Kansas, is located approximately twenty-five minutes away via KS 171 West to US 160 North.

Wildlife Ridge Winery

34751 Miller Road, Smithton, MO 65350
660-343-5493
wildliferidgewinery.com

In 2013 Kristy Long and her husband Kevin began the process of opening Wildlife Ridge Winery, the only winery in Pettis County southeast of Sedalia. They built a tasting room and gift shop on their ninety-eight-acre farm and bought grapes from Missouri growers. By 2015 they had established a vineyard to begin growing grapes for wine production. Now the winery produces five thousand gallons of wine annually. As vintner, Kristy develops blends and single-variety wines for Wildlife Ridge.

Highlights: Deceitful Red Wine won first place at the 2016 People's Choice Show-Me Wine Competition, held in Jefferson City, Missouri. This semisweet blend of three grapes is a deep red color with initial sweetness that tapers off at the finish. Other wines include Bone Dry, a straw-colored white wine with crisp Granny Smith apple flavor, popular semidry white Cricket with citrus-pear notes, and Sweet Pea, a sweet red with hints of ripe red berries.

Travel tip: From Sedalia, take US 50 to Highway M, turn south on M, and continue for 11.7 miles. Turn right on State Highway V and left on Miller Road. Or head south on US 65 to State Highway V, turn left on V, and proceed 8.1 miles. Turn right on Miller Road.

Eichenberg Winery

103 North Olive, Cole Camp, MO 65325
660-668-3511
eichenbergwinery.homestead.com

Eichenberg Winery, a charming tasting room and gift shop, is in the midst of a town with German heritage. Located southeast of Sedalia and west of Versailles, the town of Cole Camp likely rings a bell for travelers bound for Truman Lake or the Lake of the Ozarks.

Rodger and Theila Luetjen licensed the winery in 2002 and opened the tasting room a year later. Dating back to 1906, the building housed a blacksmith shop with a dirt floor until the early sixties. Rodger remembers visiting the shop as a child. Now the Luetjens and their black pug Dinky welcome guests in the refurbished space. The vineyard began as a three-acre plot in Cole Camp with an additional three acres in the Fort Leonard Wood area along the Missouri River. They grow Norton, Concord, Catawba, and Edelweiss grapes.

Rodger and Theila Luetjen sell their German-influenced wines from their quaint tasting room in Cole Camp, a town known for its German immigrant roots. Photo by the author.

Rodger, a retired rural mail carrier, learned winemaking in part from Buffalo Creek Winery's vintner. He started the winery as a hobby, loosely inspired by his grandfather Henry, a second-generation German immigrant. Grandfather Henry once made beer and wine on the family farm north of Cole Camp. Rodger's great-grandfather brought grapevines to the area from northern Germany.

Rodger processes the grapes on-site and uses a *sur lie* method that the Germans adapted from the French. With *sur lie* aging, a finished wine continues to sit on the grape lees or yeast lees in order to extract additional flavors and aromas. Theila assists as the "cellar rat" and runs the tasting room.

Highlights: Sweet wines are preferred among the town's residents and Eichenberg Winery's customers. Semisweet Festival, a bestseller, is brick-colored with bold pepper flavor easing into light cherry. Liebersaft, with a name meaning "love juice," is a light white wine with a hint of citrus. Rodger joked that the romantic "love juice" is guaranteed to work. Rubin Hausschuh (pronounced *huss-shaw*) is a blended dry red made with Chambourcin and is ideally paired with chocolate. This wine's name, meaning "ruby slipper," is a nod to a daughter-in-law and her love of *The Wizard of Oz*.

Travel tip: From US 65, take the MO 52 East exit toward Cole Camp. Turn onto MO 52, heading east for 4.2 miles. Turn left onto North Olive Street. For authentic German food, grab dinner at The German Table (111 East Main, Cole Camp; thegermantable.com).

Welpman Springs Brewery

517 Hatchery Road, Stover, MO 65078
573-377-2343
welpmanspringsbrewing.weebly.com

While Bryan and Leslie Welpman's nanobrewery and winery does not have a tasting room, the business is allowed to sell direct to customers from its office. Their beer is also on tap at Taterhoggz in Laurie, Missouri. The Welpmans, homebrewers for seven years, launched their one-barrel brewhouse operation "to bring fantastic, quality beer to our area."

Highlights: The brewery produces a rotation of Dusseldorf Alt bier, American IPA, imperial stout, American wheat, and seasonal Shubunkin Punkin, a pumpkin-flavored American amber ale.

Travel tip: Reach out to Welpman Brewing in advance for operating hours before visiting. From MO 135, take M Highway West and turn left on Hatchery Road.

Dale Hollow Winery

314 East First Street, Stover, MO 65078
573-569-0094
dalehollow.wordpress.com

Family and grapevines both draw on strong, deep roots to endure and thrive. Established in 2012, Dale Hollow Winery is the result of strong ties in the Dale family and gnarled grapevines growing deep in the soil of Stover. Initially, Asher Dale brought up an idea with his wife, Ana, to grow grapes and make small batches of wine. Later, Asher's brother Jesse and his wife, Katy, joined the discussion and talk expanded to the idea of opening a winery. "I'm from Kentucky. Small tobacco farms were converting to wineries," said Katy. "After I met Jesse, we visited Kentucky wineries near the Bourbon Trail and enjoyed meeting owners and the social aspect."

Asher, who has a bachelor's degree in aquatic ecology and chemistry, made wine for Jesse and Katy's wedding. The winery idea began to gel. Jesse and Katy visited local wineries, including Les Bourgeois in Rocheport. Asher and Jesse leased space at Grey Bear Winery in Stover (no longer commercially producing wine) to gain experience with a mature vineyard. "Dave and Marschell Fansler offered their guidance in the vineyard and with winemaking," said Jesse. "This was our first established place of business for producing wine under our own license."

Tucked in a hollow, the four-acre vineyard contains Concord, Baco Noir, Norton, Cayuga White, Vignoles, Saint Vincent, and Catawba grape. Wine sales of limited quantities of Vignoles began in 2014. Grape production and wine volume grow annually at this young winery.

"We want to produce wine that makes people think differently about American wines," said Katy, emphasizing the winery's research and focus on grape quality and yeast selection to distinguish its wines. Asher added, "Our connection to the community and family is important. The winery helps the local economy and builds the community."

Beth Dale, mother of Asher and Jesse, draws the artwork featured on each bottle's label. Imagery for the Hiawatha Peach and Lakehouse Suite labels are inspired by lake memories from grandparents on both sides of the family. The Blackberry Patch label depicts a historic road that connects old and new Stover. Rock Island Caboose's label evokes the nearby railroad that essentially built new

Created by a Dale family member, artwork on Dale Hollow's wine labels reflects scenes and family memories of places tied to the community and its local identity. Photo by the author.

Stover. Much of the town was struck by a tornado in 1916 and was rebuilt. Regarding the wine labels, Jesse said, "The idea is essentially to draw inspiration from the places and things around this community that form its identity."

Highlights: As the vineyard matures, look for dry reds and semisweet white wines made from grapes grown on-site and Missouri-grown grapes. The winery currently produces Vignoles, Catawba, Norton, Chambourcin, and Saint Vincent wines. Sweet wines such as Vignoles sell well. Fruit wines such as apple, Hiawatha Peach, and Blackberry Patch, which is blended with Concord, are also popular.

Buffalo Creek Winery

28888 Riverview Road, Stover, MO 65078
573-377-4535
buffalocreekwinery.com

Perched above the Lake of the Ozarks at the seventy-mile marker, this winery is nestled deep in Ozark woods on a twisting unpaved back road that leads to the winery's drive on a grassy hill. At the top of the 170-foot bluff, a scenic view through trees reveals lake waters. The tasting room is housed in a refurbished 1900s farm barn.

Established by James D. and Olga Stephens in 1988 as a twelve-acre vineyard and winery, the winery and tasting room was moved in 1997 to its present location. In 2009, daughter-in-law Theresa and son Matt Stephens took over operations. Seyval, Ruby Cabernet, Vignoles, and Concord grapes grown on multiple vineyards are supplemented by Missouri grapes from other growers. The wine is produced on-site below the tasting room.

Highlights: Hawthorne White, a blend of Traminette and Seyval Blanc, exhibits a floral nose and apricot finish. Old-vine Concord and fruit wines are also available.

Travel tip: GPS is recommended to navigate back roads to the winery from US 65 or Highway 135.

Shawnee Bluff Vineyard

8 Tolwood Road, Eldon, MO 65026
573-365-1100
Shawnee Bluff Winery
2430 Bagnell Dam Boulevard, Lake Ozark, MO 65049
573-365-9935
shawneebluffwinery.com

Barrett Elwyn and Gail Griswold, owners of an eco-friendly construction company, purchased the Shawnee Bluff winery and vineyard in 2015 from Gail's parents and revitalized both venues. The Lake Ozark location, a resort-meets-tasting-room situated on a bluff, offers dining, a bar, and patio with a fourteen-mile panoramic view of the lake. Lodging with pool access is also available at the inn. At the winery, the bistro space was expanded and the menu updated with tapas, pizza, and dishes using local ingredients.

Seven miles away, Eldon is the home of the working five-acre vineyard on a forty-acre property. The winery supplements its Saint Vincent grapes with Norton and Vignoles from Missouri growers such as Les Bourgeois. The winery also produces wine from juice sourced from California and Washington. The vineyard, serving as an entertainment destination, has hosted high-profile acts including Asleep At The Wheel, Grand Funk Railroad, and the Oak Ridge Boys. Both locations host weddings and community events.

Shawnee Bluff Winery's blufftop location has a premium view of Lake of the Ozarks for tasting room guests and resort visitors. Photo by the author.

Highlights: Tastings include samples of four wines. Bestselling Double Bluff, a semisweet red, blends Saint Vincent and Pinot Noir to yield a light, fruity wine perfect with pasta and pizza. The 2014 Limited Reserve Cabernet Sauvignon begins with berry and drops black pepper bite on the finish. Dry white Flappers & Philosophers dances with crisp notes of grapefruit and lemon drops. Missouri-grown Vignoles delivers a semisweet wine with citrus–green apple notes.

Ozark Distillery

1684 Highway KK, Osage Beach, MO 65065
573-348-2449
ozarkdistillery.com

Ozark Distillery owner Dave Huffman and his wife, Tiffhany, took a breather. Offering tours and assisting customers in the tasting room and gift shop kept them busy over the weekend. Dave headed to the distillery's production space to discuss his Ozark moonshines and his path toward becoming a distiller. During tours, Dave emphasized the importance of craft and attention to detail that a small-batch distiller devotes to the process. He compared distilling to baking. "You can buy a box of cookies at the store and they'll taste fine," he said, "but they are not your mom's or grandmother's cookies made with love."

Huffman's four-plate column still has a modular design so it may be con-

Distiller Dave Huffman guides guests on a tour around Ozark Distillery while his wife, Tiffhany, manages the tasting room and sales. From grain to bottle, tourists learn how Ozark moonshine is made, legal and proper. Photo by the author.

verted to a pot still for initial distillation. Simply put, distilling alcohol vapors through multiple plates in a column still is a key step to produce purer spirits.

Huffman specializes in legally making moonshine, a high-proof distilled spirit made with corn mash also known as white whiskey. Long before moonshine, he brewed beer in his younger days to drink at the drive-in movie theater. He shared homebrewed beer with girls at the drive-in, but they didn't like the yeast in it. He found an article in *Mother Earth News* about distilling and figured out how to distill beer and remove the yeast. He later realized he had made the equivalent of moonshine. It still tasted rough. Huffman hit on the idea to pilfer from his father's stash of butterscotch candies and add them to the spirit. Bingo—the girls loved it, as well as cherry, watermelon, and other Jolly Rancher–flavored versions.

Over time, Huffman learned more about distilling from the library and through practice. "That was pre-Google," he said. "It was less about drinking and more about distilling well." Huffman woke up one day and decided to open a distillery. He converted his property management office into a production facility and sold his rental company. As a successful serial entrepreneur, Huffman was more focused on the process and craft of distilling than profit and marketing a brand.

"I tell customers the story of what we do and how we do it," said Huffman. "I take two dollars of grain and produce a twenty-five-dollar bottle of alcohol. I pay the farmer, bottle maker, cork maker, and label printer. I create value from my effort and bring it to society. It's part of the American dream."

Highlights: Free tours include a view of the distillery, discussion of the distilling and aging process, and tasting. Products are available for sale at the distillery and online. The flagship Corn Whiskey Moonshine, a silver-medal winner at the American Distilling Institute Competition, is smooth and sweet with a light corn flavor and aroma. Ozark Distillery offers naturally flavored moonshines, including butterscotch, vanilla, cinnamon, apple, and blackberry, that work especially well as mixers. Sweet Tea Moonshine incorporates brewed tea and cane sugar for a taste of summer in the South. The vodka is distilled multiple times for smoothness. Bourbon whiskey is aged from nine months to two years in new charred oak barrels produced by McGinnis Wood Products in Cuba, Missouri. The distillery's products are also sold in 370 locations in Missouri.

Sugarloaf Vineyard

66 Feline Lane, Camdenton, MO 65020
573-873-2020
sugarloafwinery.com

Long before Ward and Barb Morris launched Sugarloaf Vineyard and its winery, their property was an orchard for four decades. Planted in 1958, the apple, pear, and peach orchard was based on the edge of the Big Niangua River on the Lake of the Ozarks. Once the orchard ran its course, the land was primed for growing grapes. Rich river soil, mild winds, and years of composted orchard fruit enriched the soil.

They planted Chardonel in 2007 and Norton in 2008, followed by additional plantings of these grapes and Saint Croix in a three-acre vineyard. Several years later, they began to harvest and produce wine from their grapes. In a good harvest year, the winery produces four hundred cases of wine. "We no longer produce on property, as we have grown past our 'basement' production facility," said Ward. "We do have to use grapes from other Missouri farmers as we don't grow the type of grapes that are conducive to sweeter wines."

Sugarloaf Vineyard borders about 1,200 feet of Lake of the Ozarks shoreline and is a quarter mile by water from the Onyx Cave. The Morrises rent kayaks, homes, and cottages for the day or week, offer event space for weddings, and run the winery and an outdoor tasting room with live music, pizza, and barbecue. It's an ideal spot to picnic and watch boating activity, dine, and share a glass of wine.

Highlights: In terms of wines in greatest demand, Foxxxy Red edges out the nearest competitors of Sir Ivor, Blushed Pelican, and White Pelican. Blushed Pelican is a sweet-tart pinkish wine with flavors of strawberry and rhubarb. Sugar Bella's has a Moscato-like sweetness and bouquet of honeysuckle. Semidry Vignoles offers slightly sweet tropical flavors. On the dry red spectrum, try full-bodied Sir Ivor. Sweeter palates will prefer Foxxxy Red's aromas of raspberry and cherry and ripe berry flavor. According to Ward, "Many customers like to use our Foxxxy Red in homemade sangria. It's best to marinate the fruit (oranges, apples, limes, grapes) in a bath of blackberry brandy for a day or two, and then add Foxxxy Red, ice, and a bit of club soda."

Casa de Loco Winery

442 Riverbird Lane, Camdenton, MO 65020
573-317-9695
casadelocowinery.com

The name of Casa de Loco Winery refers to the rich history of the property dating back to the late 1920s that now houses a winery, tasting room, and lodge. Construction of Bagnell Dam began in 1929 and was completed two years later. Once the Osage River was dammed to create the Lake of the Ozarks, the region became a popular tourism spot for hunting, fishing, and outdoor activity.

Businessman Hugo Urbauer and his wife, Ina, constructed The Millionaires Club, a lodge on 7.9 acres with two cottages and garage, where the Urbauers and their Saint Louis friends relaxed. When Hugo died in 1948, the property was sold and became The Mozark Club. The club and added restaurant closed in the mid-fifties due to a fire. Eventually, the property reopened as the Mozark Health Care Facility to treat elderly and mentally ill patients until the facility closed again in the late 1990s.

Now owned by Larry Owens, the winery once again operates as a lodge and float trip launch point, hosts live music from summer through fall, and serves as a venue for weddings and other events. The winery has thirty acres of vineyard in California and a six-acre Missouri vineyard. Its grapes include Zinfandel, Cabernet Sauvignon, Merlot, Syrah, Petite Sirah, Malvasia, and Saint Vincent.

Highlights: Bipolar is a semidry red blend of Pinot Noir and Saint Vincent. Casa Cooler is a lightly spritzed Moscato. Call Me A Cab, a California Cabernet Sauvignon, is aged sixteen months in a Missouri oak barrel and six months in a French oak barrel. These wines with wacky names (a riff on the property's history) are made in California and Missouri by vintner Allen Kreutzer with grapes mostly sourced outside of Missouri.

Seven Springs Winery

846 Winery Hills Estates, Linn Creek, MO 65052
573-317-0100
sevenspringswinery.com

A mere fifteen minutes from Camdenton and Osage Beach, Seven Springs Winery is a verdant oasis atop Missouri's Ozark foothills. Founder Mike Bleile, a real estate broker, bought the 160-acre property in 2007. Originally, the land was homesteaded by the Hanks family in the late 1800s. Bleile and his father spent eighteen months clearing the overgrown land, planted grapevines, and gradually transformed this former cattle farm into a breathtaking winery and tasting room with a full-service menu.

A paved drive leads through the expansive landscaped property, proceeding past a reception hall and three outdoor settings for weddings, rehearsal dinners, and other events. By the tasting room, live musicians perform regularly on the large patio. Guests relax with wine by fire pits and gaze at wooded hills in the distance. More than two miles of biking trails span the grounds. A one-room schoolhouse, cave, and seven springs on the property offer plenty to explore outdoors.

Bleile learned to make fruit wine from his grandfather. He continued the hobby through college and later learned more of the craft from professional winemakers. Approximately 4,200 Vignoles grapevines were planted in the vineyard's rocky, clay-laden soil. In 2009, one thousand Norton grapevines were planted in the vineyard. Annually, the winery grows twenty-five tons of grapes, uses eight to ten tons, and sells the remainder to area wineries. Ninety percent of Seven Springs's wines are made from Missouri grapes with some out-of-state imports.

Highlights: Dry Vignoles is a crisp white with tangerine-citrus notes and a hint of acid. A sweeter version of Vignoles, made with a different fermentation process, results in a light straw-colored wine that sings of peach nectar and melon. Chardonel's fruitiness is tempered by toasted oak. Seven's Red Heaven, a deep plum-hued wine, is fruit-forward with a sweet finish. The tasting room offers an

Owner Mike Bleile has planted 4,200 Vignole grapevines in the rocky, clay-laden soil of Seven Springs Winery. The tasting room and café, part of a verdant 160-acre estate, offers resplendent views of the Ozark Hills. Photo by the author.

extensive selection for different palates, from a sparkling Moscato to the berry-pepper combination of Syrah. The food menu includes appetizers, cheese trays, Mediterranean pizza, award-winning spicy shrimp and crab bisque, salads, paninis, and burgers.

Travel tip: A shuttle bus service is available for guests at the lake. See the website for details.

Golden Rock Winery

955 North Business Route 5, Camdenton, MO 65020
573-317-9463
goldenrockwinery.com

Jennifer and Scott Woods established Golden Rock in 2011 and named it after a large golden-hued rock near the entrance. The winery, located in a former John Deere dealership, imports grapes from California, Italy, and other parts of the world. The winery produces and bottles its wines on-site in Camdenton.

Originally, the Woodses bought the business as a franchise concept that has since disbanded. The Woodses learned to make wine in California as part of the venture, but ultimately opted to outsource the growing operation. Conveniently located off the highway, Golden Rock also operates as a restaurant with an Italian-themed menu and full bar.

Highlights: Whites include Chardonnay, Pinot Grigio, Riesling, White Zinfandel, and Bella Bianco with rich buttery aromas and balanced flavors of tropical fruit and oak. Reds include Cab Syrah Zin, a juicy blend that is well balanced and smooth; a Cabernet/Merlot blend; French Merlot; California Syrah; and Barrelicious, a barrel-aged version of Cabernet Sauvignon with ample tannin, cherry notes, and vanilla-oak aroma. Golden Rock also sells a popular six-pack of its fruit wines that may be mixed and matched.

Leaky Roof Meadery

1306 Azalea Street, Buffalo, MO 65622
417-345-1233
leakyroofmeadery.com

Located a few minutes away from US 65, Leaky Roof Meadery is a large production facility and taproom that, as the name suggests, focuses on mead. Mead, created by fermenting honey, water, and yeast for up to a month, is not classified as beer (made from malt grain) or wine (made from fruit). The term "honey wine" is a misnomer. Naturally gluten-free, mead may be produced in a range of styles from sweet to dry, still to sparkling, low-alcohol session drink to potent beverage. Wildflower, buckwheat, alfalfa, and other honeys are used to produce different characteristics in the flavor and aroma of mead. Leaky Roof ages some mead in bourbon barrels for six to eight months to add complex layers of flavor.

Founder Todd Rock's path to establishing Leaky Roof Meadery spans the United States. Born and raised in Hillsborough, New Jersey, he studied at the University of Missouri–Columbia, where he brewed beer at home and where he met his wife, Katie. They moved to Anchorage, Alaska, where Todd studied anthropology at the state university and began homebrewing again. After winning several awards for his beers, he attended the University of California, Davis, master brewing program and later secured a cellarman job for Hangar 24 Brewery in Redlands, California. The Rocks moved back to Missouri with their son. Todd worked at Mother's Brewing in Springfield and then at a meadery in Rogersville, Missouri. In time, the family (which now includes two sons and a daughter) moved to Buffalo, Missouri, where Todd and Katie founded the meadery in January 2014.

The business is named after the Leaky Roof Railroad, the nickname for the Kansas City, Clinton and Springfield Railroad (KCC&S) that hauled coal, marble, and clay tile and served as a lifeline that connected towns in the region. In a twist of fate, the rail line never made it to Buffalo. Ask the taproom staff about

Leaky Roof Meadery owner Todd Rock, one of the few modern meadmakers in Missouri, marries traditional mead with methods and influences inspired by craft beer. Photo by the author.

the backstory. However, the railroad imagery and theme struck a chord with the bygone golden era of southwest Missouri that Leaky Roof Meadery sought to capture.

Weekend visitors might find themselves smack in the middle of a jam session as talented local musicians play and harmonize. The taproom is a local hangout full of friendly customers. Ask nicely and a tour may be arranged.

Highlights: Most of the mead is canned for distribution throughout the region. The taproom has a half dozen or more selections on tap, plus packaged product. High, Dry, and Dusty is a ginger-laced, lightly carbonated mead with subtle spice and dry finish. Bourbon Barrel Blackberry Mead's sweetness is tempered by tannin and oak from aging. Spook Light uses cinnamon, nutmeg, and pie spices to evoke the fall season. Mikado's initial sweetness smooths out to reveal green tea and mint. Cyser, the semisweet flagship mead, blends honey and fresh-pressed Granny Smith apple cider. Berry Picker blends wildflower honey with strawberries, blueberries, blackberries, and red raspberries. Bond Burner Mead is accented with mesquite-smoked pineapple and jalapeño.

Leaky Roof regularly hosts jam sessions with sing-alongs by local musicians on weekends. Whether playing, singing, drinking, or applauding, the lively, communal spirit is irresistible and fun. Photo by the author.

Travel tip: US 65 turns into South Ash Street entering Buffalo. Turn west on County Road 65–172/Truman Road and turn right (north) onto Azalea Street.

Boat Town Brewing

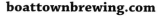

18146 Campground Road, Phillipsburg, MO 65722
417-533-2306
boattownbrewing.com

After three years of planning and building, friends and homebrewers Bart Guyer and Dale Korn founded Boat Town Brewing in 2015 on the outskirts of Lebanon, Missouri. They opened the brewery's doors in April 2016, choosing a name that reflected the interests of the community and area. "Lebanon and the surrounding county, Laclede, has five aluminum boat factories," said Guyer. "Locals once told me that it was once called the 'aluminum boat factory town of the world' by Ronald Reagan."

Between them, Guyer and Korn have homebrewed for thirty-five years. Guyer said, "Our backgrounds include many years of science and chemistry training, including a degree in analytical chemistry." Eventually, their homebrewing operations began to resemble nanobreweries. Guyer and Korn committed to opening a brewery with a seven-barrel brewhouse. They also juggle full-time professions as healthcare providers in local emergency rooms.

The fifty-seat taproom has a "wabi-sabi" industrial feel with additional seating for another fifty people in the brewery space as needed. Seating ranges from old theater seats to church pews to bar stools at custom-made cedar plank tables. Guests play board games over a beer and relax in the beer garden by the fire pit. Outdoor activities such as corn hole, Frisbee golf, and washer toss are available for fun competition.

A variety of food trucks rotate on Fridays and Saturdays, serving fare ranging from American pub food like fried pickles and burgers to Jamaican jerk-style meats. The taproom and beer garden is a family-friendly environment where old friends and new acquaintances meet.

Highlights: The taproom has up to ten beers on tap, including four barrel-aged beers, plus Missouri-made mead and cider. Wyota Wheat, a hefeweizen, is named after the Osage tribe that lived in the area before Lebanon formed. Barley's Bite, a bracing 11-percent-alcohol barleywine, is cousin to Barley's Chill, the same high-alcohol beer aged in a whiskey barrel. Brother Blue Belgian Abbey Ale, crowd favorite bourbon-barrel-aged Perficle Imperial Stout, Journeyman whiskey-barrel-aged Irish stout, and 70 H.P. East Coast–style IPA are some of the many selections available.

Travel tip: From I-44, take exit 123. The brewery is on the southeast corner of the overpass on Campground Road. Look for Jenkins the Frog on the side of the building.

7C's Winery and Meadery

502 East 560th Road, Walnut Grove, MO 65770
7cswinery.com

Drink what you like. Like what you drink.

Dwight and Jean Anne Crevelt bought 120 acres of vacant land in Walnut Grove near the home of Dwight's grandfather. Instead of farming the acreage, they

7C's Winery's flavored meads outsell its grape and fruit wines. Taste them and you'll see why the mead is popular. Guests may sample several meads and wines to find a favorite. Photo by the author.

grew interested in winemaking. Jean Anne took classes with the Viticulture and Enology Science and Technology Alliance through Missouri State University to earn certificates in viticulture and enology. The Crevelts began making wine as amateurs, entered them in competitions, and won awards before launching 7C's Winery with a five-acre vineyard.

Established in 2009, the tasting room and gift shop is housed in a large building atop a hill above a grassy field. The field is regularly booked for weddings, medieval festivals, Oktoberfest, Mead Fest, Pirate Faire, and other annual events. The business derives its name from the tally of C's of the last names of seven family members—owners Dwight and Jean Anne Crevelt, Jean Anne's mother Irene Cassens, and the Crevelts' four children.

The business makes grape and fruit wine and naturally flavored honey-based mead. Elderberry, plum, apple, and other produce used in the mead is locally sourced. Sixty percent of the business is mead, and 7C's is the top seller of mead in the state, according to Dwight. Most of the honey is sourced from Missouri, with exceptions like orange blossom honey from Florida. The mead, made with no carbonation, is aged from three months to one year before bottling to remove any harsh finish from the beverage. The mead is packaged in bottles and full-size

(750 ml) and half-size (375 ml) pouches described as "juice boxes for adults." Dwight said, "Pouches outsell bottles of mead by a ten-to-one ratio."

Highlights: Meads by 7C's won multiple awards at the 2014 Missouri State Competition, including Alfalfa Mead (gold), Wildflower Mead, Swashbuckler, and Clover Mead (silver), and Viking's Heart and Mid-Life Crisis (bronze). Wildflower Mead tastes clean and floral. Swashbuckler is made with red poplar honey sourced from Mobile, Alabama. Viking's Heart, made with buckwheat honey, stands out with wheat and caramel flavor. Pepper-infused meads include After-Burn Jalapeño Mead, Hades Ambrosia Habanero Mead, and After-Life Ghost Pepper Mead. 7C's sells a full range of red and white grape wines from dry to sweet. Elderberry and apple wine are also available.

Travel tip: Visit 7cswinery.com/directions.html for detailed directions from Springfield (forty minutes southeast), Bolivar, Historic Route 66, and other points. The winery, a quarter mile east of Highway 123 and two miles north of Walnut Grove, is also a popular stop for cyclists along the US Bike Route 76, which follows Main Street through Walnut Grove.

OOVVDA Winery

5448 North Berry Lane, Springfield, MO 65803
417-833-4896
oovvda.com

"Uff da," an exclamation of bafflement, dismay, or surprise, is the all-purpose phrase one might hear Scandinavias say when they stub a toe, spill milk, or win the lottery. That's according to Brian Overboe, the barrel-chested co-owner and vintner of OOVVDA Winery, established in 2005. Overboe, who is half Norwegian, quarter Swede, and quarter British, should know. This "Viking Vintner" can trace his family lineage back to 1179 AD in Norway. Four generations of the Overboe family have made wine. The winery's name is a variation of "Uff da." OOVVDA also stands for Overboe's Own Viking Vintners' Distinctive Alcohols.

The Viking-Norwegian heritage of the owner is evident by the outer building mural, painted by local artist Jamie Lewis. It depicts a Viking ship entering a fjord as a tiny troll sips wine in the grassy foothills of a mountain. Shadow, a shepherd dog, is diligent and friendly when greeting guests. Rows of OOVVDA's numerous white, red, fruit, and blush wines in sweet, semisweet, and dry variations are

Vikings and all manner of travelers are welcome to OOVVDA Winery. OOVVDA is a variation of an all-purpose Scandinavian phrase "uff da." Photo by the author.

displayed behind the tasting room's bar. Overboe uses grapes from Tyler Ridge and other Missouri wineries and makes wine in the back of the building.

OOVVDA's wines are sealed with easy-opening, reusable zorks, a "peel and re-seal" closure that replaces traditional and plastic corks. Overboe said, "The zork enclosure protects the wine with a foil barrier built in."

Highlights: Sweet and slightly foxy, blush-colored Reliance is made in the orange style, in which macerated grapes in contact with the skins results in an orange color. Pale blush-hued Chambourcin Blanc has raspberry notes. Cayuga White is crisp with a peppery finish. Blush options include unoaked Chambourcin Blanc and Norton Rosé. Winemaker's Red consists of 2012 Norton aging in a 2013 oak barrel. Other reds include Norton and regular and reserve variations of Chambourcin. A variety of fruit wines are made with at least one pound's worth of local fruit in each bottle. The impressive black raspberry dessert wine is comparable to Chambord, a raspberry liqueur. The unusual tomato wine, made with 4 percent lime juice, is dry and tart and bears the aroma and taste of tomato with

OOVVDA vintner Brian Overboe takes a peek at wine in a fermenter in the production area behind the tasting room. Photo by the author.

a hint of olives. Overboe suggests savoring a glass with Mexican food or salad, or sipping it on a hot summer day.

Tyler Ridge Vineyard Winery

7325 North Farm Road 171, Springfield, MO 65803
417-536-1630
facebook.com/Tyler-Ridge-Vineyard-Winery
-161562913955650

Mike and Kathy Dennis are two of the most relaxed, fun-loving winery owners you'll meet, with no interest in expanding the business. Both retired, they run Tyler Ridge Vineyard Winery as a fun hobby that enables them to make fine wine, meet interesting people, and socialize at their tasting room on the Ozark Mountain Wine Trail. "My goal is to have fun with the winery," added Mike. "It's work but it is not a job. People come here from Kansas City, Branson, and Tulsa to have a good time and make friends."

Mike and Kathy Dennis take life easy and remind guests by example why it's important not to take life too seriously. Warm hospitality, laughter, conversation, and wine are plentiful at the Tyler Ridge Winery tasting room. Photo by the author.

Surprisingly, the couple never drank a drop of wine before 2000. They visited a winery in Augusta, Missouri, and found they liked dry red wine. They used land near their home to plant Vignoles, Cayuga White, Norton, and Chambourcin grapevines. Having planted too many for their own use, Tyler Ridge supplies half of its grapes to OOVVDA Winery.

The tasting room is in a refurbished farmhouse built in 1905. Lush grapevines in a 2.5-acre vineyard, walnut trees, and cozy outdoor seating surround the farmhouse. After tasting wine, guests may purchase a bottle to enjoy on the shaded deck, on the romantic arbor swing, or in the courtyard. The grounds have a horseshoe pit and bocce ball.

Highlights: The winery offers free tastings. Dry Cayuga White is crisp and bright with citrus and green apple notes. It's also available as a semisweet and sweet white. Dry Vignoles opens with the aroma of honey and finishes with crisp minerality; or opt for the semisweet version. Dry Chambourcin offers berry-forward flavor and a light plum color. The 2009 Burnt Barn Red, a blend of Norton and Chambourcin, has smoke and oak-accented notes to balance light sweetness. The 2013 Norton, a deep purple color, has a bold, intense berry flavor with a peppery finish.

Explore Springfield

While in Springfield, explore historic Commercial Street's local shops, eateries, and nearby destinations such as Missouri Spirit Distillery, Mother's Brewing Company, White River Brewing Company, Springfield Brewing Company, and local wineries. For a great chili dog and inexpensive diner grub, pop into Casper's (601 West Walnut Street), a local institution with eclectic folk-art decor and fast, friendly service.

Missouri Spirits

507 West Walnut Street, Springfield, MO 65806
417-501-4674
missourispirits.com

Springfield's first and only distillery, Missouri Spirits, is located downtown near Mother's Brewing Company and Springfield Brewing Company. The spirit house operates as a production distillery in the rear of the building and houses a spacious cocktail bar and event room in the front. With rough-hewn wood, racks of bourbon barrels, and taxidermied game animals on display, the space has an industrial-meets-man-cave feel tempered by the cozy Ozarks hospitality of a cocktail lounge.

Founder Scott Shotts formerly worked in marketing for Budweiser and Copper Run Distillery. Also a homebrewer, he turned his skills toward making spirits using several stills in the production space.

Highlights: The 80-proof bourbon whiskey is made with a blend of corn, rye, and malted barley sourced from the Midwest, resulting in a spirit with initial heat that reveals vanilla, oak, and caramel notes and finishes with a peppery bite. The whiskey is aged for a minimum of two years in new charred Missouri white oak barrels. The vodka, distilled six times, is soft and creamy with a hint of sweetness and grain aroma. Sweet with mild heat, the unaged corn whiskey, or "moonshine," is produced with 100 percent pot-distilled corn and then blended with purified water to 80 proof.

Missouri Spirits operates as a production distillery in the back and a cocktail bar and lounge in the front. The Midwest character of Springfield is evident in the decor of the space. Photo by the author.

White River Brewing Company

505 West Commercial Street, Springfield, MO 65803
417-869-1366
whiteriverbrewingco.com

White River Brewing Company's name, design aesthetic, and taproom decor take inspiration from the active lifestyle tied to the White River, a spring-fed body of water that wends its way through the Ozarks and southern Missouri. The brewery puts its own Ozark spin on traditional styles of beer from Belgium, England, and Germany. Small-batch in operation, it produces beers with bold presence, layers of flavor, and integrity to style.

Owner and retired banker John "Buz" Hosfield purchased the building in 2007 and began renovations. By mid-2012 Hosfield and Dave Lamb, a renowned beer expert in the area, devised a business plan for the brewery. With Lamb as a veteran brewmaster, the brewery's first test batch of Table Rock Red Ale set sail in August 2012, and kegs officially shipped by January the following year.

White River Brewing Company's decor, atmosphere, and name are inspired by boating, fishing, and camping along this prominent southern Missouri river. The taproom offers classic and inventive takes on craft beer styles. Photo by the author.

The rustic taproom can comfortably seat up to fifty people—less if live music is scheduled on the weekend. The brewery is visible through glass windows from the event space adjacent to the taproom. The spacious patio (dog-friendly) is an attractive option for drinking, socializing, and watching people along busy Commercial Street.

Tour guide Steve McDonald conducts informative, adventurous tours at 2 p.m. and 3 p.m. on the first Saturday of the month. Tours are limited to twelve people, so reserve a spot early. Tourists learn about the brewing process, history of the building, and brewery staff while sampling beer often.

Highlights: Table Rock Red is an Irish red ale brewed with five malts, including German Caramel Rye, as well as German and English hops, to yield maltiness with a nutty finish. Thank coriander and orange peel used in the Belgian-style White Creek Wit for its floral aroma and hint of spice. Tavern Creek Tripel is a Belgian-style beer with notable spice and fruit followed by a dry-tart finish.

Jam Up Blackberry Ale, a Belgian Blonde fall seasonal, kicks off with blackberry flavor that drifts to a dry, tart landing. Gravel Bar IPA goes big and bold with aromas of tropical fruit meets stone fruit and an appropriate hop bite on the finish. Look for special taproom-only releases such as the herbaceous Smoked Peach and Sage, refreshing and zesty Lemon Ginger Wit, and citrusy Grapefruit C Street Pale Ale.

Springfield Brewing Company

305 South Market Avenue, Springfield, MO 65806
417-832-8277
springfieldbrewingco.com

Springfield Brewing Company's large brewpub has been a craft beer and dining destination in downtown Springfield since 1997, when the first wave of modern microbrewing was in full swing around the country. Local manufacturer Paul Mueller Company purchased the building, built a showcase for its stainless steel brewery tank line, and created a brewpub to demonstrate its handiwork to clients. In 2011, Ashton Lewis, Bryan Bevel, and a group of local partners acquired the business.

The brewery's operations are visible from the dining room and bar. English-, German-, and American-style ales and lagers constitute the brewhouse's output. Co-owner and brewmaster Lewis, a respected brewing expert and writer in the industry, oversees brewhouse operations with head brewer Bruce Johnson and brewers Steve Straub and Clayton Gatschet. The brewery underwent an expansion in spring 2016 that enabled it to triple its production capacity.

The restaurant is a staple in town for lunch, dinner, brunch, special occasions, and events, featuring classic brewpub fare including wings, pulled pork sliders, salads, street tacos, fish and chips, mac and cheese, hearty sandwiches, wraps, burgers, and brick oven–baked pizza.

Highlights: The brewery has a vast array of beers on tap, with some packaged for sale. Hop Lobster is a citrus-forward hoppy ale balanced by malt. Its red hue inspired the crustacean moniker. One of the brewery's original six offerings, Walnut Street Wheat's floral aroma comes from unfiltered wheat and wheat malt. Malty and mildly hoppy, Paul's Pale Ale is a tribute to Paul Mueller, founder of the company that first established the brewery and led the revitalization of downtown Springfield. Seasonals include West Coast–style Greene Ghost IPA, Day Pack Ale, and award-winning fall classic Oktoberfest beer Mayhem Märzen.

Made-from-scratch food and solid craft beer keep crowds coming back to Springfield Brewing Company in downtown Springfield. Credit: Rebecca Miller.

Travel tip: Parking is available in the lot south of the building or in the free public parking garage directly northeast of the building.

Mother's Brewing Company

215 South Grant Avenue, Springfield, MO 65806
417-862-0423
mothersbrewing.com

Founded in 2011 by owner Jeff Schrag, Mother's Brewing occupies a forty-five-thousand-square-foot building in downtown Springfield. More than eighty years ago, the building housed Star Bottling Works and was home to a succession of bakeries from 1926 to 2009, until Interstate Brands closed. A local craft beer destination, the popular tasting room still displays a large bakery sign on one wall as a nod to the building's past.

The brewery's name and logo is a devoted tribute to mothers and a throwback to classic tattoos that honored that dedication. While fun-loving in spirit, Mother's is committed to the art and craft of making high-quality, distinctive beer and investing in its community. The brewery revealed all-new package designs in spring 2016 to celebrate its fifth anniversary.

Mother's taproom is a prime craft beer destination with an easygoing, convivial atmosphere. Visitors line up at the taproom to buy glasses of beer, social-

Mother's Brewing is housed in a former bakery building. Tours include a walk through the production brewery and barrel room and a stop at the tasting room, where some special releases are only available at that location. Photo by the author.

ize at communal tables, and purchase merchandise and growlers to go. While beer flights aren't available, customers are welcome to sample core, seasonal, and taproom-only rotating beers on tap. Guests also relax with friends and pets, drink beer, toss Frisbees, picnic, and attend occasional live music and festivals in "The Backyard," a fenced-in outdoor grassy area by the taproom.

Highlights: Year-rounders include Towhead American Blonde, Lil' Helper Midwest Coast IPA, Three Blind Mice, Brown Ale, and Loopty Loop New World Lager. Seasonals such as summery, fruit-laced refresher Blush! Pomegranate Hibiscus Wit, classic fall Oktoberfest Lager, and bold Winter Grind Coffee Stout are beers to explore on tap and packaged in stores. Look for selections on tap from The Backyard Beers 16-ounce-can series, especially Chocolate Chili Mole and Blood Orange Saison. Other aces include Doozy Double IPA, Spiffy Britches Belgian Style IPA, Making Trouble Double IPA, and barrel-aged MILF.

Lambs and Vines Winery

228 Country View Road, Seymour, MO 65746
lambsandvineswinery.com

Marshall Snodgrass, his wife, Kristin, and their son Lucas regularly discussed the idea of growing European varieties of grapes and opening a winery. In 2005, they proceeded with a plan to focus on organically grown European grapes and wines. Meanwhile, Lucas began studying soils at Missouri State University with the intent to learn more about vineyard management and winemaking. The Snodgrasses experimented with a small vineyard while they learned winemaking basics by using boxed kits in the basement.

Over the next decade, they acquired seventy Babydoll Southdown sheep to organically control weeds in the vineyard. It took a couple of years of pasture management to determine how to prevent the cute sheep from eating ripe grapes and tender new vine growth. The family planted hundreds of grapevines for four years, losing the vines and harvest to a hard freeze, a Japanese beetle invasion, and hungry sheep. In 2012, they lost grapes again due to a late frost, but a secondary growth produced enough harvest to yield a whopping nine gallons of wine. Undaunted, the Snodgrasses hit their stride in 2013 as problems smoothed out. The sheep handled organic weed control. The vineyards produced their first full crop. Construction began on the winery building. By May 2015 the winery opened to the public, ten years after planting the first vines.

The winery's focus remains on *Vitis vinifera*, European varieties of grapes that typically don't thrive in the Midwest, rather than the French hybrid grapes that are commonly grown in Missouri. As a byproduct from the sheep flock, abundant wool is dyed and spun into yarn used by Kristin and daughter Natasha, who helps tend the sheep side of the business. The winery also sells the colorful yarn. The tasting room sells local cheeses, breads, and sausages. Guests may dine and relax with wine at picnic tables by the vineyard.

Highlights: Cabernet Franc, a dry red with tannin and hint of oak, reveals hints of leather. Chambourcin, a smooth dry red, carries a touch of smoke and fruit followed by black pepper. Mild tannins lead to light tobacco on the finish. Dornfelder, a dark-skinned grape variety of German origin, produces a dry red with an inky dark color, lush fruit with traces of plum and leather, and a subtle smoky finish. Vidal, a dry white with crisp minerality, is aged on American oak to produce caramel initially and an oaky finish.

Lambs and Vines Winery embodies the full spectrum of Missouri's agricultural beauty and splendor. After years of trial and error, the Snodgrass family found a balance to make their winery thrive. Credit: Kristin Snodgrass, Lambs and Vines Winery.

Travel tip: The winery is located thirty miles (one hour) east of Springfield. From the Springfield area, head east on Highway 60. At Diggins (between Ford-land and Seymour), turn south on Highway NN. Follow until NN ends, then turn left on Cardwell Chapel Road. Take the next left onto Country View Road.

Whispering Oaks Vineyard and Winery

520 Lucky Road, Seymour, MO 65746
417-935-4103
whisperingoakswinery.com

Tucked in the Gasconade watershed of the Ozark Mountains viticultural area of southwest Missouri, Whispering Oaks Vineyard and Winery is located above a sweeping valley with picturesque views. The Green family has owned the land since 1968. They established the vineyard in 1997 and opened the winery and tasting room in spring 2004.

Rocky Ozark soil enables the vines to grow deep and extract mineral from the land that imparts flavor to the grapes. The wines are made only from their grapes, such as Vignoles, Catawba, and Vidal, harvested from a fourteen-acre vineyard.

Highlights: Whispering Oaks offers eleven wines and two sparkling wines, including Semi-Sweet Rosé, Vidal Blanc, Saint Vincent, Norton, Vignoles, Catawba, and Cayuga White.

Mountain Grove Cellars Winery

Missouri State Fruit Experiment Station
9740 Red Spring Road, Mountain Grove, MO 65711
417-547-7500
mtngrv.missouristate.edu/mtngrvcellars

Mountain Grove Cellars Winery, a licensed winery and distillery, operates as part of the State Fruit Experiment Station of Missouri State University, a unit in the Darr School of Agriculture. The facility supports research conducted on specific winemaking problems and offers educational opportunities for Missouri State department of agriculture students interested in enology. Missouri State wines are produced and bottled by the Mountain Grove Cellars Winery from grapes grown at the Missouri State Fruit Experiment Station.

Highlights: The tasting room sells Missouri Pink Catawba, Missouri Chambourcin, Missouri Norton, Ozark Mountain Port, grappa, apple liqueur, and other products. Wine sales support research and education in viticulture and enology at Missouri State University.

Piney River Brewing Company

15194 Walnut Grove Drive, Bucyrus, MO 65444
417-967-4001
pineyriverbrewing.com

Joleen and Brian Durham founded Piney River Brewing Company on their eighty-acre farm in south-central Missouri in 2010. Let's say up front that their award-winning beer is worth the drive from all points of the United States to sample fresh and enjoy at the taproom.

The Durhams first began homebrewing beer in the basement of their one-hundred-year-old farmhouse. In 2010 they renovated a 1940s-era barn to install a brewery and taproom. Maximum capacity of 1,800 barrels was reached in the BARn in 2013. Two years later, a twelve-thousand-square-foot barn became home to a new fifteen-barrel brewhouse with sixty-barrel fermentation and bright beer tanks and an eight-head canning line to package beer in twelve- and sixteen-ounce cans sold throughout Missouri and parts of Arkansas. The original BARn is now used for mixed-fermentation and barrel projects known as "Farm Raised Funk."

Amber Powell, lead brewer at Piney River, oversees brewhouse production. In 2015 Piney River Brewing produced more than 2,200 barrels of beer. The brewery demonstrates and exemplifies the potential of craft beer to represent regional flavor and traditional styles that please the palate.

Highlights: Float Trip Ale received a 2014 gold award at the World Beer Cup. Old Tom Porter received a 2013 gold medal at the Great American Beer Festival. At the 2016 US Open Beer Championship, Black Walnut Wheat, a dark wheat brewed with hand-harvested black walnuts, won bronze in 2016 and silver in 2015. Bronzeback Pale Ale, an American-style pale ale brewed with Galaxy and Citra hops, won bronze in the international pale ale category. Seasonals include Crank-bait Cream Ale, Hobby Farm Ale with basil and honey, and Sweet Potato Ale.

Travel tip: Area lodging, floating, and shuttle information is available on the website. Tours of the brewery are available on Saturdays.

Williams Creek Winery

310 South Hickory Street, Mount Vernon, MO 65712
417-466-4076
williamscreekwinery.com

Louis and Sue Woody opened their winery and tasting room just south of Mount Vernon's historic courthouse square in February 2007. Williams Creek Winery uses Chambourcin, Saint Vincent, Seyval Blanc, and Golden Muscat grapes from their 2.4-acre vineyard located six miles away. They also purchase grapes from southwest Missouri vineyards to supplement production.

Mount Vernon was the site of a battle between Confederate and Union troops and of encampments during the Civil War. More than one hundred different regiments either camped or passed through the area during the period of 1861–1865. The town's other claim to fame is Harold Bell Wright, an early teacher at Mount Vernon Academy who went on to write *The Shepherd of the Hills*, a well-known novel about life in the Ozarks.

Highlights: The winery sells several wines under the Creekside name, including a semidry red, dry white, semisweet white, and sweet wine. A dry Vidal Blanc, semisweet Catawba pink, and other wines are also available.

The White Rose Irish Bed and Breakfast and Winery

13001 Journey Road, Carthage, MO 64836
417-359-9253
whiterosewinery.com

Jim and Jan O'Haro opened their Irish-themed bed and breakfast, restaurant, and winery in 1999 on Saint Patrick's Day. The original farmstead, built in 1900 on a two-thousand-acre cattle ranch, was downsized in the 1920s and became the thousand-acre Overlook Dairy Farm. Today the family operates its business on a ten-acre property with a four-acre vineyard off historic US Route 66. The winery produces wine from grapes sourced from their vineyard and other Missouri growers.

Highlights: Rich Chambourcin serves up intense flavors of raspberries and blackberries. Maréchal Foch's spicy aroma is followed by a spicy plum finish. Other whites include dry Chardonel, Cayuga, and citrusy Vidal. Spring River White's citrus tones are complemented by spicy apple. Notably, the Norton earned gold and Sweet Lady in Red earned bronze at the 2014 Texas Wine and Grape Growers Association's twenty-ninth Annual Lone Star International Wine Competition.

Copper Run Distillery

1901 Day Road, Walnut Shade, MO 65771
417-587-3456
copperrundistillery.com

No need to bootleg at Copper Run, the Ozarks' first legal moonshine distillery. Before he ventured into small-batch artisan distillery, Copper Run's founder, Jim Blansit, brewed beer at home in his youth and went on to refine his craft at microbreweries and wineries throughout the nineties. Next he channeled his interest, energy, and skills into distilling.

The Ozark region is blessed with limestone-rich water ideal for distilling. Charred Missouri white oak barrels, used worldwide for aging spirits, wine, and beer to impart color, aroma, and flavors of caramel, toffee, and vanilla, are made locally from wood grown in the region's forests. Further, the seasonal climate of the Ozarks—akin to conditions in Kentucky's Bourbon Belt—also provides a hospitable distilling and maturing environment for spirits. With restrictive Prohibition laws long gone, conditions made sense for Blansit to revive an Ozark tradition as Copper Run's master distiller.

Blansit and fellow distillers David Burley and Brandon Moore use a 140-gallon, direct-fire, copper pot still and distillation techniques and methods developed over the past decade. They hone in on the "heart" of the distilled spirit and use barrel aging to coax out desired qualities. From the grain mash to hand-bottling, attention to detail and dedication to small-batch distilling has earned Copper Run a growing reputation for fine spirits.

Highlights: The tasting room serves flights of spirits, single servings, crafted cocktails, flavor-infused moonshine and spirits, and beer. Overproof White Rum's bouquet brings sweet molasses to the forefront with toasted vanilla, bananas, and tropical fruit with a full, round body, and a sweet, balanced finish. It was awarded a gold medal and best in category award during the American Distilling Institute's 2015 "Judging of Craft American Spirits." Ozark Mountain Moonshine teases with delicate caramel malted tones, a result of using a 20 percent wheat mash blend with traditional corn mash. At 120 proof, Overproof Ozark Mountain Moonshine is distilled and blended from separate batches of corn, wheat, and barley. The resulting white whiskey offers a fruity grain aroma, flavors of buttery corn, toasted wheat, and caramelized barley, and a clean finish with traces of honey, cinnamon, and licorice. Small-Batch Whiskey begins with toasted oak and hints of vanilla and caramel flavors followed by sweet corn and wheat undertones and ripe banana on the finish.

Lindwedel Winery

3158 MO 265, Branson, MO 65616
417-338-0256
lindwedelwinery.com

Located in Branson West, this Ozark ridgetop winery was founded in November 2007 by pharmacists Stephen and Kim Lindwedel. The Lindwedels enjoyed visiting area wineries and decided that they would one day open a winery themselves. They acquired Frontenac grapevines, a hybrid developed by the University of Minnesota, from a former grower in the Branson area and planted them on three acres. Grapes are also sourced from Les Bourgeois Vineyards in Rocheport, Missouri, and other local growers.

Production takes place on the first floor of the building below the tasting room and deck. Vintner Adam Jett learned the trade from Les Bourgeois and also taught himself. Jett notes, "We're the only winery in Branson where you can drink on-site."

Outlet stores operated by Stone Hill and Mount Pleasant wineries in Branson offer tours and tastings in a large-scale retail environment. Meanwhile, Lind-

Tucked away on the west end of Branson on a ridge, Lindwedel Winery offers a view of rolling Ozark hills to admire while sampling wine and listening to live music on the back deck. Photo by the author.

wedel's tasting room offers live music on select weekends, jovial service, and a charming, homestyle atmosphere with a scenic view from the deck.

Highlights: Lindwedel offers free tasting for up to six wines. Table Rock Red, a sweet red blend with prominent cherry and raspberry fruit flavor, is a strong seller that works well in sangria. Sweet and fruity, the popular blackberry wine is made with local berries. Table Rock White's floral aroma is followed by honeydew and tropical fruit notes. A semidry fifty-fifty blend of Vignoles and Traminette has a honeyed flavor with subtle crispness on the finish. Pear, lemon, and grapefruit notes accent off-dry Vidal's minerality and dry finish.

Missouri Ridge Distillery

7000 Highway 248, Branson, MO 65616
417-699-4095
missouriridgedistillery.com

Open since fall 2016, this rustic distillery features a full bar and tasting room. Master distiller Greg Pope's focus is on production to supply distributors and their clients with spirits across the nation. Pope, a homebrewer for nearly a decade, began distilling around 2012. His grandfather was a distiller before and after Prohibition.

Missouri Ridge Distillery's tasting room is a rustic Ozark setting in which to drink hometown spirits and chow down on Texas-style barbecue. Courtesy of Missouri Ridge Distillery.

The distillery's production facility is built in-the-round so that tasting room customers may observe the mashing, distilling, proofing, and bottling process. With safeguards for the public in place, Pope can distill while customers are in the room. Missouri Ridge serves Texas-style barbecue pork butts and ribs, sandwiches, and salads. The distillery has live entertainment on weekends as well.

Highlights: Spirits made from family recipes include small-batch corn whiskey, Single-Barrel Bourbon, Howlin' Hounds Moonshine, and American Single Malt Whiskey.

BIBLIOGRAPHY

Books and Publications

Andreas, Alfred T. *History of the State of Kansas*. Chicago: 1883. Electronic reproduction. New York: Columbia University Libraries, 2011.

Dulin, Pete. *Kansas City Beer: A History of Brewing in the Heartland*. Charleston, SC: History Press, 2016.

Kansas State Board of Agriculture. *Transactions, 1873*. Topeka, KS: Kansas State Board of Agriculture, 1874.

Laclede County Genealogical Society. *Laclede County, Missouri: History and Families*. Vol. 1. Paducah, KY: Turner Publishing Company, 2000.

Pinney, Thomas. *A History of Wine in America*. Vol. 1, *From the Beginnings to Prohibition*. Berkeley: University of California Press, 1989.

Souter, Gerry, and Janet Souter. *The Chicago Air and Water Show: A History of Wings above the Waves*. Charleston, SC: History Press, 2010.

Websites

Bell, Dena Weigel. "Shiloh Vineyards Opens the Doors to Trego County's First Winery." *WaKeeney Travel Blog*. August 14, 2015. https://wakeeneytravel blog.wordpress.com/2015/08/14/shiloh-vineyards-opens-the-doors-to -trego-countys-first-winery/.

Egtvedt, Richard T. "Honoring Luther." *Dr. Eric W. Gritsch*. Accessed March 5, 2017. http://ericwgritsch.org/archives/archives_honoring_luther.

Kansas Historical Society. "Prohibition." *Kansapedia*. Last modified March 2014. kshs.org/kansapedia/prohibition/14523.

La Pierre, Karen. "A Different Flavor: Mo's Place Microbrewery Reopens in Beaver." *Mid-Kansas News*. August 5, 2016. http://www.midksnews .com/2016/08/05/a-different-flavor-mos-place-microbrewery-reopens-in -beaver/.

Miami County Historical Museum. "'Wine Smith,' aka John U. Smith." *Miami County Kansas History*. Accessed March 5, 2017. http://thinkmiamicounty history.com/Wine-Smith.html.

Mugler v. Kansas. Supreme Court of the United States. Argued April 11, 1887. Argued October 11, 1887. Decided December 5, 1887. 123 US 623; 8 S. Ct. 273; 1887 US LEXIS 2204; 31 L. Ed. 205. http://aalto.arch.ksu.edu/jwk plan/cases/mugler.pdf.

Neil, Denise. "River City's Craft Beers Keep Fans Coming Back for More." *Wichita Eagle*. February 21, 2013. http://www.kansas.com/entertainment /restaurants/article1109181.html.

Overland Park Historical Society. Accessed March 5, 2017. http://www.ophistori cal.org/.

Schaper, Jo. "Pennsylvanian Period." *Jo Schaper's Missouri World*. Accessed March 5, 2017. members.socket.net/~joschaper/penn.html.

Schnyder, MeLinda. "Person of Interest: Cereal Entrepreneur." *Wichita Magazine*. May 1, 2014. http://wichitamag.com/blogsearch/issues/0205/cereal -entrepreneur.

Seneker, Don. "History." *Mt. Vernon, Missouri*. Accessed March 5, 2017. http:// mtvernon-cityhall.org/index.cfm?content=44.

Strengell, Teemu. "Fermentation Waters." *Whisky Science*. April 16, 2014. http://whiskyscience.blogspot.com/2014/04/fermentation-waters.html.

US Department of Agriculture, Kansas Department of Agriculture. *Kansas 2010 Grape Production: Kansas Agricultural Statistics*. Topeka, KS: National Agricultural Statistics Service, Kansas Field Office, 2011. https://www.nass .usda.gov/Statistics_by_State/Kansas/Publications/Economics_and_Misc /Winery/2010GrapeRelease.pdf.

Wilschke, Nancy. "The Brenner Vineyards Historic District, Doniphan County, Kansas." *Pluot*. January 24, 2014. http://atfirstglasspluot.blogspot.com /2014/01/the-brenner-vineyards-historic-district.html.

ABOUT THE AUTHOR

Pete Dulin is the author of *Kansas City Beer: A History of Brewing in the Heartland*; *KC Ale Trail*; and *Last Bite: 100 Simple Recipes from Kansas City's Best Chefs and Cooks*. He also writes about food, beer, wine, and spirits; business; travel; and other subjects for *Flatland, Feast Magazine, Kansas City Star, Visit KC, Riverfront Times, Thinking Bigger,* and other publications. He lives in Kansas City, Missouri.

BREWERIES, WINERIES, AND DISTILLERIES

INDEX

Yeager, Emily, 134

Zinfandel
  Casa de Loco Winery, 221
  Golden Rock Winery, 224

Isinglass Estate Winery, 72
Tipple Hill Winery, 170
  See also grapes
Zweigelt, Prairie Fire Winery and, 38. *See
  also* grapes